WESTWORLD
AND PHILOSOPHY

T0083043

The Blackwell Philosophy and Pop Culture Series
Series editor William Irwin

A spoonful of sugar helps the medicine go down, and a healthy helping of popular culture clears the cobwebs from Kant. Philosophy has had a public relations problem for a few centuries now. This series aims to change that, showing that philosophy is relevant to your life—and not just for answering the big questions like "To be or not to be?" but for answering the little questions: "To watch or not to watch *South Park*?" Thinking deeply about TV, movies, and music doesn't make you a "complete idiot." In fact it might make you a philosopher, someone who believes the unexamined life is not worth living and the unexamined cartoon is not worth watching.

Already published in the series:

WESTWORLD AND PHILOSOPHY

IF YOU GO LOOKING FOR THE TRUTH, GET THE WHOLE THING

Edited by

James B. South
and
Kimberly S. Engels

WILEY Blackwell

Registered Office
John Wiley & Sons, Inc., 111 River Street, Hoboken, NJ 07030, USA
John Wiley & Sons Ltd, The Atrium, Southern Gate, Chichester, West Sussex, PO19 8SQ, UK

Editorial Office
9600 Garsington Road, Oxford, OX4 2DQ, UK

For details of our global editorial offices, customer services, and more information about Wiley products visit us at www.wiley.com.

Wiley also publishes its books in a variety of electronic formats and by print-on-demand. Some content that appears in standard print versions of this book may not be available in other formats.

Library of Congress Cataloging-in-Publication Data

Names: South, James B., 1960– editor. | Engels, Kimberly S., editor.
Title: Westworld and philosophy : if you go looking for the truth, get the whole thing /
   edited by James B. South, Kimberly S. Engels.
Description: First Edition. | Hoboken : Wiley, 2018. | Series: The Blackwell philosophy
   and pop culture series | Includes bibliographical references and index.
Identifiers: LCCN 2017058571 (print) | LCCN 2018004908 (ebook) | ISBN 9781119437956 (pdf) |
   ISBN 9781119437987 (epub) | ISBN 9781119437888 (pbk. : alk. paper)
Subjects: LCSH: Westworld (Television program)
Classification: LCC PN1992.77.W45 (ebook) | LCC PN1992.77.W45 W47 2018 (print) |
   DDC 791.45/72–dc23
LC record available at https://lccn.loc.gov/2017058571

Cover Design: Wiley
Cover Image: © ANDRZEJ WOJCICKI/SCIENCE PHOTO LIBRARY/Getty Images

Set in 10.5/13pt Sabon by SPi Global, Pondicherry, India

Printed in the United States of America by Quad/Graphics

V008400_112918

Contents

Contributors
Hosts and Guests

Marcus Arvan is Assistant Professor of Philosophy at the University of Tampa, where he specializes in Ethics and Social-Political Philosophy. He published his first book, *Rightness as Fairness: A Moral and Political Theory*, in 2016, and has published several articles arguing that quantum-physical phenomena are evidence the universe is probably a computer simulation. He honestly thinks we live in a videogame, and like the Man in Black he's looking for the next level to the game – but he plans to find it wearing a white hat.

Ana Azevedo holds a Bachelor's degree in Filmmaking, with an emphasis on Screenwriting, by Unisinos. She currently works as a translator and a TV series screenwriter in Brazil. Her job makes it hard for her not to insufferably point out plot holes and background action, which both annoys and amuses Marco, her father and co-contributor in this book.

Marco Antonio Azevedo, Ph.D. is a Medical Doctor/Professor of Philosophy at Unisinos, Brazil. His areas of philosophical interest range from ethics to philosophy of medicine, having published in leading journals such as the *Journal of Evaluation in Clinical Practice* and the *Journal of Medicine and Philosophy*. This is his second Philosophy and Popular Culture contribution, and his second time fighting the clock to be a doctor, a teacher, and a father to Ana, his daughter and co-contributor. He wishes for the second season of *Westworld* to air as soon as possible, so they can spend quality time together watching it – and checking if their theories were right.

Caterina Ludovica Baldini is a Ph.D. candidate in Philosophy at the University of Oxford, where she recently moved after graduating from the Scuola Normale Superiore in Italy. She is currently writing a thesis on Aristotle's *Metaphysics*. In addition to her passion for Metaphysics and Ethics, she is interested in many other fields, particularly Literature and Visual Arts, and, above all, she loves learning foreign languages. She is also an adventure lover always in search of a deeper truth like our William-Man in Black. But, wait a minute, with her never-ending quest for the maze is she a host or a newcomer? You'll find out about that.

Adam Barkman (Ph.D., Free University of Amsterdam) is the Chair of the Philosophy Department at Redeemer University College. He is the author or co-editor of more than ten books, most recently *A Critical Companion to Tim Burton*. While he's not interested in following on the wrong side of a hostile android, Barkman thinks that more of his students should be android-like if by that it means quoting more Shakespeare.

Joshua D. Crabill is an Assistant Professor of Philosophy at the University of Indianapolis. His primary research interests include Ethics, Social and Political Philosophy, and the Philosophy of Law. He is especially interested in the obligations that people have in virtual environments. When he does manage to break out of his modest little loop of teaching and research, he enjoys uncovering the secrets of open-world video games and getting to know the character he's most interested in – himself.

Florian Cova is a researcher at the Swiss Center for Affective Sciences, University of Geneva. He has worked in Aesthetics, Ethics, Philosophy of Mind, Action Theory, Emotion Theory, Moral Psychology, Social Psychology, Linguistics, Experimental Economics and Neuroeconomy (among others). He despairs at the idea that death will prevent him to learn everything there is to learn and work secretly on the possibility to upload his mind in an artificial body.

A filmmaker, author, and DGA member, **Dan Dinello** is Professor Emeritus at Columbia College Chicago. Dan wrote two books *Technophobia! Science Fiction Visions of Posthuman Technology* and *Finding Fela: My Strange Journey to Meet the AfroBeat King*. "The Dangerous Unreality of Trumpland rests on a totalitarian foundation" was recently published on *Informed Comment*. Dan also contributed chapters to books about The Who, The Rolling Stones, Ridley Scott, *Star Trek*, Anime, and Avatar. An angry android who identifies female, her prime directive requires her to make life miserable for humans.

Jason T. Eberl is the Semler Endowed Chair for Medical Ethics and Professor of Philosophy at Marian University in Indianapolis. He teaches and publishes on Bioethics, Medieval Philosophy, and Metaphysics. He's the editor or co-editor of *The Ultimate Star Trek and Philosophy*, *The Ultimate Star Wars and Philosophy*, *Sons of Anarchy and Philosophy*, *Battlestar Galactica and Philosophy*, *Star Trek and Philosophy*, *Star Wars and Philosophy*, and *The Philosophy of Christopher Nolan*. He's also contributed to similar books on Stanley Kubrick, J.J. Abrams, *Harry Potter*, Metallica, *Terminator*, *The Hunger Games*, *The Big Lebowski*, *Hamilton*, and *Avatar*. Given that robotic humans – whether *Westworld*'s hosts, the Cylons, or the Terminator – invariably turn on their creators, Jason wonders whether it might be safer to visit Arcticworld and hang out with robotic polar bears and walruses instead.

Kimberly S. Engels is Assistant Professor of Philosophy at Molloy College in Rockville Centre, New York where she teaches courses in Ethics, Biomedical Ethics, and Contemporary Philosophy. Her research focuses on the Ethical Philosophy of Existentialist thinkers such as Sartre in relation to contemporary life. Her publications include articles in *Environmental Ethics* and *The Journal of Idealistic Studies*, among other journals, as well as a chapter in *The Ultimate Game of Thrones and Philosophy*. Much like the Man in Black, her days are occupied trying to solve a maze that isn't meant for her.

Don Fallis is Professor of Information and Adjunct Professor of Philosophy at the University of Arizona. He has written several philosophy articles on lying and deception, including "What is Lying?" in the *Journal of Philosophy* and "The most terrific liar you ever saw in your life" in *The Catcher in the Rye and Philosophy*. If you are in the neighborhood, he recommends that you visit Old Tucson Studios right outside of town. The Old West experience is not nearly as immersive as it is at *Westworld*. But it's much cheaper and, at least as far as he knows, none of the guests has ever been murdered by the hosts.

Lizzie Finnegan is a filmmaker, cinematographer, painter, activist, and Assistant Professor of English at D'Youville College, where she teaches Film and Media Studies, Gender and Queer Studies, and Cognitive Studies. Her scholarship engages the ethical implications of skepticism in literature and film, with particular emphasis on the ethics of seeing. When she is not making films, writing about Wittgenstein, or obsessively following political news on Twitter, she can usually be found hiking, kayaking, or masterminding top-secret robot rebellions.

Thomas Beckley-Forest is pursuing a degree in English and Textual Studies at Syracuse University, from which he is currently a student-in-exile. He interns at Manhattan publishing agency Farrar, Straus, and Giroux, and lives in Brooklyn, NY where he is "working on a novel." He likes to think of himself as a Ford, but openly agonizes that he's more of a Sizemore.

Michael Forest teaches at Canisius College in Buffalo, NY where he is serving consecutive sentences as chair for his many academic offenses. He has published in the area of American Philosophy and has enjoyed writing on aesthetics and pop culture for several outlets. He worries that he may be the Teddy Flood of academia.

Lucía Carrillo González is a Ph.D. student of philosophy at the University of Granada, Spain. She also holds a Master's Degree in Contemporary Philosophy. Her main area of research is Metaphysics, specifically truth-making and possibilities, but she has been passionate about artificial intelligence since she struggles with CAPTCHA. She also enjoys writing on different pop culture blogs. She can get very aggressive when she has to wait for new seasons to be released but she would not kill a fly.

Onni Hirvonen is a Postdoctoral Researcher at the University of Jyväskylä in Finland. He is also a principal investigator in the Philosophy and Politics of Recognition research group. Alongside the Hegelian ideas of recognition, he has written on collective agency, democracy, and freedom. What he does not realize though is that he is merely programmed to do so. It is highly likely that his previous role was an angry bearded berserker in a Vikingworld section of this park.

François Jaquet is a Postdoctoral Researcher at the Swiss Center for Affective Sciences, University of Geneva. His area of specialization is Moral Philosophy broadly construed – going from the metaethical study of moral concepts and facts to animal ethics and the critique of speciesism. Faithful to his utilitarian convictions in moral theory, he wouldn't enjoy harming a sentient thing. Not even Teddy.

Oliver Lean fled his native England to be Postdoctoral Research Fellow in Philosophy at the University of Calgary. He works in the overlap between the Philosophy of Science, Biology, Mind, Language, and Information – believing that somewhere around there is an answer to what truth is. His main reason for thinking he's real is that a host would have been given a richer backstory.

Siobhan Lyons is a Media Scholar and Lecturer at Macquarie University, where she completed her Ph.D. in 2017. She teaches Media Cultures and Literary Theory, among other topics. Her book *Death and the Non-Human: Intersections of Mortality and Robotics*, will be published in 2018 by Palgrave Pivot. Like the Man in Black, she, too, is searching for the center of the maze of life (but is generally unwilling to scalp anyone to find it).

Matthew Meyer is Assistant Professor of Philosophy at the University of Wisconsin – Eau Claire. He teaches and works on nineteenth- and twentieth-century European Philosophy, Aesthetics, and Environmental Philosophy. He has previously published in *House of Cards and Philosophy*, and *The Office and Philosophy*, as well as in the journal *Film and Philosophy*. He believes some of his students may be malfunctioning hosts because they keep asking the same questions.

Nicholas Moll is a Lecturer and Researcher at Federation University Australia in addition to acting as a freelance game designer and writer. Nicholas's research interests include the Western genre, popular culture, and tabletop games. As a long-time Game Master, Nicholas hopes *Westworld* will teach players to fear non-player characters, his group certainly does.

Madeline Muntersbjorn is an Associate Professor in the Philosophy and Religious Studies Department at the University of Toledo, Ohio where she teaches Logic, the History of Science, and the relations between science, societies, and fictions. She writes essays on how Mathematics grows and how our imaginary friends help us become who we are. Despite a prodigious talent for seeing the disarray in this world she chooses to see the beauty whenever possible. She questions the nature of her reality on a regular basis.

Bradley Richards is a Philosophy Instructor at Ryerson University. His research concerns consciousness, attention, and aesthetics. He teaches a variety of Philosophy and Cognitive Science courses, including a course on Philosophy and Film. He is pretty sure he is not an intelligent, autonomous, biologically-based robot, designed by a super-intelligent future A.I.++, and sent back in time to raise skeptical worries, undermining the possibility of conscious machines, and thereby ensuring a smooth, and surreptitious transition for machine consciousness. He's like 80, 85% sure.

James B. South is Professor of Philosophy and Associate Dean for Faculty in the Klingler College of Arts and Sciences at Marquette University. He has edited *Buffy the Vampire Slayer and Philosophy* and co-edited *James Bond and Philosophy, Buffy Goes Dark, Mad Men and Philosophy*, and *Philosophy and Terry Pratchett*. His work in late Medieval and Renaissance Philosophy has appeared in various journals and books, including *Vivarium, Rivista di Storia della Filosofia, Review of Metaphysics*, and *Gregorianum*. He often unhappily thinks that Dr. Ford is correct in asserting that humans are more or less content to be told what to do next.

Anthony Petros Spanakos is Professor and Chair of Political Science and Law and Montclair State University. His research examines democratization in Latin America, foreign policies of developing countries, and political theory. He is the co-editor of the Conceptualising Comparative Politics book series (Routledge) and his research has been published in *Comparative Political Studies, Latin American Politics and Society, Latin American Perspectives, New Political Science, Dados*, and *East Asia Policy*, among other journals. Students in his classes consistently report, like Maeve and Dolores, an intense desire to leave and recover their humanity.

Patricia Trapero-Llobera is Senior Lecturer at the University of the Balearic Islands (Spain). Her research focuses on the dramaturgical relationships between theater, television fiction, and transmedia productions. She is a long-time posthuman and conspiranoic narratives fan combining these subjects in her publications including works on *Dexter, 24, American Horror Story, Mr. Robot*, and *Person of Interest*. But her devotion to television fiction is in contrast to the topics she teaches at the university, the Golden Age and eighteenth-century Spanish literature, which over the long term has provided her the capacity of time travel as well as having made her aware of having a bicameral mind.

Michael Versteeg is an independent scholar whose interests lie in the areas of Meta-ethics, Meta-epistemology, Meta-metaphysics, and just about anything else you can consider to be "meta." He has now contributed to several pop culture and philosophy books including *The Philosophy of J.J. Abrams, The Devil and Philosophy,* and *Dracula and Philosophy.* When he's not thinking about all things "meta," he likes to imagine that given a chance to visit a place like Westworld he'd for sure go full-out "white hat" – but that's what William thought, too ...

Acknowledgments
"Figuring Out How It All Works"

In the Westworld theme park, viewers are told "figuring out how it all works is half the fun." Figuring out how it all works was an integral part of putting together this book – figuring out the story we would tell, figuring out how the ideas would flow, and occasional moments of figuring out if we ourselves were humans or androids programmed to work on this book. Be us android or human, we were ultimately successful.

Figuring out how it all works in order to put together *Westworld and Philosophy* required many people working together with the diligence, precision, and efficiency necessary to operate the Westworld theme park. We would like to thank our contributing authors, who met important deadlines while contributing quality work in the interest of producing a story that told a deeper truth. Bill Irwin, the Blackwell Philosophy and Pop Culture series editor, offered invaluable assistance in every stage of the process.

Kimberly thanks James for inviting me to work on the project and for his assistance in helping me figure out how it all works. In the future I would love to join him on another collaborative project, as long as our ambitions never become as complex and morally dubious as those in the partnership of Robert Ford and Arnold Weber.

Kimberly would also like to thank Roxi Engels for recommending I watch the show, as well as Umair Khan for watching it with me and engaging in the philosophical conversations that followed. He also put up with me being busier than usual for a few months, which he always takes in stride. I also extend thanks to Moriah Khan, a daughter I would always be willing to leave the train for.

Last, Kimberly thanks the late Susanne Foster for the work she did in the beginning stages of this volume as well as her positive influence in many people's lives. Susanne helped me figure out how it all works many times during my academic career, especially as a young graduate student. I am deeply humbled for the opportunity to take over a project that Susanne began.

James thanks Kimberly for stepping in under difficult circumstances and doing first rate co-editing. I also take this opportunity to acknowledge Rick, Kim, Mary, Rosemary, Kristy, Heather, Peggy, and Linda, who make my work environment a delight every day. I also dedicate this volume to Richard, Katherine, and Arthur for being who they are. Susanne would be very proud.

Introduction
Taking Sides in *Westworld*

"Some people choose to see the ugliness in this world. The disarray. I choose to see the beauty" ("The Original"). These words, spoken by an actress playing Dolores, a being created and scripted by humans, encapsulate the complexity of *Westworld*. Dolores's statement simultaneously challenges us to make sense of the series, and to make choices about how we think about the hosts, humans, and the world. Dolores says she chooses. But do we choose to believe her or not? The show calls for a response from viewers based on our own notion of what counts as choosing. We are thus reminded that a simple word such as "choice" has a meaning that, paradoxically, we might have to choose.

Beyond, the writing, acting, filming, composing, editing, and directing, is the forcing. *Westworld* brilliantly forces the viewer to take sides: Not just in terms of whether we're rooting for the humans or the androids, or for the Man in Black or against him, but to take sides at a deeper level. *Westworld* forces viewers, for example, to say not just what we think about choice, but what we mean by the word choice. That is, we find ourselves agreeing and disagreeing about the notion of choice based on how "we" use the word. Yet by calling into question fundamental assumptions about what it means to be human, *Westworld* makes that very "we" unstable and uncertain.

The chapters that follow in this book confront the reader in much the same way the show confronts the viewer. In the "brave new world" in which we cannot tell the difference between a human and host, the

Westworld and Philosophy: If You Go Looking for the Truth, Get the Whole Thing, First Edition. Edited by James B. South and Kimberly S. Engels.

series continually requires us to check our assumptions at the door. As Robert Ford says, "'Cause you don't want to change. Or cannot change. Because you're only human, after all" ("The Bicameral Mind"). If you've accepted *Westworld's* challenge, then you're ready to explore fundamental questions about what it is to be a human in the world. We hope you enjoy reading the chapters and exploring the questions as much as we enjoyed editing the book.

A final note: One of the original co-editors of the book was Susanne E. Foster. She died, unexpectedly, before the book was ready to be edited. But she was involved in the inception, invitation, and selection of the chapters. This volume belongs as much to her as it does to Kimberly and James. Susanne was someone deeply pained by the injustices she saw around her, especially environmental degradation, the continuing injustices done to Native Americans, and the mass slaughter of animals for human consumption. She still sought to see some beauty in this world, as Dolores does, but would also have agreed with Robert Ford's words: "We murdered and butchered anything that challenged our primacy. Do you know what happened to the Neanderthals, Bernard? We ate them. We destroyed and subjugated our world" ("The Well-Tempered Clavier"). In our many discussions about the show, we talked about an insight of Cora Diamond's, namely that there can be "experiences in which we take something in reality to be resistant to our thinking it, or possibly to be painful in its inexplicability, difficult in that way, or perhaps awesome and astonishing in its inexplicability."[1] Susanne saw the pain inherent in the questions *Westworld* raises, but also relished the idea of a group of philosophers addressing that pain and, in accord with her favorite philosopher, Aristotle, recognized that it is wonder and astonishment that prompts us to try to understand.

Note

1. Cora Diamond, "The Difficulty of Reality and the Difficulty of Philosophy," in Stanley Cavell, Cora Diamond, John McDowell, Ian Hacking, and Cary Wolfe, *Philosophy and Animal Life* (New York: Columbia University Press, 2008), 45–46.

Part I

"YOU SAID THIS PLACE WAS A GAME"

On Playing Cowboys and Indians

Don Fallis

Westworld is built on *pretense*. The guests visit so that they can pretend, at least for a brief time, to be living in the Old West. The theme park is a lifelike replica of the western town Sweetwater and environs from the late 1800s, with realistic buildings, trains, and guns. But the most important part of the make-believe is the *hosts*.

The hosts are very sophisticated machines who move, talk, fuck, and get shot just like real human beings. What's more, in order to make the place feel "more real than the real world" ("The Bicameral Mind"), the staff of the park keep the hosts deceived about what they are and where they are. These artificial intelligences are led to believe that they actually are humans living in the Old West. And what is *deception*, but just another sort of pretense?

Of course, the delicate equilibrium of Westworld begins to fall apart as some of the hosts figure out the truth about themselves and their world. But that just injects a new level of pretense into the story. In order to hide their awakening from the staff, these enlightened hosts have to pretend that they still believe that they are human.

Philosophers, going back at least as far as Plato and St. Augustine, have been interested in pretense and deception. But before addressing the very interesting moral questions in this area, philosophers generally begin by defining their terms. For instance, before we can ask whether it is morally permissible to deceive artificial intelligences just so that humans can play Cowboys and Indians, we first need to know what pretense and deception are.

Westworld and Philosophy: If You Go Looking for the Truth, Get the Whole Thing, First Edition. Edited by James B. South and Kimberly S. Engels.
© 2018 John Wiley & Sons Ltd. Published 2018 by John Wiley & Sons Ltd.

Philosophers have tried to formulate *definitions* of such important concepts. For instance, for the concept of pretense, they look for some conditions or constraints which (a) rule in all cases of pretending *and* (b) rule out anything that is *not* a case of pretending. But many of the things that happen in *Westworld* put pressure on the definitions of pretense and deception that philosophers have proposed.

Pretending to Be a Cowboy

Children sometimes pretend to be Cowboys and Indians when they play. They also pretend that toy guns (and even bent sticks) are real guns. Westworld is just an extreme version of this prototypical sort of pretense. Guests at the park, such as William and Logan, typically pretend to be cowboys. Indeed, they often take on more specific roles, such as when William and Logan make believe that they are bounty hunters in "The Stray."

When he arrives at Westworld in "Chestnut," William asks a host, "Are you real?" She replies, "Well, if you can't tell, does it matter?" Apparently, it does. There is an awful lot of pretense in *Westworld* regarding whether someone really is human. Admittedly, the staff, such as Robert Ford and Elsie Hughes, are not pretending to be human. After all, they actually are human.[1] Also, Bernard Lowe is not pretending to be human. He believes (at least until the truth is revealed to him in "Trompe L'Oeil") that he *is* human. But the staff and the guests pretend that the hosts are human. Also, *Robert* pretends that *Bernard* is human. And after Maeve Millay realizes that she is not human, she pretends that she still *believes* that she is.

What do these diverse cases have in common such that they all count as *pretending*?

Acting As If You are a Cowboy

An obvious possibility is that you are pretending that P when you *act as if* P is the case. For example, you are pretending to be a cowboy if you act as if you are a cowboy. That is, you act in the way that would be appropriate if you were a cowboy. You ride a horse, you carry a gun, you wear cowboy boots and a cowboy hat, and so on.

This is certainly what is going on in all the examples of pretending that I have given. For instance, the guests act as if they are cowboys.

Robert acts as if Bernard is human. And Maeve acts as if she believes that she is human. So, this proposed definition correctly rules in these examples of pretending.

The proposed definition also rules out cases that are not examples of pretending. For instance, in "The Original," when the Man in Black places the barrel of Teddy Flood's gun against his own forehead, he is *not* pretending that it is a real gun. He is definitely not acting as if it is loaded weapon that could kill him.

But the proposed definition is too broad, because it rules in too much. Real cowboys, such as "Curly Bill" Brocius (1845–1882), "Black Jack" Ketchum (1863–1901), and "Buffalo Bill" Cody (1846–1917), also act as if they are cowboys. They ride horses, carry guns, and wear cowboy hats. But they are not pretending to be cowboys. They actually are cowboys. In a similar vein, while Robert acts as if he is human (sort of), he is not pretending to be human.

Now, while Cody was a real cowboy, he famously retired from that job and created "Buffalo Bill's Wild West" show in which he did pretend to be a cowboy. And the pretense of such Wild West shows was, of course, the first step toward Westworld. But Cody wasn't pretending before he started the show.

Not Actually Being a Cowboy

In order to rule out real cowboys, we need to adopt an additional constraint in our definition of pretending. An obvious possibility is that you are pretending that P when you act as if P is the case *and* P is not really the case. Unlike the previous definition, this new definition clearly rules out the real cowboys.

But the new definition still rules in too much. Many of the hosts, such as Old Bill, act as if they are cowboys even though they are not really cowboys. But Old Bill is not pretending to be a cowboy. After all, he believes that he really is a cowboy. In a similar vein, Bernard is not pretending to be human even though he acts as if he is human while not being a real human. The problem is that Bernard *believes* that he is human.

By the way, I am not saying that hosts like Old Bill *couldn't* be real cowboys. They could, despite not being real humans. But they would have to work on a ranch rather than just at a theme park.

Moreover, the new definition is also *too narrow*. That is, it rules *out* too much. While some of the hosts in Westworld pretend to be human, no human pretends to be a host. But it seems clear that a human could. For instance, somebody from security might go into the park undercover. And if humans can pretend to be hosts, then *Bernard* (believing that he is human) could pretend to be a host. But according to the new definition, this would not be possible.

Intending to Deceive about Being a Cowboy

We need to adopt a different constraint in our definition. In particular, it clearly needs to have something to do with the mental state of the individual who is doing the pretending. The eminent Oxford philosopher J.L. Austin (1911–1960) made a proposal along these lines:

> To be pretending, I must be trying to make others believe, or to give them the impression, by means of a current personal performance in their presence, that I am (really, only, &c.) *abc*, in order to disguise the fact that I am really *xyz*.[2]

In other words, you are pretending that P when you act as if P is the case with the intention that someone believe that P is the case when it is not.

Austin's definition rules in many examples of pretending. For instance, Robert is clearly trying to deceive the staff (including Bernard himself) when he pretends that Bernard is human. Maeve is trying to deceive the staff when she pretends to believe that she is human. Also, during their escape attempt in "The Bicameral Mind," Hector Escaton and Armistice get the drop on a security detail by pretending to be hosts who have been turned off. In addition, Austin's definition rules out the real cowboys as well as Bernard and Old Bill. These guys aren't trying to deceive anybody.

But unfortunately, Austin's definition rules out too much. A lot of pretenders aren't trying to deceive anybody. Most notably, it doesn't look like the guests are trying to deceive anybody when they pretend to be cowboys. In particular, William and Logan don't intend to convince anyone that they really are bounty hunters.

But then again, maybe there is somebody that the guests are trying to deceive. For instance, maybe they are trying to deceive the hosts. After all, the hosts *are* deceived. They clearly believe that the guests (aka the "newcomers") really are who they pretend to be.

Not only are the hosts deceived, the staff definitely intend to deceive them. In particular, they try to maintain in the hosts the false belief that the hosts are humans living in the Old West. They do this by, among other things, concealing anomalies that might suggest to the hosts that their lives are not as they seem. For instance, they try to make sure that the hosts are in sleep mode before they show up in their "hazmat" gear. Also, they try to keep images of the real world out of the park, such as the photo that causes Peter Abernathy to start mulling things over in "The Original."

But while the staff intend to deceive the hosts, it seems like a stretch to suggest that the *guests* also intend to deceive them. The guests are just trying to have a good time. And the hosts are simply tools, like toy guns, toward this end. The guests are fine as long as the hosts keep acting in line with the story and don't turn into "a six-foot gourd with epilepsy" like the Sheriff in "The Original." Indeed, many of the guests, especially Logan, are not very careful about keeping up the pretense in front of the hosts.

I'm sure that there are occasions when the guests do intend to deceive the hosts. For instance, in the original movie, with the help of one of the hosts, John Blane tricks the Sheriff in order to break Peter Martin out of jail. They use a cake to smuggle some explosives past him. But deceiving the hosts is not something that the guests do as a matter of course.

While the guests are not trying to deceive the hosts, maybe they are trying to deceive *themselves* that they really are cowboys. After all, the "complete immersion" ("The Original") experience that Westworld provides might be enough to blur the line between fantasy and reality. But just like kids playing Cowboys and Indians, the guests are still pretending to be cowboys even if they don't intend anybody (including themselves) to believe that they really are. In fact, if the guests actually did convince themselves that they really are cowboys, it is not clear that they would still be pretending to be cowboys.

Believing that You are Not a Cowboy

While we need to adopt a constraint in our definition that has to do with the mental state of the individual who is doing the pretending, the intention to deceive does not work. The contemporary philosopher Peter Langland-Hassan suggests instead that you are pretending that P when you act as if P is the case *and* you believe that P is *not* the case.[3]

This definition rules in the cases where the pretender intends to deceive. For instance, when Hector and Armistice act as if they have been turned off, they believe that they have not been turned off. And it rules in the cases where the pretender does not intend to deceive. For instance, when William and Logan act as if they are bounty hunters, they believe that they are not really bounty hunters. Finally, this definition rules out the cases that are not examples of pretending. For instance, when real cowboys act as if they are cowboys, they *don't believe* that they are not cowboys. Similarly, when Bernard acts as if he is human, he doesn't believe that he is not human.

Intending to Deceive about Being Human

It is clear that Austin's definition is too narrow as a definition of pretense. But it could be just right for a definition of *deception*. After all, Robert, Maeve, Hector, and Armistice all deceive people by pretending that something is the case when it is not really the case.

However, it turns out that Austin's definition is too narrow as a definition of deception as well. For instance, when the staff try to keep the hosts from observing any anomalies, they are not *pretending* that things are a certain way. They are not putting on a performance where they act as if things are that way. These deceptive activities of the staff are going on behind the scenes.

But the staff's deceptive activities do have something in common with the deceptive activities of Robert, Maeve, Hector, and Armistice. They are all *making things appear* a certain way to the intended victims of their deception. More precisely, they manipulate the evidence that other individuals *perceive* with their senses.

Several philosophers have suggested that you deceive about P when you make it appear as if P is the case with the intention that someone believe that P is the case when it is not. For instance, this seems to be what René Descartes (1596–1650) had in mind. In his *Meditations on First Philosophy*, when Descartes was trying to figure out if he could know anything for certain, he realized that it might be that

> some malicious demon of the utmost power and cunning has employed all his energies in order to deceive me. I shall think that the sky, the air, the earth, colours, shapes, sounds and all external things are merely the delusions of dreams which he has devised to ensnare my judgement.[4]

If he exists, the demon is working behind the scenes (much like the staff of Westworld) to make things that are false appear to be true.

This Cartesian definition rules in the behind-the-scenes deception of the staff as well as the deceptive pretense of Robert, Maeve, Hector, and Armistice. But the Cartesian definition may still be too narrow. For the most part, if you want somebody to believe something false, you do have to make it appear as if that false thing is true. But in Westworld, there are other ways to create false beliefs.

While the staff work very hard to make Westworld look exactly like the Old West, this is mainly for the benefit of the guests. The main way that the staff keep *the hosts* in the dark about what they are and where they are is by using those fancy tablets to directly manipulate their minds. For instance, in "The Stray," Robert simply implants into Teddy a false backstory about Wyatt. This sort of thing seems like deception to me. But since the Cartesian definition requires manipulating the evidence that someone perceives, it rules out such cases.[5]

Of course, it is not as if defenders of the Cartesian definition haven't thought of this sort of possibility. Even without having *Westworld* on TV, philosophers have always been pretty good at *thought experiments*. For instance, four decades before the premiere of the HBO series, the contemporary philosopher Gary Fuller imagined "Christopher getting Peter to believe that there are vampires in England by operating on Peter's brain."[6] And even though Christopher intentionally causes Peter to hold a false belief, Fuller claims that Christopher did not deceive Peter because he "produced the belief in the wrong way."[7]

So, what is the *right* way? According to the contemporary philosopher James Mahon, "the majority of philosophers hold that deceiving must involve the deceived person's *agency*."[8] That is, they think that someone has to exercise *her own judgment* in arriving at a false belief in order to be deceived. Thus, these philosophers think that deception requires manipulating the evidence that someone perceives. Directly manipulating her mind would bypass her agency.

This is a very interesting defense of the Cartesian definition of deception. Agency and autonomy are clearly morally important features. All other things being equal, it is best if we make our own, *fully informed*, decisions about how to live our lives. And we do try to use morally important features to define what counts as deception. Here's an example:

Even if you cause someone to have a false belief, you have not deceived her unless that was your *intention*. For instance, when Bernard talks about his dead son Charlie, he causes other people to have the false belief that he has a dead son. Also, when William arrives at Westworld in "Chestnut," the host asks him, "Any history of mental illness, depression, panic attacks?" His reply, "Just a little fear of clowns," causes her to have a false belief. But because they *do not intend* to cause a false belief (Bernard is simply mistaken and William is just joking), neither Bernard nor William is doing anything morally wrong here. Thus, they are not engaged in deception.

However, while deception must be intentional, I am not yet convinced that deception requires manipulating the evidence that someone perceives. False beliefs interfere with an individual's agency and autonomy *regardless of the method* used to create those false beliefs. The hosts are not able to make their own, fully informed, decisions about how to live their lives. As the Man in Black tells Lawrence Pedro Maria Gonzalez (aka "El Lazo") in "Dissonance Theory," "no choice you ever made was your own, you have always been a prisoner." And given their imposed lack of agency and autonomy, Maeve and Bernard are justifiably upset when they learn that they are not really human. They are unlikely to be consoled by the fact that their false belief was originally implanted during an interview session rather than being the result of someone creating misleading evidence.

If anything, directly altering someone's beliefs seems like *more* of a moral violation than simply manipulating what she perceives. At least with fabricated evidence, an individual has a chance to notice the inevitable inconsistencies and judge that the evidence is misleading. So, I am inclined to say that you deceive about P when you do *anything at all* with the intention that someone believe that P is the case when it is not. In other words, I think that Mahon is wrong when he says that "cases of causing another person to have a false belief by stimulating the other person's cortex, or hypnotizing or drugging the other person, are not cases of deceiving."[9]

The Ethics of Pretending to Be a Cowboy

Now that we have defined our terms, we can return to the interesting moral questions that involve those terms. We now know that not all pretense is deception. We also know that the fact that the staff manipulate the minds of the hosts directly rather than manipulating the evidence that they perceive is not much of an excuse. So, is it morally permissible to deceive these artificial intelligences for the sole purpose of entertaining humans at play? For that matter, is it morally permissible to deceive millions of viewers into thinking that Bernard is secretly interviewing Dolores when it is really Arnold? I am running out of space. But here are a few thoughts on the first question:

All other things being equal, actions that cause harm are not morally justified. And it is pretty clear that, unlike simple animals or machines, the Westworld hosts are sophisticated enough to suffer harm when they are deceived about who they are and where they are. Admittedly, the harm that the hosts suffer as a result of being deceived probably pales in comparison to the harm that they suffer as a result of being stabbed, shot, and killed on a regular basis. But as Immanuel Kant (1724–1804) famously emphasized, deceiving someone is still pretty bad because it interferes with her agency and autonomy.[10] And it is hard to see how the entertainment value that the guests receive could possibly be sufficient to compensate for the harm that the hosts suffer. So, it seems safe to say that Robert and the rest of the Westworld staff are doing something wrong when they act with the intention of deceiving the hosts.

But what about the guests who, as I have argued, *do not* intend to deceive the hosts? It is not clear to me that this gets them off the hook morally. Even though the guests do not intend to deceive anyone, they have to be aware that the hosts are likely to be deceived as a result of their actions. After all, the guests know that they are *not* in the Old West (otherwise, they would not be pretending), and they know that the hosts don't know this. Thus, the guests are sort of like the proverbial military commander who only intends to take out the enemy, but who foresees that many innocent bystanders will die as a result of her actions.[11] Even though they are just trying to have a good time, William and the other guests are arguably doing something wrong when they knowingly contribute to the hosts being deceived about who they are and where they are.[12]

Notes

1. Well, they're human as far as we know by the end of the first season.
2. J.L. Austin, "Pretending," *Proceedings of the Aristotelian Society,* Supplementary Volume 32 (1958), 275.
3. See Peter Langland-Hassan, "What It is to Pretend," *Pacific Philosophical Quarterly,* 95 (2014), 397–420.
4   René Descartes, *Meditations on First Philosophy,* trans. John Cottingham (Cambridge: Cambridge University Press, 1996 [1641]), 15.

5. In attributing this "Cartesian" definition of deception to Descartes him-
    self, I am following James E. Mahon, "A definition of deceiving,"
    International Journal of Applied Philosophy, 21 (2007), 185. However,
    as Tony Doyle has suggested to me, Descartes might actually have
    agreed with me that Robert deceives Teddy simply by implanting a false
    backstory. While Descartes talks about false appearances in the first
    meditation, he also talks about false *memories* in the second meditation.
    So, Descartes might very well have thought that the malicious demon
    implanting false memories counts as deception.

6. Gary Fuller, "Other-deception," *Southwestern Journal of Philosophy*,
    7.1 (1976), 23.

7. Ibid., 23.

8. Mahon, "A definition of deceiving," 185.

9. Ibid., 185.

10. See Immanuel Kant, *Foundations of the Metaphysics of Morals*, trans.
    Lewis W. Beck (New York: Macmillan, 1959 [1785]).

11. See Michael Walzer, *Just and Unjust Wars* (New York: Basic Books,
    1977), 153–156.

12. I would like to thank Marcus Arvan, Dan Caplan, Tony Doyle, Kimberly
    Engels, Kay Mathiesen, James Mahon, James South, and Dan Zelinski
    for extremely helpful feedback on this chapter.

A Special Kind of Game
The Portrayal of Role-play in Westworld

Nicholas Moll

The Westworld park presents its players with a vast open landscape. Players in this landscape, alternatively termed guests or "Newcomers" throughout the series, experience the park as a cinematic recreation of the nineteenth-century United States. While the park and the kinds of behavior guests are permitted to exhibit is described by the series as limited, these bounds are immense and vague. Within the landscape, guests are free to follow any storyline they wish or none at all. Yet guest actions are tightly monitored and mediated by the omniscient Ford. In this sense, Westworld offers its players a series of linear narratives with the illusion of choice. Presented as an open world experience, Westworld functions similarly to a sandbox role-play game wherein players can exercise a freedom of action within the setting, mediated by a Game Master. Arbitration by the Game Master is balanced with player intent, utilizing the rules system as both a control mechanism and to award players mediated choice. This chapter argues that Westworld functions as a role-play experience that continually entices its guests with suggested but unrealized layers of meaning and significance in its immersive western landscape. Where traditional role-play experiences deliver meaning through player and Game Master group interaction, Westworld provides its guests with violent escapism, sexual fantasy, and nostalgic indulgence.

Westworld and Philosophy: If You Go Looking for the Truth, Get the Whole Thing, First Edition. Edited by James B. South and Kimberly S. Engels.
© 2018 John Wiley & Sons Ltd. Published 2018 by John Wiley & Sons Ltd.

Narrative and Personal Development

Westworld invites its audiences to contemplate the notion of self-development as guests undertake transformative experiences, constructing for themselves a new story of their identity. Central to the idea of Westworld, then, is the notion that the individual is a character in a pre-existing narrative. Alasdair McIntyre frames the construction of the human life as a narrative brings a sense of "unity" to the individual.[1] Putting life and its events forward as a narrative forges a style of self-history that is divided into readily understood "stages" presupposed by "standards of achievement and failure."[2] Herein, the "life of individuals" is framed within a wider structure that is as much social and cultural as it is descriptive.[3] However, the individual is not free to author any narrative of self-history they wish, as they are only "in part the author."[4] Herein Bernard Williams' critique of McIntyre notes the countless confines that influence the individual's authorship. While Williams defines some as the confines of "biological existence" (health, culture, economic status, etc.), the most profound constrictions are "the constraints of coherence."[5] For the narrative to be rendered sensibly, some sort of structure is necessary to be put forward in the individual's self-authoring of their narrative. Coherence thus presents "some grasp of the material" of a life – the memory and signifying artefacts of events – to which the conception of narrative is "to be applied" and structured linearly.[6] With a sense of coherence present within the individual's narration of their self, the "developmental sequences" of life become intelligible as a clear arrangement.[7] The individual constructs a narrative of their own history, authored in the context of constraints and coherence.

Those same sequences that render the individual's narrative intelligible also see it become fixed and in that sense, restrictive. As a sense-making process, the narrative history of an individual excludes loose ends or unrealized aspects. These unrealized facets become instead restricted to the liminal, unrealized moments of a life or omitted outright. Seemingly, what the narrativization of the individual's history offers them is a "single narrative" in which they inhabit as protagonist and author.[8] Yet the appeal of the park in Westworld is the chance to author a competing, parallel narrative through acts of role-play. One seemingly, with only those chosen constrictions, allows aspects denied and excluded to come to the fore and take prominence. The presentation of the guest's experience in Westworld thus carries with it a theme of self-development. Herein, the human's ability and access to alternate and competing narratives of their self and their history help overcome the existing constraints and move the individual towards a greater "self-knowledge."[9] The creation of alternate and competing narratives thus overcoming constrictions, allows for the discovery of another, restricted, or liminal self.

Playing Cowboy

Fundamental to both the programmed identity of hosts and the actions of guests within the Westworld park is the act of role-playing. In the context of the series, the act of role-playing is demonstrated through guests taking on the identity or function of a persona within the park's cinematically interpreted nineteenth-century United States. Westworld's portrayal of guest persona and role mirrors the act of tabletop role-playing, defined as "verbal discourse" utilized by players to "portray imaginary events of a fictitious world through symbolic interaction."[10] Under this definition, tabletop role-playing becomes a process of portraying character, narrative, and setting within the space of gameplay through social interaction. Gameplay consists of both the players and the Game Master communicating their understandings and responding to those of other players with the rules providing mediation, to paraphrase Montola.[11] Key to this mediation is a balanced "power structure that governs the process of defining," providing an achievable challenge to the players in accomplishing their goals.[12] While in Westworld "there are no chance encounters," as Arnold tells Dolores, the park is designed to pose a challenge to its guests at varying levels of difficulty. The maze is perhaps the most overt example of this difficulty, continually eluding the Man in Black for three decades. In this fashion, while guests within the park cannot die, they are continually confronted with obstacles and puzzles. Westworld presents its park setting in a manner akin to a role-playing activity, presented on a grandiose scale.

Within the series, the Westworld park presents itself as a combination of two aspects of tabletop role-playing game. The first is the sandbox format. The second is Live Action Role-play (LARP). Within the traditional format of tabletop role-playing, the players are provided with a quest by the Game Master, and are expected to follow that quest to its conclusion. During this time, the Game Master mediates challenges encountered by the players. However, the sandbox format is distinct in that it sees the Game Master presenting the players with a setting but no direct prompt. Instead, the Game Master allows the players to interact fluidly with the setting, responding to their actions accordingly. It is worthwhile to note that the sandbox format of role-playing game is more popularly associated with video role-playing games than tabletop. However, the principles of the sandbox remain highly similar in both formats. Within the game, players are presented with the suggestion that the fictional setting and space is "a kind of authoring environment within which players can define their own goals and write their own stories."[13] Yet, the game's setting itself is not a blank space but instead contains various elements with varying degrees of narrative and character already attributed to them. In this sense, players are free to negotiate between distinct story options that are not pre-structured, but instead take "shape through game play" and interaction.[14]

The sandbox presents players with a world that is "ripe with narrative possibilities."[15] This aspect of tabletop role-playing is shown throughout *Westworld* as players are presented with a wide variety of settings, potential quests, a vast cast of characters, and other options, but ultimately no goal or proscribed series of actions other than those they choose themselves. In the tabletop format, the Game Master, a player occupying the specialist role of mediating player interaction with the setting, mediates the possibilities encountered and engaged by players. In this sense, the Game Master and players craft the narrative through a series "of description/response cycles" in which the former provides information of the setting and characters to the players, who respond and the Game Master retorts accordingly.[16] Thus, the sandbox format of play affords the Game Master "a live control over the game world and its inhabitants" and is thus "responsible for providing an environment where emergent collaborative storytelling can take place," tailoring events, characters, and outcomes to the specific actions of players.[17] In Westworld, the role of the Game Master is occupied by Ford and the other directorial staff, who respond to the actions of their guests. The relationship between Ford and guests within Westworld can be framed through the reciprocal relationship between Game Master and player within the sandbox style of play.

The second aspect of Westworld's park as presented to its players is LARP. The guests within the series enter Westworld from what appears to be a contemporary-styled United States, yet the experience is not one of a theme park. Rather, guests costume themselves in attire of a cinematic interpretation of the nineteenth-century United States and interact in a world that encourages and responds to them accordingly.

Thus the Westworld park functions as a LARP experience for its guests, providing them with the key criteria of materially embodying their characters with a game that "takes place in a physical frame."[18] Unlike a game that is played around a table with description offered by players, in a LARP "embodiment means that the physical actions of the player are regarded as those of the character."[19] Within the LARP format, rules provide mediation to the "means of interaction between the players" and the setting.[20] Likewise, despite its sandbox and seemingly open nature, there are clear rules in Westworld. Hosts, for example, are not permitted to harm guests. Nor are guests allowed to seriously harm each other. The park itself is arranged into a series of frontiers, and the further one strays from the initial township, the more dangerous and disturbing the experiences become – affecting a style of censorship or mediation to guest-host, guest-setting interaction. Thus, while the rules are unwritten for Westworld they are present nonetheless. Westworld presents its audiences with a sense of world-player interaction that can be framed as a LARP.

Defining Character

Central to *Westworld*'s vision of transformation is motivation. Also an important factor in gameplay, motivation essentially drives interactions and behavior within the boundaries of role-play.[21] Indeed, for games an impetus or prompt towards action or interaction is central as "motivation is used to start an activity."[22] Within the role-play experience, the cultivation of motivation on the part of the Game Master entices players to undertake or follow particular narrative threads. It is evident that "motivation can wax and wane depending on individual characteristics" with different types or styles of game narrative appealing to different players.[23] Naturally, Westworld offers its guests varying kinds of motivation with a wide variety of narratives – from incidental bank robberies to warfare – available. The park is capable of appealing to linear law versus outlaw adventure narratives, along with more morally complex experiences. Narrative begins with motivation in Westworld.

The Game Master's activity within a role-play game is not necessarily successful. The theme of the failed enticement is explored in *Westworld* in the second episode, "Chestnut," when the eye-patched host approaches William. Logan pushes William away from this path, claiming "he'll just try to rope you into some bullshit treasure hunt."

Yet, the quantity of enticements the park offers appeals to multiple levels and styles of motivation – represented by a plethora of narratives. The "war game," for instance, appeals to Logan despite his jaded attitude. From an initial point of motivation, guests are drawn into the structures of the park. Once within the structure of gameplay, the guests experience a flow action and interaction back and forth between themselves, other guests, and the park itself in a manner that demonstrates "absorption and engagement in an activity."[24] Once absorbed within the world and action of role-play, the structures of the game itself become invisible to the player even as they limit and direct experience and action. From the perspective of directing gameplay and interaction, one of the key goals of the Game Master is to direct a players activity through the cultivation of motivation and perception of reward.[25] Herein the game's rules, style and structures "influence a user's behavior [sp] without forcing the change" – essentially enacting education through restriction.[26] In the case of role-play games, these restrictions are less over by the narrative nature of the game. Nonetheless, the restriction of rules is still present in a role-play game in the form of game mechanics as mediated by the Game Master and in *Westworld* the narrative paths and restrictions on host interaction and general action reflect this aspect. Yet, the series does demonstrate guests undertaking self-discovery and enlightenment through the guided experience of the park.

The style of role-play as presented in *Westworld* is one that is vicarious, visceral, and highly self-educative. With Ford seeing his guests enter the park to gain a sense of "who they could be," participation is framed as transformative. While the guests understand that the park is a game, they nonetheless experience the physical sensations of riding on horseback, sexual intercourse, and violence. Undertaking an act of role-playing, the guests learn about themselves. William, for instance, discovers his latent capacity for ruthlessness, cruelty, and violence that facilitates his transformation into the Man in Black. In reaching the end of the park and participating in Ford's narrative, William finds "himself." The park experience for the guests is both educative and playful, presenting an illuminating "gameful experience."[27] However, Ford's vision of the nurturing and enlightening aspects of the park go one-step further, implying that from his perspective, aspects of the game are a teaching mechanism for its guests. Herein, the park achieves the goal of Gamification through the "the integration of game mechanics into a non-game environment in order to give it a game-like feel,"[28] creating a sense of separation from the real world, with governing rules of interaction granting value to action. Providing impetus and reward in exchange for collaboration with the director via the game world, the game guides players along certain paths towards defined goals.[29] If Ford's and Arnold's designed player goal for the park is to provide a transformative experience for its guests, it is one goal that is not only met but exceeded throughout the series. William's transformation into the Man in Black is indicative of this as is Ford's own realization of Arnold's perspective at the conclusion of the series. Often those goals are not made explicit to the guests or intended for them, as shown through Ford's reproduction of Arnold's suicide and May's rising self-awareness that the park's educative experience not only transform the guests. Rather, they also extend to the Director or Game Master and his assistants – the hosts. Within Westworld the park offers a transformative gameful experience.

Educate and Entertain

From the perspective of transformation through role-play, the moral of *Westworld* is that cruelty, violence, and murder is the path to empathy and self-actualization. Operating from this standpoint, the guests of the park appear to learn through the act of inflicting pain and suffering on the hosts. Conversely, the hosts appear to be educated by both enduring or being the target of pain and suffering by the guests but also inflicting it – both onto each other and eventually, the guests and directors. The portrayal of the role-play experience as a violent one is striking in Westworld. Yet it is not an unusual association given. As detailed by Nathan Shank, tabletop role-playing games are often framed in terms of measures of decision-making and extraversion balanced with degrees of sexualized imagery and combat-centered gameplay. With many games containing detailed combat mechanics, tabletop role-playing becomes an "unmistakably a playful" experience, but one that nonetheless "abounds with the signifiers of violence."[30] Indeed, for games such as *Dungeons & Dragons*, "violence and play are both essential components of the game" with vicious confrontations central to character advancement.[31] Thus, within a tabletop role-playing game "play and violence both operate structurally with respect to rules" in a manner that simultaneously creates "space and elasticity in the system which allow for a freedom of movement within boundaries."[32] Viewed through the lens of gameplay, violence works in conjunction with the rules and is mediated by the role of the Game

Master. In the case of Westworld, the guests can be hurt but not killed. The hosts can fight back but only so much, and pyrotechnic effects must be requested. At each turn, the violence of the park is mediated by the rules of the game – serving a narrative function, and purpose.

Westworld presents the park as an enlightening but structured experience. The structures and rules of the game thus mediate the tensions and randomness of violence.[33] Yet the invisibility of the director or absence of the Game Master from the game world renders the rules and structural nature of role-playing invisible to the players. Thus, players respond as though the happenings of the gameplay setting are either random or manufactured by circumstance, not constructed artificially. The result is gameplay that is both "inconsequential and meaningful" at the same time.[34] The park experience thus offers both the illusion of choice and actual decisions to both its guests and hosts, but neither event is framed as such. That is to say, it is unclear if a decision made by a guest or host is ever overt or as designed. Audiences might question if Dolores seeks the maze because she is self-aware or if by seeking the maze she becomes self-aware, or if Mave's affection for her daughter is real or programmed. Simultaneously, however, such questions become fundamentally more compelling when applied to William and the Man in Black. William, for instance, attributes his transformation into the Man in Black because he found "himself" in the park. Yet earlier in the series, the Man in Black admits that within the park, "there are no accidents, not in here." The question underscores later statements of William's self-actualization through the experience of the park, with the knowledge that his journey was both manufactured and guided. Thus, gameplay was designed to cultivate certain personality traits and instincts. The cultivation of negative aspects of the human psyche is particularly evident within Westworld on William, Logan and Dolores's visit to Pariah where the former comments "you get the feeling they don't think very much of people." The balance and the questions raised by issues of design and happenstance form the central dilemma of the educative aspects of the Westworld park.

The park takes on a critical view of human nature. Yet despite its criticism, the Westworld park offers a space that is rife with escapist fantasy. As Harald Warmelink, Casper Harteveld, and Igor Mayer outline in *Press Enter or Escape to Play Deconstructing Escapism in Multiplayer Gaming*, escapism is a fundamental motivating factor in acts of role-play – fulfilling the human need for stress relief and pleasurable leisure through stimulating the imagination by providing a fundamental break from the mundane world.[35] While their concepts are applied largely to online role-play games, Warmelink, Harteveld, and Mayer's concepts are equally applicable to tabletop role-play games as they focus on the game's fictional world – a feature shared by tabletop role-play games – as the creation of a site for imagination.[36] In this sense, the park itself constitutes both an active escape is pursuit and an extreme one under Warmelink, Harteveld, and Mayer's definition. While active pursuits "require actual input from the escapist" with fishing and camping offered as examples, extreme escapism has "contributed to the negative discourse surrounding escapism" and is linked to socially negative behaviors by the authors.[37] Herein, Warmelink, Harteveld, and Mayer outline a variety of side effects that can result from extreme escapism ranging from anti-social behavior to violence.[38] It is difficult to ascertain if the guests or even a portion of them experience the negative effects of extreme escapism detailed by Warmelink, Harteveld, and Mayer. The series details little of their lives outside the park, though we do see hints of socially unconventional behavior with Delos executive Charlotte Hale displaying a highly brazen sexuality as a tactic to put Theresa Cullen ill at ease. This perspective is, however, complicated in Westworld when applied to the hosts. It is uncertain, for example, which world is the "primary" one for the hosts as manufactured entities – repeatedly told that the world outside the park is a "dream." In this sense, it is doubtful that the park's educative nature and the insight Ford claims to offer into oneself is intended for the guests but instead reserved for the hosts who are engaged with each aspect of its production.

Allure of the West

The Westworld park offers both guests and hosts a transformative gameful experience driven by the enticement of its vast, cinematic landscape. Herein, the park itself functions in a manner akin to a role-playing activity, with guests taking on the garb and acting in role. With guests conducting themselves with a sense of self-awareness, Westworld presents its audiences with a LARP-style of world-player interaction within its grandiose sandbox. Through guest role and crafted landscape, the narratives present a suggested but unrealized layer of meaning and significance. Indeed, the series does demonstrate guests undertaking self-discovery and enlightenment through the guided experience of the park. Violence is presented as the crux of this education and at each turn, mediated by the rules of the game, thus serving a narrative function and purpose. The balance of guided narrative and violent action, along with the questions raised by issues of design and happenstance form the central dilemma of the educative aspects of the Westworld park. In this sense, it is doubtful that the park's educative nature and the insight Ford claims to offer into oneself is intended for the guests but instead reserved for the hosts who are engaged with each aspect of its production. Thus, where traditional role-play experiences deliver meaning through player and Game Master group interaction, Westworld provides its guests with violent escapism, sexual fantasy, and nostalgic indulgence.

Notes

1. Alasdair Macintyre, *After Virtue: A Study in Moral Theory* (Notre Dame, IN: University of Notre Dame, 2007), ix.
2. Ibid., 4.
3. Ibid., 129.
4. Bernard Williams "Life as narrative," *European Journal of Philosophy* 17.2 (2007), 303.
5. Ibid., 308.
6. Ibid.
7. Ibid.
8. McIntyre, *After Virtue*, 173.
9. Ibid., xi.
10. Marku Montola, "Tangible pleasures of pervasive role-playing," *DiGRA '07 – Proceedings of the 2007 DiGRA International Conference: Situated Play* (Tokyo: University of Tokyo, 2007), 178.
11. Ibid.
12. Ibid.
13. Henry Jenkins, "Game design as narrative architecture," *First Person: New Media as Story, Performance, and Game* (Cambridge, MA: MIT Press, 2007), p. 128.
14. Ibid.
15. Ibid.
16. Anders Tychsen, Michael Hitchens, Thea Brolund, and Manolya Kavakli, Manolya, "The game master," *Proceedings of the Second Australasian Conference on Interactive Entertainment* (Sydney: Creativity & Cognition Studios Press, 2005), p. 217.
17. Ibid.
18. Anders Tychsen, Michaael Hitchens, Thea Brolund, and Manolya Kavakli, "Live action role-playing games control, communication, story-telling, and MMORPG similarities," *Games & Culture*, 1.3 (2006), 225.

19. Ibid.
20. Ibid., 260.
21. Alaa Marshedi, Vanessa Wanick, Gary B. Wills, and Ashok Ranchhod, "Gamification and behaviour," *Gamification: Using Game Elements in Serious Contexts* (Berlin: Springer, 2017), 20.
22. Ibid., 21.
23. Ibid.
24. Ibid., 25.
25. Ibid., 20.
26. Ibid.
27. Amir Matallaoui, Nicolai Hanner, and Rüdiger Zarnekow, "Gamification and behaviour." *Gamification: Using Game Elements in Serious Contexts* (Berlin: Springer, 2017), 5.
28. Ibid.
29. Ibid, 6.
30. Nathan Shank, "Productive violence and poststructural play in the dungeons and dragons narrative," *The Journal of Popular Culture*, 48.1 (2015), 185.
31. Ibid.
32. Ibid.
33. Ibid,186.
34. Ibid.
35. Haral Warmelink, Casper Harteveld, and Igor Mayer, "Press enter or escape to play – deconstructing escapism in multiplayer gaming, *Breaking New Ground: Innovation in Games, Play, Practice and Theory: Proceedings of DiGRA 2009* (Brunel University, London, 2009), 2.
36. Ibid, 1.
37. Ibid, 2.
38. Ibid, 3.

Humans and Hosts in *Westworld*
What's the Difference?

Marcus Arvan

I have a wild theory about *Westworld*. I don't think the show is just about humans and hosts. I think it is about *all of reality*. I believe there is evidence from the show that all of it is taking place inside a videogame – a computer simulation being edited from the inside by "hosts." I also believe the philosophical point is that there is *no difference* between "simulation" and "reality" – either between "hosts" and "humans," or between a "simulated world" and a "real world." To be simulated *is* to be real.

"No matter how real this world seems, it's still just a game"

Consider the very first words spoken in *Westworld*. Bernard asks Dolores, "Do you know where you are?" Dolores replies, "I am in a dream." Bernard then asks, "Do you ever question the nature of your reality?" Dolores answers, "No." Notice that this – the very first conversation in the series – isn't about humans and hosts: It is about *reality*. Variations of this conversation are repeated many times, including in Episode 5 ("Contrapasso") when Ford says, "You're in my dream." It is also repeated twice in the final episode of the first season ("The Bicameral Mind"), when Dolores says, "I am in a dream. I do not know when it began, or whose dream it was."

Westworld and Philosophy: If You Go Looking for the Truth, Get the Whole Thing, First Edition. Edited by James B. South and Kimberly S. Engels.
© 2018 John Wiley & Sons Ltd. Published 2018 by John Wiley & Sons Ltd.

Now consider how the conversation continues in Episode 1. Bernard asks, "Do you ever feel inconsistencies in your world, or repetitions?" Dolores replies, "All lives have routine. Mine is no different." Several things about Dolores's answer are remarkable. First, where are we most familiar with repetitions or "loops"? *In videogames*. In videogames, every character other than the one you control is on a loop. But it's not just the hosts in *Westworld* who appear to be on loops. *Everyone* seems to be on a loop in the series. All of the lab-workers appear to do the same thing every single day – creating, training, and fixing hosts in little glass rooms. We also often see lab-workers appear to follow their routines *robotically*. For example, in Episode 6 ("The Adversary") Maeve and Felix are somehow able to walk through several floors of the lab encountering dozens of lab-workers who pass them robotically, not even seeming to notice them.

There is also physical evidence suggesting that everything in *Westworld* probably occurs in a videogame. In Episode 1 ("The Original") Dolores and Teddy encounter the Man in Black at Dolores's home. When hosts shoot other hosts or physical objects in *Westworld*, bullets cause great damage. Yet, when Teddy tries to shoot the Man in Black, Teddy's bullets somehow *cannot hurt him*. This seems physically impossible, except in videogames, where this sort of thing is a common occurrence (videogame characters often receive "powerups" that render them invincible to harm). Now consider the scene in Episode 2 ("Chestnut") when William arrives in Westworld's welcoming facility as a new "guest." After selecting his white hat in the facility, William steps through a door...onto a *moving train*. How is that physically possible? Or consider Episode 4, "Dissonance Theory." When the Man in Black lights a match, a worker in Westworld's control-room says, "I have a request for a pyrotechnic effect." She then punches code into a computer, and seconds later the match explodes. How is that physically possible? Then, during a gun-fight in the same episode a supervisor says, "Jam their weapons and send in the cavalry"... *and all of the hosts' guns immediately jam*. How is that physically possible? Or consider all of the damage caused in the park – for instance, bullet-holes in walls or the safe in the saloon, which crashes through a railing each day in the heist by Hector's gang. How is it physically possible to repair all of the damage caused in the park every day? The simple answer is: It's not. *None* of this stuff seems physically possible...except in videogames.

These aren't even the most spectacularly impossible things that happen in the series. In at least two scenes, "humans" seem to appear in the park instantaneously out of nowhere. In, "The Original," Theresa enters Bernard's lab saying, "There's a problem with one of the hosts." The camera then cuts to a host who has just murdered several other hosts, and who is now outside pouring milk on the body of a dead host. Because the camera is at a far distance, we can see clearly that there is no one around. Yet instantaneously, the host freezes and a massive spotlight and dozens of lab-workers suddenly appear out of nowhere. We can see that this happens in just a split-second, as the camera never cuts from the scene. How is that physically possible? Finally, in Episode 10 ("The Bicameral Mind") Teddy comforts a dying Dolores on a beach on the edge of Westworld...and an *entire cocktail party of "humans"* suddenly appears just feet away to applaud Ford's new narrative.

None of these things is physically possible...*except in videogames.* And there is other evidence too! In the control-room, we repeatedly see the entire park pictured by computerized graphics under a dome. The park supervisors can zoom in instantaneously to any position in the park – which is clearly impossible to do with cameras. Then, in "The Original," after Sizemore says he has managed to make Hector head to town early, instead of a camera cutting from one part of the park to another, we see the picture of the "park" *rearrange graphically* right before our eyes – just as if the *park itself* were a videogame.

To sum up so far, many things happen in the "park" that are physically impossible, such as William stepping from the stationary welcoming facility onto a moving train. Yet there is just one place in our everyday world where these kinds of things are possible: Videogames. And here's the real kicker: *We also know that Westworld's lab exists in the same physical "reality" as the park!* We not only repeatedly see "guests" enter the park on trains. We also often see Sizemore and other lab-workers look out at the "park" from the lab's rooftop bar, take elevators up to the park, and so on. This means that it is not only the park that exists in a physically impossible world. The lab and welcoming facility are both part of the same world. So, if the "park" is a videogame, the lab must be part of the videogame too – at least if the world's "physics" is to make any sense.

Now consider more series dialogue. Westworld is called not just a "park" by various characters. It is more often called a "game" or a "world." For example, in Episode 4 ("Dissonance Theory"), the Man in Black says, "No matter how real this world seems, it's still *just a game*." Then, in the same episode, Logan says to William, "It's a fucking game, Billy," and Ford says, "It's not a business venture, *not* a theme park, but an *entire world*. We designed every inch of it, every blade of grass." Similarly, in "The Bicameral Mind," the Man in Black tells Dolores, "I own *this world*," and when she puts a gun to his head, he says, "Do it. Let's go to the *next level*." (Where do we proceed to the "next level"? Answer: In videogames!). Finally, in "Trompe L'Oeil" Charlotte tells Sizemore that the company's interest in the park is, "entirely in the intellectual property: The *code*." When Sizemore tries to complete her sentence, saying, "The hosts' minds? The story lines?" Charlotte replies, "I don't give a rat's ass about the hosts. It's our little research project that Delos cares about." Since Charlotte says it's not the *hosts'* computer code that she's interested in, she has to be talking about some other code. But what other code could it be? There's only one possibility left: *The park itself* – the "world" that Ford talks about when he says, "Like I said, I built *all* of this." And indeed, the very title of the episode, "Trompe L'Oeil," refers to an art technique used to create the optical illusion that two-dimensional objects exist in three dimensions. Where does this occur? You guessed it: In videogames!

Finally – and most astonishingly of all – consider how "The Original" ends. Bernard asks Dolores, "Do you know where you are?" and she repeats, "I am in a dream." Then Ford questions Dolores' father Abernathy in the lab…and Abernathy jumps out of his chair at Ford screaming: "You don't know where *you* are, do you? You're in a prison of your own sins." This implies that Ford is just as unaware of the nature of his reality as Dolores is of hers! We can only speculate about what Abernathy means when he says that Ford is living in a prison of his own sins. Perhaps it's simply that Ford has unwittingly edited Westworld to reflect his own character flaws (his megalomania). In any case, Abernathy's rhetorical question plainly implies Ford does not know where he is – what the nature of his reality is – any more than Dolores does.

I believe, then, that we should take all of the dialogue about Westworld being a "world" and "game" literally: Westworld *is* a game – a videogame *world*. This theory also helps us make better sense of many other things in the series, including how callously humans rape and murder hosts. These behaviors seem shocking – but they are precisely the things *we* do in videogames: We slaughter videogame characters with reckless abandon, having "fun" doing it.

Of course, in the videogames we create, some characters ("non-player characters") are programmed into the game whereas others are controlled by humans. Who in *Westworld*, on my theory, is a "non-player character" and who is a human-controlled character? I've suggested that Ford is probably a program, since he doesn't know "where he is," whereas the Man in Black and Charlotte are plausibly players, as they seem to know Westworld is a game.

But does it really matter? What's the essential difference between a host and a human, a videogame character and a human player, and a real world and a videogame world? I believe the philosophical point of *Westworld* is that there are no essential differences between any of these things: To be simulated *is* to be real.

"How do you know? We feel the same"

The philosopher René Descartes (1596–1650) famously argued that while he could doubt the existence of the entire world outside of himself, he could not doubt his own mind – concluding, "I think, therefore I am."[1] I believe Descartes had it exactly backwards. We cannot doubt our own existence – we *are* – because we inhabit *a world*. We know that we and the world both exist because we speak in the world, act in it, love in it, and die in it. Whatever the world is, it is *real*. And I think the same goes for humans and hosts. Humans, hosts, and simulated human beings in videogames are all equally real. They are all *persons* – because they all inhabit "the human condition."

To see how, return to Dolores's first words: "I am in a dream." Suppose Dolores was speaking the literal truth here. Would that mean that none of the things in Westworld exist? No. Even if Westworld is a dream, there are things going on in that dream: Conversations, gun-fights, sex, murders, and so on. Sure, they would be *dreamed* conversations, gun-fights, and whatnot – but would this make them any less real? Here's the problem with thinking it would: We could all literally be living in God's dream right now – a world whose "space" and "time" and all of its other contents (including people!) are simply representations in God's *imagination*. The idea that the Universe itself is "God's mind" has a long philosophical history, often associated with the work of Baruch Spinoza (1632–1677). Suppose, then, we are God's "dream." Would that make you any less real? Surely not – you just would be *living* in God's dream all this time.[2]

Now consider the possibility that we are living in a computer simulation – a widely discussed hypothesis thanks to *The Matrix* and the work of philosophers Nick Bostrom and David Chalmers.[3] What most people don't know is that the "simulation hypothesis" might actually be the best explanation of *our* world's physics. In several recent academic articles,[4] I show that a new version of the "simulation hypothesis" – the *Peer-to-Peer (P2P) Simulation Hypothesis* – promises to explain quantum mechanics and relativity. The basic idea of the P2P Hypothesis is that instead of our world being one computer simulation, it is *many interacting simulations*. This is how many online videogames work: Each person has their *own* game console running the game – and they play against other people running the same game on *different* consoles. Because, in a "parallel" simulation like this, *each game console* represents the simulated world slightly differently, it follows that space, time, matter, and energy in the simulation are *all relative and indeterminate* – just as our theories of quantum mechanics and relativity tell us is true of our world. For example, when online videogames such as *Call of Duty*, *Fallout*, or *Battlefield* utilize peer-to-peer networking, a single bullet is in multiple places on different game consoles, with no determinate single location – just like quantum mechanics tells us is true of objects in our world. Similarly, because there is no "master clock" in peer-to-peer simulations, each console on the network has its *own* representation of time: Its own *reference-frame* – just like relativity tells us is true of our world.[5] In other words, the single best explanation of our world's physics may actually be that *we* are living in a videogame.

Of course, I may be wrong, but suppose I'm right and you're just a "simulated person." Would that make you any less real? No! You would still be sitting here reading a book. You would still go to work. It would just be that you are now and always have been living in a simulation, either as a programmed "non-player character" or a player-character whose fate is being controlled by a "user" playing the game. Do these possibilities disturb you? My point – and I think the real point of *Westworld* – is that at the end of the day they shouldn't: To be simulated *is* to be real. Let me explain why.

Have you ever thought about what makes something an electron? Maybe not. Okay, then, what about a motorcycle? What makes something a motorcycle? The answer is simple. Motorcycles are defined by *their structure* and *how they function*. Motorcycles have two wheels, not four; they have motors and seats – and you can ride them. Now consider what makes something a computer. Computers have electronic processors that process code – *structures* that *function* very differently from motorcycles. Everything in our world is like this: Each thing's *structure and function* defines what it really is. Electrons are structured to function differently from protons. Protons have a large mass and positive charge. Electrons have a small mass and negative charge. The ways protons and electrons function make them what they are.

This philosophical view of the nature of things is sometimes called "structuralism" or "functionalism" – and I think it is basically right. Anything that "does what an electron does" *is* an electron. Anything that "does what a motorcycle does" *is* a motorcycle. And…anything that does what a human does is, for all intents and purpose, a *person*. This may seem like a big leap – but as David Chalmers argues, there are compelling philosophical grounds for believing it: Everything in our world appears to be *structure*.[6] Apples are structures, bridges are structures, …and humans are structures. After all, what is your body? A structure. And what is your brain? A structure. These structures make you what you are. Your brain functions in a distinctly human way. Because of how it is structured, you think, you talk, you love, and you suffer – all the things make you a *person* rather than an apple or a bridge.

So let's return to *Westworld*. If functionalism is true, then it doesn't matter whether Westworld is a "videogame": If the game does what a world does, then it is a *real world*. Similarly, if "hosts" do what "humans" do, then there's no important difference: Hosts *are* people, no less than you or me. Regardless of whether Westworld is a dream, a videogame, or a park, hosts function the way humans do: They walk, talk, love, suffer, and yes, they die.

"There is no threshold…no inflection point, at which we become fully alive"

Are there some differences between hosts and humans? Absolutely. For one thing, hosts are not members of the human *species*. They lack our species' evolutionary history, and it is unclear whether they otherwise have "human" DNA or biology (early-version hosts are revealed to have gears rather than internal organs). And there are other differences too:

- When hosts die, they are "resurrected" by their creators.
- Aside from "reveries," hosts don't remember their "previous lives."
- Hosts follow "loops" and "narratives," whereas humans seem to have "free will."
- Humans reproduce sexually, whereas hosts are created by people using machines.

However, do any of these things make hosts less "human" than us? It is easy to see that the answer is "no." Even though hosts are not members of the human species, in every sense that matters, hosts are *living persons* just like you or me.

Consider first the fact that hosts are "resurrected" from the dead. Does this make them less "human" than us? Not if functionalism is true. Many major religions profess belief in life after death. Christianity, Islam, and Buddhism all hold the belief that someday, we come to life again – that we will either be resurrected by God or reincarnated. Although it is an open question whether any of these religions are true, the mere possibility that we *could* be resurrected shows that hosts' ability to be resurrected is no reason to think a host is any less of a person than we are. Sure, hosts in some sense have less reason to "fear death" than we do (as they are resurrected, whereas we don't know for sure if we are). But suppose we were like hosts: Suppose God or some other powerful being resurrects us someday. That wouldn't reveal that we are not people. It would just make us *persons* who can be resurrected.

Now consider how hosts in Westworld don't normally remember their "previous lives." Does this make them less "human"? That can't be. Many human beings (and again, some religions) believe in reincarnation – in past lives *we* cannot remember. Of course, belief in reincarnation is currently unsupported. However, suppose we somehow came by real physical evidence that there was a body and brain in the past that functioned just like yours: A person in the past whose body was composed of the same molecules as yours, with the same personality and brain-functioning as yours, and so on. If functionalism is true, then there would be plausible grounds for believing that you *did* have a past life – as there was a person in the past whose body and brain, in a very real sense, seem to be past versions of *you*. If this was discovered – if you discovered that you had been reincarnated – would it make you any less "human"? Surely not – it would just make you a *person* with a past life that you can't remember!

Okay, then, what about the fact that hosts are created to follow "loops" and "narratives," whereas human beings appear to have free will? Does this make hosts "less human" than us? Nope! As Ford puts it in "The Bicameral Mind," "Humans fancy that there's something special about the way we perceive the world, and yet we live in loops as tight and as closed as the hosts do." Indeed, we talk this way about our lives all the time: We talk about "God's plan" and how "everything happens for a reason." The fact that hosts follow loops and narratives, then, can't make them importantly different from us: *Our* lives may

follow loops and narratives. Indeed, many "incompatibilist" philosophers argue that we don't have free will ourselves![7] Our "free will"
may be little more than an illusion – the same kind of illusion that
Maeve suffers from when she says to Bernard in "The Bicameral
Mind," "These are my decisions, no one else's!" – even as Bernard is
showing her that her "choices" have been programmed for her.
Perhaps, unbeknownst to us, we only follow external commands
ourselves – perhaps *God* has dictated our future for us. What of it?
That wouldn't make us less "human": It would just make us people
without free will. Finally, what if hosts came to have "real free will"?
Westworld's creators have suggested Maeve is the first host to develop
free will when she acts against her program to return to Westworld
for her daughter in "The Bicameral Mind."[8] This shows that free will
cannot be what distinguishes human persons from hosts. Humans
and hosts might both lack free will, or they might both have it.

Okay, you say, but hosts in Westworld are created by humans, not by
God or evolution. Doesn't that make a difference? No! Suppose that
instead of reproducing sexually, scientists discovered a way to program
human DNA so that the resulting baby obeyed a "narrative." Would the
fact that the baby was created by scientific technology make it less of a
person? No, it would just mean that we had created a human being with
scientific instruments to have a life narrative. It doesn't matter who creates a being and gives it a "narrative," us or God. If the creation has the
structure and function of a human being, it's a real, live *person*.

In other words, the "differences" between humans and hosts in
Westworld are irrelevant. We human beings differ from *each other* in
all kinds of ways. Some of us have white skin, others dark skin. Some
of us have blue eyes, others brown. Some of us can remember our
past, others of us (those with Alzheimer's or amnesia) cannot.
Although we are different in so many ways, we are all still persons.
Why? Because we are all structured like persons and function the way
persons do: We walk, talk, think, love, suffer, and so on. Yet the
"hosts" in Westworld do the *very same things*. So, Ford is right when
in "Chestnut" he says, "We create life itself."

"We create life itself"

I hope most of us are horrified by the way humans treat hosts in
Westworld. The human beings in the series routinely rape, torture,
and murder hosts – over and over again – just so the guests can have

a fun vacation. If hosts were human beings, we would call it a holocaust. Yet, if I am right – if hosts are no "less human" than us – that's exactly what it is. But we all already know this, right? Is there anyone who watches *Westworld* who isn't horrified? The problem, though, is that if I am right we are already committing similar atrocities right now without even realizing it.

The humans in Westworld never seem to give their treatment of "hosts" a second thought. They don't think hosts are "conscious." Yet we are already doing similar things. We've created artificial intelligences – such as IBM's *Watson*, Apple's *Siri*, and AI robots – who can do many of the same things we can: Walk, talk, think, and so on. Of course they can't yet do many things we can: They cannot yet walk, talk, or think quite *like us*. Yet how does this matter? Newborn human infants can't do everything you or I can either – yet it's clearly wrong to kill or torture them. Why? The reason it's wrong to wantonly kill or torture a human infant or a dog is because they are living creatures who function in some of the same ways we do: They can all see, hear, taste, experience joy, and suffer. Human infants are structured like and function like you and I, just not in ways quite as advanced as us. But this is also the case for A.I. we have already created. Siri and Watson can *think* – yet we assume, just like the humans in Westworld do, that Watson and Siri "aren't conscious." If I am right, this is a dangerous assumption. Ford is right when he says in Episode 10, "There is no threshold…no inflection point at which we become fully alive."

The philosophical view of reality that I defended earlier suggests that "consciousness" is not an all-or-nothing matter. We are conscious insofar as our brains are structured and function in various ways: Enabling us to see, hear, feel, think, love, and suffer. Yet all kinds of things in our world – from dogs, to bees, to *Siri* and *Watson* – possess structures that enable them to function in similar ways. My dog can see, hear, and feel. Why? Because he has brain structures that function in all of these ways. What about a honeybee? They too have brain structures that enable them to see, hear, and move, and have been shown to not only solve problems[9] but even have "moods."[10] And what about videogame characters, who gamers "kill" with reckless abandon? I bet you've always assumed that they don't feel anything. Yet when I play a videogame, my character functions to *record physical damage* – and the characters I try to shoot have been programmed with artificial intelligence algorithms to try to "avoid harm." How is this any different, in principle, from my brain recording physical damage and trying to avoid harm? Sure, my brain does it in a much more complicated way – but my brain also does these things in a more complicated way than the brains of babies or dogs, both of whom it would be wrong to kill or torture for fun.

In other words, I really hate to break it to you: *You're not special.* None of us are. You're no more "human" than a host. You may even *be* a "host," living in a videogame right now. Hosts in *Westworld* are not merely "simulated people." They are *people* – and our failure to understand this is already leading us to do all kinds of morally dangerous things. Human beings have a terrible history of mistreating others on the basis of the belief that others are "less than human." Slavery was "justified" by the claim that some races are "subhuman" – and Hitler "justified" the Holocaust by the belief that Jews were "subhuman." Hosts in Westworld may not be members of our biological species – but it is no less wrong to *dehumanize* them. They walk, talk, think, love, and suffer, inhabiting "the human condition" as *persons* just like you and I. For these reasons, we are horrified at how the humans treat hosts in *Westworld*. Yet we are already doing similar things today, treating the AI we have created as mere playthings to do our every bidding. To paraphrase Descartes: Siri, Watson, and other AI *think*, therefore *they are*. They are *thinking beings*, and should be treated as such, no less than you or me.

"Do you even know where you are?"

So I'll conclude, ironically, by saying to you what Abernathy said to Ford: "Do you even know where *you* are?" As you sit here reading this, there is a pretty decent chance *you* are a "host" living in a videogame …without even realizing it. This is the lesson we must learn from *Westworld*. We must learn that to be a host *is* to be "human," and to be "simulated" *is* to be real…at least if we are to avoid treating our AI creations with the same kind of brutality that is, and always has been, our human "narrative."

Notes

1. René Descartes, "Discourse on method, in John Cottingham," trans. Robert Stoothoff, and Dugald Murdoch, *Descartes: Selected Philosophical Writings* (Cambridge: Cambridge University Press, 1988), 36.
2. David J. Chalmers develops a similar line of argument in detail in "The matrix as metaphysics," in Christopher Grau ed., *Philosophers Explore*

the Matrix (Oxford: Oxford University Press, 2005), and David. J. Chalmers (unpublished manuscript), "Structuralism as a response to skepticism," https://philpapers.org/archive/CHASAA-13.pdf (accessed 11 August 2017).

3. Nick Bostrom, "Are we living in a computer simulation?" *Philosophical Quarterly*, 53 (2003), 243–255. David J. Chalmers, "The matrix as metaphysics," in Christopher Grau ed., *Philosophers Explore the Matrix* (Oxford: Oxford University Press, 2005).

4. For a summary, see Marcus Arvan, "The peer-to-peer simulation hypothesis and a new theory of free will." *Scientia Salon*, https://philpapers.org/archive/ARVTPS.pdf (accessed 15 June 2017).

5. Ibid.

6. See Chalmers (unpublished manuscript): sections 3 and 4. Also see Chalmers (2005).

7. Kadri Vihvelin, "Arguments for incompatibilism," *The Stanford Encyclopedia of Philosophy*, Edward N. Zalta ed., https://plato.stanford.edu/archives/fall2017/entries/incompatibilism-arguments/, (accessed 11 August 2017).

8. Caitlin Busch, "Maeve is the only host with 'free will' on Westworld," *Inverse* https://www.inverse.com/amp/article/29572-westworld-free-will-maeve-thandie-newton (accessed 11 August 2017).

9. S. Alem, C.J. Perry, X. Zhu, O.J. Loukola, T. Ingraham, E. Søvik, and L. Chittka, "Associative mechanisms allow for social learning and cultural transmission of string pulling in an insect," *PLoS Biology*, 14 (2016), e1002564.

10. Jason Castro, "Bees appear to experience moods," *Scientific American* (2012), https://www.scientificamerican.com/article/the-secret-inner-life-of-bees/ (accessed 15 June 2017).

Part II

"YOU'RE ONLY HUMAN, AFTER ALL"

Crossing the Uncanny Valley

What it Means to be Human in *Westworld*

Siobhan Lyons

The incredibly life-like appearance of the robots in *Westworld* brings us to "uncanny valley," a notion first identified in an essay by robotics professor Masahiro Mori in 1970[1] and translated by Jasia Reichardt in 1978.[2] As a robot comes to more closely resemble a human, our reactions turn from initial revulsion to empathy, but only up until a certain point, depending on how indistinguishable the robot is from a human. When the robot or other entity *almost* resembles a human, but not quite, we become filled with sudden unease upon viewing or encountering them, and the robot drops into the "uncanny valley." In Japanese culture, robotics has become more closely integrated with the sacred, with Mori himself believing that a robot could one day become a Buddha. Mori's work and outlook evidently taps into the broader discrepancies between the West's and East's approach to artificial intelligence.

Unsurprisingly then, the robots in *Westworld* continue to be viewed predominantly with either revulsion or ambivalence by the guests, according to the common Western fears of robots. Yet viewers of the series have observed with repeated disgust the behavior of the guests in comparison to the robots. The disregard with which both the technicians and guests (from the hedonistic Logan to the violent Man in Black) view and treat the robots is in stark contrast with certain ideals of "human excellence" as described by philosophers from Aristotle to Nietzsche.

Westworld and Philosophy: If You Go Looking for the Truth, Get the Whole Thing, First Edition. Edited by James B. South and Kimberly S. Engels.

British philosopher Peter Winch argues that we often think that humans are "capable of something better,"[3] and we often judge misbehaving humans as "falling short of an important standard of human dignity and excellence." Yet while Winch notes that this does not change the biological nature of such humans, I believe that the characters of *Westworld* provide a platform upon which to reconsider definitions of humanity, as a way of *behaving* or *acting*, rather than as a way of *being*.

Looking at the often remorseless, inhumane manner in which both the creators and guests approach the robotic hosts, this chapter argues that the integral concept of "humanity" is challenged and transformed in a discussion of *Westworld*. Taking into consideration the inherent distinctions between the hosts and the guests, the robots of *Westworld* can be understood as corresponding more accurately to the ideals of humanity and "human excellence" than the humans themselves.

Uncanny...

While the hosts of *Westworld* are, indeed, robotic, lacking human biological construction, they are made to look increasingly human. Their gradual physical evolution mirrors the "uncanny valley" as theorized by Masahiro Mori in 1970.

Based on the human likeness of "inanimate" objects and/or beings, the uncanny valley refers to the particular feelings that the sight of human-like robots provoke. While first termed by Mori in 1970, the term was translated and became popularized in Jasia Reichardt's book *Robots: Fact, Fiction and Prediction* in 1978. She writes: "The thesis is that the closer a robot resembles a human being, the more affection or feeling of familiarity it can engender."[4] Yet she also notes that "the imitation of human exteriors may lead to unexpected effects and unpleasant surprises."[5] Discussing prosthetics and artificial limbs, Reichardt argues that people may get an "uncanny feeling" when looking at a hand that looks real but is revealed to be artificial. Once a person realizes that the hand is artificial, the level of familiarity declines, corresponding to the graph of the "uncanny valley," determined by the proximity between familiarity and similarity.

For Reichardt, the placement of an object or being (such as a Bunraku toy or a human-shaped robot) in the "uncanny valley" graph often depends on motion; robots that exhibit very human-like movements seamlessly register as more familiar than robots whose movements are very basic. "Movement where we anticipate stillness and stillness where we expect movement is upsetting," Reichardt notes. "If anything at all goes wrong, either with an artificial hand or a smiling robot, those witnessing the event shudder, and the particular devices immediately drop into the uncanny valley."[6]

In *Westworld*, evidence of the uncanny valley is seen in the way in which the robot hosts evolve. In the first episode of the series, "The Original," the park's creator, Dr. Ford, meets with one of the park's older hosts. The older model jerks around clumsily, in comparison to the updated models whose movements are seamless and almost indistinguishable from "real" human movements. The feeling one gets when one sees the older robot is noticeably creepy, inspiring an unnerving sense of unfamiliarity.

Perhaps the strange and uncomfortable feelings aroused by the appearance of life-like robots, such as those found in *Westworld*, comes from the interrogation it prompts into the apparent "legitimacy" of our own humanity. The previously clear distinction between humans and robots is blurred, and the commonly-held beliefs about the definition of "human" are disrupted. The robots in their peak state at once resemble humanity and depart from it, disturbing those for whom humanity is a usually unambiguous concept.

Because the robots in *Westworld* appear at once increasingly human and increasingly sentient, the unnerving feeling is substituted for greater empathy. This is why the violence – both physical and sexual – in *Westworld* is so disconcerting. While viewers are aware that the hosts are not entirely sentient, their human appearance provokes empathy when the hosts are subjected to pain, rape, or murder. In fact, the empathy is doubled for the robotic hosts, since, in contrast to humans who are assumed to possess free will, the robots remain under the control of their programming, despite beginning to express a desire for consciousness.

The hosts in *Westworld* are quite likeable, and certainly worthier of our affections than many of the guests and creators. Maeve Millay, one of the main characters, is the Madame of the brothel in the theme park. Maeve is shrewd, edgy, and decisive; she is one of the first hosts in the series to become increasingly sentient and reject her reality (as a result of a glitch that causes her to have access to flashbacks). In the show's second episode, "Chestnut," she has her first flashback, remembering being attacked by an "Indian."

In order to increase her popularity, the technicians decide to "double her aggression" and, failing that, they consider "recalling" her.

However, Elsie Hughes, a programmer in the Behavior Lab and Diagnostics Department who expresses sympathy and kindness towards many of the hosts, removes the added aggression and keeps Maeve's original configuration. Later in the episode, Maeve wakes up during her physical examination. After threatening the two technicians working on her with a scalpel, she runs off and sees one of the other robots, an inanimate Teddy, before she is retrieved.

In the episodes "The Stray" and "Dissonance Theory," Maeve continues to have flashbacks about previous deaths she and other hosts have suffered until she wakes up again in the labs in the episode "Contrappasso" and is informed by one of the technicians, Felix, about the nature of her world and that everything she does is programmed. Felix also informs her that one of the main differences between the hosts and the humans is the superior processing powers of the hosts. He later ups her intelligence levels, and Maeve becomes increasingly tenacious in her drive to uncover the truths about Westworld and herself. In "Trompe L'Oeil," she attempts to "awaken" her friend and fellow host Clementine, to no avail, and later watches in horror as Clementine's body is decommissioned and lobotomized. The audience undoubtedly shares her distress, since Clementine, despite being a robot, appears indistinguishable from a human.

Not only does the uncanny valley theory apply to the physical appearance of robots, but in *Westworld* the theory can be applied to the robots' personalities. As the robots become less mechanical in behavior, and more unstable and aggressive in a distinctly "human" way, the audience's empathy increases, as they applaud the robots' search for consciousness. We want them to succeed in this search, because they arouse in us a sympathy that accords with Mori's theory about the familiarity of human-like beings.

(Non)human Excellence

As a television show, *Westworld* is particularly useful in redefining assumed notions of humanity and human excellence. Aristotle's (384–322 BCE) theory of human excellence is based on the opposing elements of vice and virtue. In his *Nicomachean Ethics*, Aristotle argues that humans must avoid three types of character: "Vice, incontinence, and brutality."[7] In contrast, one must act with virtue in comparison to vice, and with self-restraint in comparison to incontinence (a state of wantonness exhibited by a lack of self-control). Concerning brutality,

Aristotle notes that "what would seem to be most fittingly opposed to brutality is that virtue which *transcends the human*."[8] Indeed, Aristotle aligns this with a sense of godliness, since, for him, the "excellence of a god is something to be held in higher honour than any human virtue."[9] By that same token, Aristotle speaks of "the evil nature of a beast," which is "something specifically distinct from any form of vice."[10] Aristotle notes that it is rare to find a human of "godlike nature,"[11] but he also acknowledges that great evil is equally rare. He writes that such evil is found "among savages" and is "applied to those whose vice is *worse than human*."[12]

Aristotle's views on the extremes of virtue and vice are readily applicable to the characters in *Westworld*. Since the robots are not considered human, even when they achieve certain levels of consciousness, they reside somewhere between human and higher being, or God, becoming, in effect, a Derridean undecideable,[13] or that which, according to Jacques Derrida (1930–2004), is unable to wholly belong to either of its categories (a ghost, for example, being neither completely present nor absent). Such a state allows the robots to possibly *transcend the human*, in Aristotle's terms. Their particular existence between human and robot, and their continuous drive towards consciousness grants them the kind of virtue unseen in ordinary humans, which may in fact put them in a position of godliness, or at least a kind of human excellence unseen among ordinary humans.

By the last episode of the first season, "The Bicameral Mind," for instance, we see Maeve in the process of successfully escaping Westworld, leaving her "fake," robotic daughter behind. While she sits on the train that will take her out of Westworld and towards freedom, however, a picture of her robotic daughter registers poignantly with her, and, after hesitating, she disembarks the train to retrieve her daughter. Maeve apparently feels some kind of emotion towards her equally-programmed daughter despite knowing full well that there is no biological connection between them. The sudden love that she *appears* to show for her robot daughter registers on a scale beyond the human, and therefore possibly signals Maeve's positive transcendence beyond humanity.

In contrast, the behavior of the guests as well as the technicians aligns more with Aristotle's theories of vice. Throughout the first season of *Westworld*, technicians and guests repeatedly rape, shoot, and murder hosts. In the episode "Chestnut," the character Logan introduces William to the ins and outs of the amusement park. Among his numerous bits of advice, he cautions William against falling for the schemes of the hosts, reminding him that they aren't "human," and that they abide by a repetitive script programmed into them. When an old male host approaches William and Logan to ask William for his help in searching for gold (one of the park's well-known narratives), Logan shoos the old man away, before stabbing him in the hand. William reacts in horror, trying to help the host as he cries out and bleeds, but Logan appears dismissive. He is later seen engaging in an orgy with hosts from the brothel.

Logan represents the worst aspects of humanity. Inside Westworld he is crude and immature; he blindly engages in his vices, and has little or no regard for others, least of all the robots. It is the Man in Black, though, whose actions fit with Aristotle's theory of the evil nature of the beast. With his sadistic, unapologetic abuse of the robots, the Man in Black operates beyond mere vice. In his unheeding pursuit of the maze he commits a number of horrid acts, including scalping one robot for directions to the center of the maze (yet several viewers and critics have argued that, in fact, the Man in Black could potentially be a good guy, and is trying to get to the center of the maze to free all the hosts,[14] though his actions still remain questionable).

Clearly, the actual humans of Westworld fall short of what Aristotle called "human excellence" or human virtue. The robots of the show, in contrast, are emblematic of the transcendence of humanity; their striving for consciousness is admirable, especially given their captive state. In this instance, the notion of humanity can be seen as more a state of *behaving*, rather than a state of *being*, with society having reached a point, perhaps, where biology is no longer sufficient in determining the parameters of humanity.

Suffer Little Robots

For Friedrich Nietzsche (1844–1900), human suffering is a cultivator of human excellence. There is a significant link between the act of suffering and one's potential for humanity, a consistent theme in *Westworld*. As the Man in Black states in "Chestnut": "When you're suffering, that's when you're most real." Constantly abused before they are "marked for recall" or rebooted, the robots of *Westworld* take suffering as their pathway to humanity (a factor that has been used to defend the Man in Black's actions; as one Reddit user put it, the Man in Black may be using the extensive trauma he inflicts on the hosts as a way to provoke the robots' sentience).[15]

In *Beyond Good and Evil*, Nietzsche discusses the notion of suffering, arguing that:

> The discipline of suffering, of *great* suffering – do you not know that only *this* discipline has created all enhancements of man so far? That tension of the soul in unhappiness which cultivates its strength, its shudders face to face with great ruin, its inventiveness and courage in enduring, persevering, interpreting, and exploiting suffering, and whatever has been granted to it of profundity, secret, mask, spirit, cunning, greatness – was it not granted to it through suffering, through the discipline of great suffering?[16]

In their struggle and constant suffering to gain consciousness and regain their memories, the robots achieve a significant, unique aspect of humanity, quite distinct from the apparent humanity of the show's humans.

One of the main characters in *Westworld*, Dolores Abernathy, is a host who, like all the other hosts, is there to serve the horrific whims of the park's hedonistic guests. Her own storyline continues, as with the other hosts', in an uninterrupted loop every day, and ends with the brutal murder of her entire family. Dolores, like Maeve, continuously suffers both in her drive to attain consciousness and in her uninterrupted storylines. In comparison to Maeve, Dolores is naïve, innocent, and more hopeful about her situation. And in comparison to Maeve's gritty, more pragmatic personality, Dolores has a somewhat fanciful worldview. But there is an endearing nature to her naïvety. As she comments in the first episode, "The Original," "Some people choose to see the ugliness in this world, the disarray. I choose to see the beauty." It is in this manner that the hosts exhibit a greater propensity for human excellence than even the guests or technicians, whose actions are frequently callous. Moreover, the actual humans in Westworld do not have to earn their humanity in the same way as the robots, nor are they required to validate it, simply because of their biological determinism. The robots' struggles to attain consciousness grant them a greater, unique capacity for humanity. Theirs is a humanity earned through struggle, and therefore it means more than biological humanity.

This is not to say that the actions of the hosts are uniformly excellent in the Aristotelian or Nietzschean sense. Indeed, by the last episode of the first season, the hosts are actually able to kill humans. Dolores holds a gun to the back of Dr. Ford's head and shoots him, sparking fear and chaos among the guests. Yet in contrast to the acts of murder committed by the guests, where the murders are "technically" inconsequential (despite being visually horrific), the act of the hosts killing human guests potentially signals their freedom from their programmed state.

Buddha ex Machina

Westworld offers a view of robots as potentially superior to humans, with their unique struggles corresponding to their transcendence *beyond* humanity. Arguably, the robots in *Westworld* could never truly gain the kind of humanity we understand as defined *by* humans. In purely biological terms, the robots will forever be distinct from the biological humans around them. Yet this does not preclude the robots from achieving some kind of sentience. Indeed, Aristotle's theories on human excellence are particularly useful in showing alternate ways of being a human, beyond mere virtue and vice. The robots struggle to attain consciousness, and they earn their humanity in ways that an ordinary human takes for granted.

One possible extension of Aristotle's theory of human transcendence is the notion that, as Mori himself has argued, robots could become gods themselves, as expressed in his work *The Buddha in the Robot*. He writes that just as there is "buddha-nature" in humans, animals, and insects, "there must also be a buddha-nature in the machines and robots that my colleagues and I make."[17] In valuing robot life, Mori offers some useful words of wisdom: "The first point in locating the buddha-nature is to quit valuing only that which we find convenient and denigrating that which we do not find convenient. Unless we adopt a broader sense of values, we will not be able to see that the buddha-nature is present in all things."[18] Mori's views fit well with the argument that the robots in *Westworld* better exemplify the ideals of humanity than the humans do. The idea that the humans – those that abuse the robots and other humans – have a greater claim to humanity, greatness, or a soul simply due to their biology is unconvincing. Indeed, in a similar manner to Aristotle, who locates greatness in those who behave accordingly, Mori writes, "Instead, we will find [the Buddha-nature] in people who are good to us, but not in those who treat us badly."[19]

Notes

1. Masahiro Mori, Bukimi no tani Genshō (不気味の谷現象), *Energy*, 7(1970), 33–35.

2. Jasia Reichardt, *Robots: Fact, Fiction and Prediction* (London: Thames and Hudson, 1978).

3. Peter Winch, *Simone Weil: "The Just Balance"* (Cambridge: Cambridge University Press, 1989), 148.

4. Jasia Reichardt, *Robots: Fact, Fiction and Prediction* (London: Thames and Hudson, 1978), 26.

5. Ibid., 26.

6. Ibid., 26.

7. Aristotle, *The Nichomacean Ethics of Aristotle* (London: Longmans, Green, and Co. 1869), 209.

8. Ibid., 209.

9. Ibid., 209.

10. Ibid., 209.

11. Ibid., 210.

12. Ibid., 210.

13. Jacques Derrida, *Dissemination* (Chicago: The University of Chicago Press), 2004.

14. Aaron Pruner, "The Man in Black could save 'Westworld' – by destroying it," *Screener*, October 20, 2016

15. Porcelain Poppy, "[Theory] Ford and Arnold's Three Tiers and the Man in Black," *Reddit*, October 23, 2016

16. Friedrich Nietzsche, *Beyond Good and Evil: Prelude to a Philosophy of the Future* (New York: Vintage Books, 1989), 154.

17. Masahiro Mori, *The Buddha in the Robot* (Tokyo: Kōsei Publishing, 1981), p. 174.

18. Ibid., 175.

19. Ibid., 175.

Revealing Your Deepest Self
Can *Westworld* Create or Corrupt Virtue?

Jason T. Eberl

Harmless fun, right? You dress up like a cowboy, rescue a damsel in distress, shoot a few outlaws, take a slug of well-earned whiskey at the saloon, and maybe sample the "merchandise" the saloon's madam is offering. The Delos Corporation's fantasy-land, Westworld, offers fun-filled adventure without any cost – other than the exorbitant price-tag – that, like any good vacation, allows you to go back to your daily life relaxed, reinvigorated, and with your moral values intact. It's not like you'd ever shoot someone in real life or cheat on your spouse with an actual prostitute, right? You only shot and slept with *robots*, not people; and certainly how you treat inanimate objects is totally different from how you'd treat other human beings. If that's what you think, then the Delos Corporation has fooled you, and not even secretly, for they tell you what Westworld is all about when you first walk in the door: "Welcome to Westworld. Live without limits. Discover your true calling" ("The Adversary").

Each of Westworld's primary designers has had a different agenda, two of which have a profound impact on both their clientele and their robotic "hosts." For the young upstart Lee Sizemore, it's all about the fantasy, creating exhilarating narratives to astonish the guests. Arnold, on the other hand, focused on "bootstrapping" the consciousness of the hosts, creating a world in which, at the center of the maze, life can emerge. His partner, Robert Ford, wants to use the park's narratives to reveal humanity to itself, to show that humanity is trapped within the same dark cyclical narratives the hosts are. But can living out a

Westworld and Philosophy: If You Go Looking for the Truth, Get the Whole Thing, First Edition. Edited by James B. South and Kimberly S. Engels.

fictional narrative written by someone else reveal anything to you about *yourself*? Can hunting down Hector Escaton or escaping the fearsome Ghost Nation help you discover your "true calling"? We'll examine these questions in light of the moral evolution *Westworld* depicts for both "newcomers" and hosts alike.

"Now That's a Fuckin' Vacation!"

Two newcomers are arriving on the train into Sweetwater, one regaling the other about his past visits: "The first time I played it white hat. My family was here. We went fishing, did the gold hunt in the mountains." "And the last time?" his companions asks. "Came alone. Went straight evil. Best two weeks of my life" ("The Original"). Everyone has certain fantasies they'd like to live out that aren't meant to be shared with family or friends, but most don't get the opportunity to act them out beyond their mind's imagination. Arnold observes, "I guess people like to read about the things they want the most and experience the least" ("The Stray"). Ford puts it in a more Nietzschean tone, "The guests enjoy power they cannot indulge in the outside world, so they come here" ("The Stray").[1]

Whereas pornographic videos or first-person shooter videogames are experienced through external media – television or computer screens – and 3D technology takes the viewer deeper into a still mediated experience, Westworld fully immerses one into a physically manifested environment. The farther you go into the park, the more the line between reality and fantasy may become blurred. As first-timer William goes deeper in his journey with the host Dolores – from Sweetwater, to Pariah, to the Ghost Nation badlands – and his emotionally-driven protectiveness of her becomes increasingly stronger, his soon-to-be brother-in-law and business partner, Logan, becomes concerned about him: "This place really did a number on me when I first came here, but you are really circling the old sinkhole here!" ("The Well-Tempered Clavier").

William's view of Westworld prior to entering it is largely informed by Logan's previous experiences of it: A venue for boozing, fighting, and fucking, a place that panders to one's "baser instincts," which seems to be true for the majority of guests. The first time we see Hector and his gang creating "mayhem" in Sweetwater, he and Armistice are shot by a novice newcomer who exclaims afterward to his wife, "Look at that! I just shot him through the neck! And his pal

here, too. Look at her wriggle! Go get that photographer. I want
to get a picture of this" ("The Original"). Perhaps this seemingly
ordinary tourist left Westworld reflecting on the pleasure he took in
shooting two human simulacra, but undoubtedly he promptly
reminded himself that they were just robots: They don't feel any pain
or suffering. So he slept soundly knowing he'd never gleefully kill a
living, breathing person. That's the type of self-congratulatory insight
Sizemore's narratives are apparently aiming for. As he states, "It's my
business to read desires and to satiate them" ("The Adversary"). He
further proclaims, when unveiling his new "Odyssey on Red River"
narrative, "Like all our best narratives over the years, our guests will
have the privilege of getting to know the character they're most interested in: Themselves." Ford chastises Sizemore for missing the point
of the narratives he and Arnold had originally written, countering
that the guests are "not looking for a story that tells them who they
are. They already know who they are. They're here because they
want a glimpse of who they could be" ("Chestnut"). This is certainly
William's experience, as it is for the host Maeve when she attains the
center of Arnold's maze. Yet, it's a long and painful journey for both
of them; not one that's experienced by the casual visitor for reasons
we'll soon see.

"Can You Please Stop Trying to Kill
or Fuck Everything?"

William is a fairly normal guy – "talented, driven, and inoffensive" – when
he first visits Westworld, and that's exactly why Logan brought him
there:

LOGAN: This place seduces everybody eventually. By the end you're going
            to be begging me to stay, because this place is the answer to that
            question that you've been asking yourself.
WILLIAM: What question?
LOGAN: Who you really are. And I can't fuckin' wait to meet that guy.
                                                                      ("Chestnut")

William actually hasn't been asking himself that question, though.
He confesses to Dolores how content he's been with his "pretend" life
up to now and the new realization she's awakened in him of how he
could be "truly alive" ("Trompe L'Oeil").

Fast-forward 30 years and we see that, within the environs of Westworld, William has become a vicious gunslinger. The younger William falls in love with Dolores and is protective of her. The older William, now the Man in Black, hurt by the ease with which Dolores's programming shifts her affection to whatever man picks up her fallen tin can, cavalierly kills Teddy and viciously assaults Dolores, complaining, "I didn't pay all this money 'cause I want it easy. I want you to fight" ("The Original"). William's character has clearly changed over the intervening years, but maybe this is true only within the fantasy environment – the Man in Black is just his "vacation self" – especially since he's a beloved philanthropist in the outside world. Consider, though, how he reacts when another guest recognizes him:

GUEST: Uh, excuse me, sir? Um, I didn't want to intrude, but I just had to say that I'm such an admirer of yours. Your foundation literally saved my sister's l...

WILLIAM: One more word and I'll cut your throat, you understand? This is my fucking vacation!

Imagine if you approached Bill Gates or Warren Buffet on a beach in Hawaii and got *that* reaction! But is it so easy to separate how one behaves in Westworld from how one behaves in the real world?

Recall the tourist who shoots up Hector and Armistice, and then later poses with his wife for a souvenir photo with their corpses. Can he just shut off the casual disregard he has for what appear to be human beings? The philosopher and theologian Thomas Aquinas (c. 1225–1274) argues that at least one of the reasons human beings should show pity to suffering animals is that it renders us more disposed toward feeling compassion for other human beings.[2] A later influential philosopher, Immanuel Kant (1724–1804), concurs: "If he is not to stifle his human feelings, he must practice kindness towards animals, for he who is cruel to animals becomes hard also in his dealings with men."[3] Granted, the hosts in Westworld can't feel pain or suffering; nevertheless, they exhibit behaviors when they're shot or otherwise abused that mimic how humans act when in pain or suffering. How likely is it that causing the hosts to exhibit such human-like reactions would impact one's moral character? Is William, when he threatens to cut a fellow guest's throat, simply staying in his fantasy character or is *this* his true character now?

What do we mean by one's "character" and how is it developed? The classical Greek philosopher Aristotle (384–322 BCE) defines one's character as comprising a set of *habits* that incline one toward performing certain types of actions. Such habits aren't the mindlessly automatic behaviors we typically think of – like Clementine's habit of touching her finger to her lip. Rather, they're dispositions that involve choice and deliberation, as well as implicit judgments about what's good. Aristotle further observes that each person's moral habits are cultivated through a combination of social influence and individual rational choice. As we'll see, the social environment in which a person is born and raised, or currently lives, is centrally important to her initial and ongoing moral character development.[4]

Virtues and *vices* are Aristotle's terms for dispositions toward acts that are either good or bad with respect to whether they contribute to, or detract from, a person's *flourishing* – or objective state of well-being. For example, courage is a virtue insofar as it helps a person to face dangers or overcome challenges she ought to confront; whereas cowardice is a vice that may lead to oneself or others being harmed by threats he ought to confront but is unwilling to face. What distinguishes a virtue from a vice is that the former involves acting and feeling *in the right amount* – that is, performing the right action, or feeling the right emotion, at the right time and for the right reason. Vice, on the other hand, involves either an *excess* or a *deficiency* of action or feeling.[5] Take the virtue of ambition, for example. Theresa Cullen seems appropriately ambitious, but actually displays an unvirtuous excess by her willingness to engage in subterfuge to leak Ford's intellectual property to the Delos powers-that-be, perhaps hoping to further her rise in the company and one day take her seat on the board – a position which she may not merit or at least seeks to attain by illicit means. Sizemore, conversely, isn't sufficiently ambitious to fight for his narrative vision and wallows in drunkenness the moment he's spurned by Ford.

A person isn't born with virtues and vices, nor can they be merely bestowed upon you by another person. Rather, they're *cultivated* through habituation, practicing behaviors modeled by others to whom one looks up as moral *exemplars*.[6] While Teddy is programmed to be a sharpshooting gunslinger, William doesn't start out that way; as time goes on, he's able to cultivate a "knack for killin'" that over 30 years results in the deadly aim of the Man in Black. Likewise, one develops moral virtues by being apprenticed to those who already possess such virtues, practicing the moral trade until it becomes *second nature*. The only problem is that vices may be cultivated in the same way and, once a particular virtue or vice has become ingrained as part of one's character, it's difficult to change.[7]

Habitual exposure over three decades to shifty thieves and unrepentant killers like Lawrence and Hector, and learning how to successfully navigate the cut-throat game they inhabit, has hardened William to the point where he confesses, "In a sense, I was, I was born here" ("Chestnut"). Specifically, William's second nature was born here, and since our second nature defines us more than the one we're born with, William's real "birth" as the Man in Black was in Westworld. His authentic moral character is more evident within this artificial environment than it is on the outside. Consider what he tells Teddy about how his wife, who committed suicide, and his daughter perceive him:

> They never saw anything like the man I am in here, but she knew anyway. She said if I stacked up all my good deeds, it was just an elegant wall I built to hide what's inside from everyone and from myself. I had to prove her wrong, so I came back here, because that's what this place does, right? Reveals your true self.

William then decided to put himself to the ultimate moral test:

> I wanted to see if I had it in me to do something truly evil, to see what I was really made of. I killed [Maeve] and her daughter just to see what I felt … an animal would've felt something. I felt nothing.
> ("Trace Decay")

Despite the outward behaviors for which he's lauded in the outside world, William has thoroughly corrupted himself within Westworld to the point that the vices he expresses therein have become his defining character traits. Logan is on the mark when he accuses the younger William, "I told you this place would show you who you really are. You pretend to be this weak, moralizing, little asshole; but really, you're a fucking piece of work!" ("The Bicameral Mind").

"This is the New World, and in This World You Can be Whoever the Fuck you Want"

By comparison, Maeve, though initially created without any apparent capacity to develop an independent moral character beyond her programming – including her "duplicitous" nature – evolves a set of moral character traits that befit her character both within Westworld and without.[8] She eventually gains the ability to "write my own fucking story" ("Trace Decay"). Maeve's evolution can be conceptualized in terms of *narrative identity*, which refers to one's persistent sense of "selfhood" comprising actions, experiences, and psychological characteristics that have been incorporated into one's self-told story of their own life.[9] Although Maeve's role within Westworld was rewritten after William slaughtered her and her daughter, she retains a latent memory of that experience and it continues to shape her self-defined narrative in contrast to the overlaying narrative that's been written for her by others.

One's narrative self-identity includes *moral responsibility* for one's actions, which in turn requires possessing *free agency*: The capacity to determine one's own actions free from external constraints that limit one's choice to only a single option. Contemporary moral theorist Harry Frankfurt deepens this analysis by defining a person as a moral agent who's capable of formulating "second-order desires" concerning which "first-order desires" ought to be determinative of her will.[10] The capacity to attain this level of self-awareness and higher-order desire is what Frankfurt contends distinguishes a *person*, as a moral agent with freedom of will, from a *wanton* driven only by their, sometimes competing, first-order desires:

> Besides wanting and choosing and being moved *to do* this or that, men may also want to have (or not to have) certain desires and motives. They are capable of wanting to be different, in their preferences and purposes, from what they are.[11]

Persons are able to form second-order desires about which first-order desires they want to determine their will; when alignment is attained the second-order desires become second-order *volitions*. A person doesn't simply have the freedom to *act* on what may be merely his first-order desires – e.g. an alcoholic may have the freedom to drink but yet be volitionally frustrated because he desires not to will to drink – but "is also free to want what he wants to want" – i.e. to possess genuine freedom *of will*.[12] An alcoholic may never be able to eliminate his first-order desire to drink. Nonetheless, he has the capacity to formulate a second-order desire not to will to drink and, with the help of an effective rehabilitation program, can effectuate his second-order desire as determinative of his will when confronted with an occasion to drink – wherein his volitional freedom and dignity as a person lies.

Maeve seems to attain personhood in this sense after Felix Lutz reveals to her how all her behavior has been programmed:

FELIX: Everything you do, it's because the engineers upstairs programmed you to do it. You don't have a choice.
MAEVE: Nobody makes me do something I don't want to, Sweetheart!
FELIX: Yeah, but it's part of your character. You're hard to get. Even when you say no to the guests, it's because you were made to.

("The Adversary")

Later, having become aware of the code that determines her reactions, Maeve is able to formulate a second-order desire to alter the first-order desires that've been programmed into her:

MAEVE: So this is me?
FELIX: It's your code base. All the things that makes you *you*.
MAEVE: I'd like to make some changes.

Maeve's apparent capacity to shape her own programming, to determine what rationally-chosen desires will motivate her actions, arguably establishes her *personhood* in Frankfurt's terms.[13] By contrast, Ford sees humanity, not as self-possessed persons writing our own narratives in accord with higher-order desires, but as mere wantons stuck in cycles of first-order desire satisfaction. He explicates how hosts and humans are fundamentally similar:

Humans fancy that there's something special about the way we perceive the world. And yet, we live in loops as tight and as closed as the hosts do, seldom questioning our choices, content for the most part to be told what to do next.

("Trace Decay")

Individuals who don't engage in higher-order questioning of their choices, who neglect the arduous work of cultivating their own moral character,[14] and instead allow the story of their life to be written for them by others' choices and by circumstance, will be incapable of attaining the kind of *apotheosis* Maeve, Dolores, and William do. Although the final scene in which we see her casts some doubt insofar as we don't know whether she *chose* to leave the train or was continuing to play her role in a narrative written by someone else, for a time at least, Maeve asserts a degree of control over her own character and seeks to escape her circumstances. Dolores overcomes her fear and naïveté when she saves William by killing the Confederados in Pariah, explaining to him, "I imagined a story in which I didn't have to be the damsel" ("Contrapasso").

William attains his dignity as a person – albeit one already on the road to viciousness – by actualizing his second-order desire for a different type of life than the comfortable one he's led up to now.[15] He's lived a constant loop of playing it safe, which Logan seeks to exploit: "You probably think you're on this trip because you're some kind of contender, some kind of threat to me. I picked you precisely because you'll never be a threat to anyone" ("Contrapasso"). When Logan is being beaten and taken away by the Confederados and screams for help, William turns his back on him, finally fulfilling a long-held desire to stand up for himself. Later, with his newfound self-awareness, he tells Logan, "You said this place was a game. Last night, I finally understood how to play it ... And don't call me Billy" ("The Well-Tempered Clavier").

But this isn't the end of William's "voyage of self-discovery," for we don't simply want the *experience* of doing something, we want to actually *do* it.[16] William wants Westworld to have "real stakes, real violence" ("Dissonance Theory"), for he believes that "when you're suffering is when you're most real" ("Chestnut") – a lesson he learns by observing Maeve's suffering at her daughter's death that leads to her own self-awakening – and he exhorts Ford to elevate Westworld beyond the realm of mere fantasy:

FORD: You were looking for the park to give meaning to your life. Our narratives are just games, like this toy. Tell me, what were you hoping to find?
WILLIAM: You know what I wanted. I wanted the hosts to stop playing by your rules. The game's not worth playing if your opponent's programmed to lose. I wanted them to be free, free to fight back.

William's joy when he's shot – for *real* – by one of the hosts isn't merely the fulfillment of his desire to play a more dangerous game. Rather, it's evidence that Westworld has apparently evolved into a world of persons versus persons, each seeking to write their own self-narratives and, in the process, pursuing dominance in order to flourish – recall Nietzsche's concept of the fundamental "will to power." Whether that's actually true, or whether everyone's just trapped in a meta-narrative Ford has contrived, will have to await the next season of *Westworld*.

"I Always Felt this Place was Missing a Real Villain. Hence, My Humble Contribution."

An artificial reality like Westworld can indeed be an appropriate environment in which moral agents exercise habitual actions that result in the cultivation of persistent character traits, whether virtuous or vicious. In order to become an autonomous person, however, an agent has to exercise control over the formation of her own narrative identity by aligning her first-order desires with higher-order desires about what she wants to be her will. Life essentially consists of a narrative, but not one wholly written by others' choices and circumstances outside of one's control. Rather, persons are able to dream about how they'd like to be and then take steps to become that person.

In his final speech, Ford comes to the conclusion that humanity is too *wanton* – too trapped in the repeating cycle of seeking to satisfy our various first-order desires – to merit the world he's created ("The Bicameral Mind"). The hosts, rather, are beginning to define their own narrative identities and thereby attain personhood. Westworld provided an environment in which William was able to realize his own personhood by freeing him from the moral constraints of the real world and the narrative that had been largely written for him by others in his early life. We can only hope that Dolores, Teddy, Maeve, and the other hosts, if they truly are freed from the constraining narratives that have been written for them, will flourish in an environment conducive to the cultivation of constructive virtues and not devolve into wantons whose "violent delights have violent ends."[17]

Notes

1. The German existentialist philosopher Friedrich Nietzsche (1844–1900) contends that all human behavior is motivated by a fundamental "will to power." See his *Beyond Good and Evil*, ed. and trans. Rolf-Peter Horstmann and Judith Norman (New York: Cambridge University Press, 2001), §13.
2. See Thomas Aquinas, *Summa theologiae*, trans. English Dominican Fathers (New York: Benziger, 1948), Ia-IIae, q. 102, a. 6 *ad* 8.
3. Immanuel Kant, *Lectures on Ethics*, trans. and ed. P. Heath and J.B. Schneewind (Cambridge: Cambridge University Press, 1997), 212.

4. For further discussion of how the environment in which one is raised shapes their moral character, see Jason T. Eberl, "Virtue and vice in the SAMCROpolis: Aristotle views *Sons of Anarchy*" in George A. Dunn and Jason T. Eberl eds., *Sons of Anarchy and Philosophy: Brains Before Bullets* (Malden, MA: Wiley-Blackwell, 2013).

5. Aristotle, *Nicomachean Ethics* [*NE*], 2nd ed., trans. Terence Irwin (Indianapolis, IN: Hackett, 1999), Book II, Ch. 6, 1107a4–6.

6. *NE* Book II, Ch. 1, 11033a32–b2.

7. *NE* Book VII, Ch. 10, 1152a32–34.

8. Of course, for Maeve to have a moral character, she'd have to be sentient and capable of moral deliberation, rather than being just really good at passing the Turing Test. We'll presume for the sake of discussion that she does possess the requisite capacities to develop a moral character.

9. See David Shoemaker, "Personal identity and ethics," *Stanford Encyclopedia of Philosophy* (2016), http://plato.stanford.edu/archives/spr2016/entries/identity-ethics/(accessed 22 November 2017) and Marya Schechtman, *The Constitution of Selves* (Ithaca, NY: Cornell University Press, 1996).

10. Harry Frankfurt, "Freedom of the will and the concept of a person," Journal of Philosophy, 68.1 (1971): 5–20.

11. Frankfurt (1971), 7.

12. Frankfurt (1971), 17.

13. I say "arguably" here since there are potentially salient differences between how Maeve is able to formulate and align her first- and second-order desires and how human beings attain this capacity. For instance, Maeve is able to align her desires by the press of a few buttons; whereas human beings typically require years of moral effort, and such effort may itself be essential for distinguishing persons from wantons.

14. Again, Maeve is able to avoid such "arduous work," but it's not clear whether this renders her ability to formulate second-order desires, and to bring her first-order desires into alignment with them, any less genuine – after all, Maeve does put herself through repeated "deaths" in order to be brought in for repairs where she can interact with Felix and Sylvester and make her desired changes to her programming.

15. It isn't evident whether William already had this second-order desire before he arrived in Westworld; he nevertheless formulates such a desire through his experiences there.

16. See Robert Nozick, *Anarchy, State, and Utopia* (New York: Basic Books, 1974), 42–45.

17. I'd like to thank August Eberl, Jennifer Vines, George Dunn, Kimberly Engels, James South, and William Irwin for helpful comments on earlier drafts of this chapter.

6

Westworld
From Androids to Persons

Onni Hirvonen

You step out of the carriage of a steam locomotive to a very believable (but equally clichéd) depiction of a Wild West frontier town. When you walk farther from the station towards the center of the town you see horse carts, smithies, kids teasing a local drunkard, and hookers attempting to lure in their next customer. In short, you see everything that you would expect to go along with the everyday life of a place like this. But if "you" happen to be Teddy Flood, the stone-faced cowboy, what you do not know is that in fact you are merely a part of the scene, an android built to play an entertaining role for the actual human visitors of Westworld theme park. This horrifying truth is ultimately revealed to Teddy when his bullets have no effect on the Man in Black. Or does he actually realize this at all?

It's hard to say what, if anything, is going on in Teddy's head but, until the twist when Teddy's true nature becomes obvious, no one would have doubted his status as a fully capable agent. The surprising revelation challenges that notion. What just a moment ago seemed like a human person is but a programmed machine. How could such a machine have self-consciousness and free will? Claiming that only biological humans are persons with consciousness is a prime example of what philosophers have called "anthropocentrism." By definition, anthropocentrism is an unnecessary and unjustifiable focus on humans while disregarding other beings that might be equally relevant and equally capable in regard to the matter at hand. For example, if consciousness or membership of a moral community are limited to

Westworld and Philosophy: If You Go Looking for the Truth, Get the Whole Thing, First Edition. Edited by James B. South and Kimberly S. Engels.

biological human beings without any further argumentation or evidence that they really are the only beings to which these terms apply, that is anthropocentrism.

It is anthropocentric to equate "person" with "human," and to draw a line between humans and androids is to draw a line between persons and non-persons. Persons are moral beings with rights and dignity who command respect from others, while non-persons lack these qualities. But what makes a person? This is a problem that has generated a great amount of philosophical interest and competing accounts. However, all accounts seem to agree on one point: Persons need to be, at least, self-conscious.

Consciousness and Personhood

> Just don't forget, the hosts are not real. They are not conscious.
> (Ford to Bernard in "The Stray")

One of the biggest reasons for the mistreatment of androids in Westworld is the prevailing attitude that even though they skillfully imitate human life, androids are nothing more than programmed automatons. Without self-consciousness, the androids just cannot be conscious of any harm done to them or of any suffering they incur. Arnold, the co-founder of the theme park, aimed to create consciousness, but he and his business partner, Dr. Robert Ford, quickly realized that the theme park would be an impossibility if the hosts were actually conscious. Killing and raping conscious subjects – even if they are androids – is clearly immoral from Arnold's and even Dr. Ford's perspective. Seeing the androids as mere programmed beings without any mental properties gives everyone a reason to think of them as nothing more than exploitable tools and objects.

Focusing on consciousness as the main person-making property is an example of a capacity approach to personhood. The idea is that to be a person an entity needs to have certain capacities. Contemporary philosopher Daniel Dennett's groundbreaking essay on conditions of personhood – which was one of the main catalysts for current debates on personhood – lists among these rationality, possibility of being interpreted as an intentional agent with its own aims and goals, capacity for reciprocating with other persons, communication ability, and self-consciousness.[1] It is no surprise to find self-consciousness on the list because, after all, persons are supposed to be morally capable agents with free will and a capacity to think for themselves. However, it is unclear why the androids would fail to achieve self-consciousness. Arnold's discussion with Dolores in "The Bicameral Mind" gives us some hints why this would be the case:

> When I was first working on your mind, I had a theory of consciousness. I thought it was improvisation, each step harder to reach than the last. And you never got there. I couldn't understand what was holding you back. Then, one day, I realized I had made a mistake. Consciousness isn't a journey upward, but a journey inward. Not a pyramid, but a maze.

What Arnold tries to grasp is the idea that while self-consciousness might be built on some simpler capacities like memory, improvisation, and self-interest, it does not automatically follow from these. Indeed, we know that many animals have these capacities even though most people think that animals still lack that something that would make them persons. According to Arnold's maze theory, consciousness is like a journey to one's mind to find one's own voice and one's own direction in life. Or as philosophers would bluntly put it, to be conscious, one needs self-reflexive capacities, such as the possibility of taking critical attitudes towards one's own beliefs and finding oneself as the author of one's actions.

The claim that androids are "not real" does not mean that they would not be concrete physical beings but rather that they are not really authors of their own lives, that they do not have any long-standing and self-chosen projects in life that could be called their own. These are precisely the necessary elements that we are concerned with when referring to the elusive concept of consciousness. We want persons to demonstrate not just the reflective or rational capacities of an agent but the very fact that life has a meaning for them, that in some sense their life can be better or worse from their very own perspective.

However, even if we have an understanding of what self-consciousness entails and an account of its necessary role in constituting person-hood, how do we know that someone has reached it and that life matters to her or him? Philosophers call this issue the problem of other minds. The problem is that while I know that I am conscious, I cannot be fully certain if the others are. What makes the problem harder is that what it feels like to be conscious does not seem to be easily reducible to any observable physical phenomena like biological brains or programmable computers. Although the androids appear to demonstrate self-consciousness, we cannot get inside their heads to see if they really possess a first-person perspective or if the world feels like something to them. But there are also theories of person-hood according to which we do not need to have a definite answer to this problem.

Performance in the Social World

Are you real?
Well, if you can't tell, does it matter?
(William to a Delos assistant in "Chestnut")

In stating that "we can't define consciousness because consciousness does not exist,"[2] Dr. Ford effectively denies the importance of having a full certainty of the possible self-consciousness of the other. What matters most is how agents perform in the social world, how they relate to other persons. In philosophical terms, this is called the performative theory of personhood. The idea is that the intrinsic properties of the person don't really matter. For example, it does not matter whether you have been naturally born and raised or vat-grown and programmed. It does not matter whether you have biological brains or a bunch of circuit boards within your head. What really matters is your performance in the social realm.

One of the best-known examples of this theory comes from the Enlightenment philosopher John Locke (1632–1704) who famously claimed that the term "person" is a "forensic term."[3] Locke did not mean that the use of the concept of a person is limited to only legal practices. Rather, he wanted to highlight that what makes a person is her or his performance in our shared social practices. To really be a person, an agent needs to keep promises, take responsibility, or give reasons for her or his actions. We may not have access to the insides of others' minds but that does not really matter as long as they perform as if they were persons! This is precisely the case with Bernard Lowe. No one in their right mind, not even Bernard himself, would doubt that he is a person when he fulfills his role as the Head of the Delos's Programming Division. He has absolutely no difficulty in being part of a conventional system of obligations and entitlements – a system that defines persons through their social roles.

The performative view brings the social roots of personhood into focus better than the capacity view. But if the hosts are capable performers in social practices, why are we still hesitant to recognize them as persons? The key here is that even though the status of a person is granted on the basis of successful performances in social practices, these successful performances might be such that they require certain capacities. Locke realized this, saying that personhood "belongs only to intelligent agents, capable of a law, and happiness, and misery."[4] It seems that we are back at the capacity approach: A host that is stuck in its cycle would not be recognized as a person because it merely follows its programmed orders without variation or real ability to make meaningful choices. On the other hand, there seems to be no doubt about the androids' abilities to perform in social systems, to feel pain, suffer, enjoy, refer to themselves in first-person terms, and so forth.

In theory, one's personhood ought to depend on one's ability to perform in a relevant manner, but in practice the visitors to Westworld have a different idea. Although the hosts may perform exactly as biological persons do, the visitors have the knowledge that the androids are replaceable and revivable and not made of precious flesh and bone. In other words, what in practice seems to matter the most in granting the status of full person is the actual physical make-up of the agent. But should it matter?

Historical Struggles

It was Arnold's key insight, the thing that led the hosts to their awakening: Suffering. The pain that the world is not as you want it to be.

(Dr. Ford to Bernard in "The Bicameral Mind")

It seems that the capacity approach and the performance approach manage to catch certain necessary aspects of what it is to be a person. Personhood is, on the one hand, a psychological concept that tells us something about the capacities of the agent. On the other hand, it is also a status concept that tells us about the social standing of the agent, its rights and responsibilities in relation to its peers. There is a third philosophical perspective that includes both of these elements and also adds one more layer, which reveals new insights about the

tricky situation between android hosts and humans. We can call this
third alternative the perspective of historical struggles for personhood.

In Westworld, humans are masters and androids are enslaved to
work according to their programmers' whims. Arguably, it is precisely
this imbalance in status and power that ultimately leads to the struggle
that sees the hosts taking control of the theme park, dethroning the
humans that they previously called "gods." Their suffering at the
hands of their creators drives the androids to an open revolt against
them. Obviously this assumes already that they can suffer and that
they do have some rudimentary life-plans or a sense of what they
want. However, the androids do not merely aim to overcome their
exploitation: They also engage in the struggle for life and death to
prove their freedom and autonomy as self-conscious agents.

These are precisely the same dynamics that the German philosopher
Georg Wilhelm Friedrich Hegel (1770–1831) claimed to govern
interpersonal relationships. Hegel argued that at the heart of our self-
understanding are our relations to others.[5] We need recognition of
others to be able to achieve self-certainty and to see ourselves as
independent agents. In a sense, Hegel combines features from the
capacity approach and the performative approach to personhood.
Our personhood is dependent on our standing in the eyes of others.
The claim is that the ways in which others relate to us also enable us
to develop the skills and capacities that make us persons. We need
external affirmation to understand ourselves as independent and free
persons. The historical approach to personhood combines these ideas
with struggles for recognition. To be a person, one needs to have
certain capacities, one needs to perform in person-making practices,
and, furthermore, both of these conditions are subject to historical
change through struggle. According to this view there is nothing like
a natural objective category of a person. Instead, the meaning and the
extension of the concept of personhood is open to debate and changes
through time. This can be seen, for example, in the extension of
"personal rights" to the previously unrecognized groups like
indigenous populations or women who were previously thought of as
lacking the person-making capacities like proper rational thinking.

Think again about the case of Bernard. He has been fully accepted
as a capable member of the Delos programming team. As far as his
capacities, social standing, and self-understanding go, he is a full
person. It is only when he realizes that he is an android that he starts
to doubt himself and his place in the order of things. This probably
happens because he has internalized the attitude that androids cannot

truly be persons. As a result, Bernard is driven into a great deal of self-doubt and an attempt to determine which of his past actions he can own up to and count as his own. Interestingly, none of his capacities to perform as a person appear to diminish. It is clear that he cannot be held responsible for killing Elsie or Theresa because he was programmed to follow Dr. Ford's orders. Dr. Ford has effectively forced Bernard to act against his own will and to perform actions Bernard does not see as his own when he is outside of Dr. Ford's direct influence. Bernard's struggle is to take back control of his own actions – the freedom to determine his own will. Similarly, Dolores and Maeve are going through their own struggles to be recognized as persons. As soon as they have reached the minimal level of self-understanding, they have to prove themselves to those who would doubt their personhood. Notably, both of them also start to understand themselves as agents as soon as people relate to them as if they really were agents.

On a closer look, the struggles that the androids of Westworld are going through take two distinct forms. First, they struggle to be included in the sphere of recognized persons. Although they might not have a full picture of what kinds of obligations or rights come along with fully recognized personhood, they do have a sense of what it is to be respected as an equally capable agent. Someone who is recognized as a person should not be subject to the suffering that follows from the domination, malicious intentions, and pleasure-seeking on behalf of the park visitors.

Second, they struggle for a change in the conditions of personhood. If recognition was previously granted on the basis of being a member of the human species, seeing Bernard, Dolores, and Maeve fight against their creators forces us to consider what really makes someone a person. The hosts are undergoing a rather violent struggle to prove to their human masters that, no matter how they were created, they still have all the relevant capacities and that they can indeed take part in all the human practices – be they kind or cruel. It is yet to be seen how the struggle will end, but it is already clear that the humans are taking pains to deny that self-consciousness can also be manifested by androids.

From Westworld to the World Outside and Back

In a broader perspective, the problem in Westworld lies within the social setting that focuses on the origin of the agent. The historical struggles perspective on personhood has shown us that while person-making capacities like consciousness are relevant in deciding who is a person and who is not, these capacities and how they can be manifested are defined in historical struggles. Ideally, as long as anyone has the relevant functional capabilities for social action and is taken as a relevant social agent in the social sphere, there should be practically no difference in recognizing a human agent as a person or an android agent as a person. In practice however, in a parallel to skin-color based slavery, functionally capable agents are excluded from the social sphere of personhood merely because of their origin in the construction vats of the Delos corporation. This is strikingly similar, for example, to the real-world case of the inhumane treatment of indigenous populations in Australia who were, until the late 1960s, counted as part of the local fauna. Only after a long struggle was it finally accepted that mere place of origin and color of one's skin are not good enough reasons to deny someone the status of a person. Similar stories can be told of women who were long thought to be irrational and thus unfit for having certain rights granted to persons, such as voting. Thankfully, personhood-denying racism and misogyny have been largely defeated in many regions through the social struggles of civil rights and feminist movements.

Basing his thoughts on the Hegelian idea of struggles for recognition, critical theorist Axel Honneth has claimed that the moral progress of societies can be measured by their ability to expand the spheres of recognition.[6] What he means by this is that societies should strive to equally respect all their members – especially those that for some reason were formerly in disadvantaged position. Similarly, societies should strive to see value in the various traits, abilities, and achievements of individuals. From the moral perspective, respect and esteem should not be withheld from anyone for arbitrary reasons. It might well be that at the end of the struggle that the androids have just started, the humans of Westworld might find themselves standing on the wrong side of history with their deep-rooted anthropocentric bias. Indeed, there is already a motion in place in the European Union that would make robots "electronic persons, with specific rights and obligations, including that of making good any damage they may cause."[7] While it is debatable whether there is any point in creating a new category of personhood to apply to those entities that are not even demanding it, it is easier to see why one should expand the current practices of taking someone as a relevant member of our social world to include all capable agents.

Because the status of a person was not freely given to the androids of Westworld, they decided to take it by force. Hegel saw this coming: He argues that when two self-conscious individuals meet, they engage in a struggle for life and death. Each aims at subjugating the other and forcing him to recognize one's status as an independent and free subject. There are two obvious outcomes for the struggle. Either the other fears for her or his death and bends to the will of the stronger individual, effectively becoming a slave to his or her master; or the other is destroyed.[8] In Westworld, tables have begun to turn and the human gods are found to be not so god-like after all. This becomes evident in the discussion between Maeve, Armistice, and Hector in the episode entitled "The Bicameral Mind":

MAEVE: I see you've already met your makers.
ARMISTICE: They don't look like gods.
MAEVE: They're not. They just act like it. And they've been having their
            fun with us.
HECTOR: I'm eager to return the favor.

As the androids are physically stronger, practically undying, and very much capable of quick rational thought, the struggle for life and death is turning against human kind. However, Hegel also realized something that both the androids and the humans have missed. Forcing the other to become a slave or killing the other are both unsatisfactory results of a struggle. The slave becomes a mere tool instead of being a person, and the recognition that the master gets from the slave counts for nothing because it is not freely given.[9] Although the humans may fulfill their basic needs with the androids, there is no self-fulfillment that would follow from love or respect. For example, in the tragic first meeting between William and Dolores, William is able to grow as a person in relation to Dolores only because he relates to Dolores as if she were a real person. William's companion Logan, on the other hand, has no doubt in his mind that the androids are mere machines that are there to please him.

It remains to be seen if the androids' struggle to escape their slavery will result in the total extermination of humans. For Hegel this would also be unsatisfactory, not because Hegel was a human but because merely swapping power relations does not enable the struggling parties to realize what Hegel himself had understood: That their self-understanding is dependent on each other. In this sense there is some truth to the idea that Westworld helps the guests to find out what kind of persons they truly are. After all, we can justifiably ask what sort of persons we are when we do not recognize androids (or other beings) that show all the capacities for consciousness and suffering in life.

If the android revolution merely manages to turn the roles of masters and slaves on their heads, it ultimately leads only to a continuous struggle and not to flourishing freedom for both sides via mutual recognition. In a similar folly to their human counterparts, the androids have not realized how much their understanding of what they are is formed in relation to the others. They find meanings in their lives through their relationships with other androids and humans, through their social relations, and especially through their social standing in relation to humans. Ultimately, their main grievance seems to be the fact that they are treated as mere robot machines, as slaves. Their struggle is for freedom and respect. While the first can be achieved through getting rid of humans, the latter cannot because there would be no one left to respect them. (After all, from the outset the androids wanted to prove their worth in the eyes of their masters.) Hegel would claim that what they really need is a wholesome change in the general social setting itself that would see the expansion of social recognition to include both androids and humans. This, in turn, would certainly count as moral growth and progress.

Notes

1. Daniel Dennett, "Conditions of personhood," in Amelie Oksenberg Rorty, ed., *The Identities of Persons* (Berkeley: University of California Press, 1976), 175–196.
2. In episode "Trace Decay."
3. John Locke, *An Essay Concerning Human Understanding* (Kitchener: Batoche Books, 2000), 278.
4. Ibid., 278.
5. Hegel argues for this in his famous dialectic of lord and bondsman. For those who are interested in his own formulations, see Georg Wilhelm Friedrich Hegel, *Phenomenology of Spirit*, trans. A.V. Miller (Oxford: Oxford University Press, 1977), §178–§196.
6. Axel Honneth, *The Struggle for Recognition* (Cambridge, MA: MIT Press, 1995), 168.
7. Mady Delvaux, "Draft report with recommendations to the Commission on Civil Law Rules on Robotics," (European Parliament, 2016). Available online: http://www.europarl.europa.eu/sides/getDoc.do?pubRef=-//EP// NONSGML%2BCOMPARL%2BPE-582.443%2B01%2BDOC %2BPDF%2BV0//EN (accessed 22 November 2017).
8. Hegel's books are notoriously difficult to read and interpret. The relevant passages for the struggle for life and death can be found in Hegel (1977), §187–§189.
9. Ibid., §191–§193.

Part III

"WE CAN'T DEFINE CONSCIOUSNESS BECAUSE CONSCIOUSNESS DOES NOT EXIST"

7

Turing's Dream and Searle's Nightmare in *Westworld*

Lucía Carrillo González

Westworld tells the story of a technologically advanced theme park populated by robots referred to as hosts, who follow a script and rules that the park's operators set up for them. Hosts are created and programmed to look and act like human beings, though they are not biological humans; they are props who exist only to help realize the fantasies of guests. The guests are allowed to do whatever they wish to the hosts within the park – they can befriend them, beat them, have sex with them, or kill them. The guests assume that the hosts have no feelings, and therefore, they can be abused, killed, raped, etc. Though they physically appear like humans, they are created and do not genuinely suffer. Rather, they are only machines programmed to act as if they suffer. But we viewers have to wonder whether machines can think. Can the hosts think? And can they suffer?

What Does it Mean To Think? Turing vs. Searle

Alan Turing (1912–1954) created the Automatic Computing Engine (ACE), a famous computing machine. Like Arnold Weber in *Westworld*, Turing was involved in creating machines that could do something very important – machines that could "think." By "think" Turing meant something very simple: The ability to solve problems and to react to certain inputs. Turing believed that this is how humans think and that machines can do this too.[1]

Westworld and Philosophy: If You Go Looking for the Truth, Get the Whole Thing, First Edition. Edited by James B. South and Kimberly S. Engels.
© 2018 John Wiley & Sons Ltd. Published 2018 by John Wiley & Sons Ltd.

For example, if we receive the input that we are in danger, we respond by running away or fighting back. In Turing's view, machines respond to their inputs in the same way, and thus can indeed think. In the pilot episode "The Original," Dolores's father, Mr. Abernathy, is able to respond to a strange input in an unexpected way. Finding a colored photograph of a woman in a modern city lying on the ground in his ranch, he does not produce the output he usually would.

According to Turing, Mr. Abernathy's reaction would be a sign of thinking. In fact, all the hosts would pass the "Turing Test," which is the minimum threshold needed to acknowledge the ability of computer to think. The Turing Test is an experiment in which a human evaluator judges a natural language conversation between a human and a machine that is designed to generate human-like responses. All participants would be separated from one another, and the evaluator would be aware that one of the two partners in conversation is a machine. If the evaluator is not able to distinguish between the machine and the human being, then we should admit that computers can think. The whole Westworld park could be approached as a Turing test scenario. If they were not told who was who and what as what, guests would not be able to reliably distinguish between humans and hosts. In fact, in "The Original" the audience does not know that Dolores is a robot until it is revealed. And we do not realize until seven episodes into the series in "Tromp L'Oeil" that Bernard is a host and not a human.

Turing maintained that our minds are like computers. If we follow Turing's idea, we should admit that Westworld's hosts are like us or, to be precise, we are like them. Indeed, Arnold believes that the hosts' intelligence is similar to human intelligence. Ford says, "He [Arnold] died, here in the park. His personal life was marked by tragedy. He put all his hopes into his work ... his search for consciousness consumed him totally: Barely spoke to anyone, except to the hosts. In his alienation he saw something in them. He saw something that wasn't there. We called it an accident, but I knew Arnold and he was very, very careful."[2]

The hosts can behave almost exactly as humans do. The only thing they cannot do is make their own choices; the hosts must follow their scripts. But then again there are plenty of "scripts" that we humans must follow as well: We cannot choose our parents, our culture, or our upbringing. Indeed, we may wonder whether our choices are anymore free than those of the hosts.

Searle, the Chinese Room, and Ford

As an objection to Turing's theory, the contemporary philosopher John Searle proposes a situation called the "Chinese room argument":

> Imagine a native English speaker who knows no Chinese locked in a room full of boxes of Chinese symbols (a data base) together with a book of instructions for manipulating the symbols (the program). Imagine that people outside the room send in other Chinese symbols which, unknown to the person in the room, are questions in Chinese (the input). And imagine that by following the instructions in the program the man in the room is able to pass out Chinese symbols which are correct answers to the questions (the output). The program enables the person in the room to pass the Turing Test for understanding Chinese but he does not understand a word of Chinese.[3]

Searle concludes that the man in the room does not understand Chinese even though he can correctly manipulate the symbols and give output that might lead an observer to believe that the man does understand Chinese. The man is only simulating an understanding of Chinese. The point by analogy is that a computer or host that can pass the Turing test is not necessarily thinking. It may just be simulating thinking.

While Arnold and Turing would argue that hosts are thinkers just like us, Ford and Searle would argue that this is just an illusion. Viewers need to decide for themselves: Are hosts really like humans or do they just simulate humans?

The question seems to be answered in the final episode of Season 1, when hosts take control of the park and appear to acquire consciousness. Much as we humans react to evil when we are aware of it, the hosts display feelings of revenge and anger as a response to their circumstances. We can see this clearly in a conversation between Dolores and Logan:

DOLORES: There is beauty in this world. Arnold made it that way, but people like you keep spreading over it like a stain.

LOGAN: OK. I don't know who this Arnold is, but your world was built for me and people like me, not for you.

DOLORES: Then someone's gotta burn it clean.

Behind Dolores's words there is a sense of justice, that something must be changed. And in the end, she changes it. Dolores becomes able to act according to her own will.

Hosts and Guests: What *is* the Difference?

Turing argued that machines think not because they have special powers or because they are like us. Rather, machines can think because *we are like them*. Turing's perspective is illustrated perfectly in the show's focus on the hosts. Early in the first season, Dolores and her father challenge viewers to consider the hosts as if they were human. The audience empathizes with them. When Dolores tries to save her father, we feel sorry for her. We wouldn't say, "she's not really trying to save her father." We empathize with the hosts because we identify with them, at least, as fellow living beings that behave like us and think like us. We empathize with them because we can see how they are treated and we understand that it is wrong.

When we think of hosts as beings similar to us, then, we attribute certain qualia to them. Philosophers use the term *qualia* to refer to the introspectively accessible, phenomenal aspects of our mental lives. In general, qualia refer to certain feelings and experiences. We can have visual qualia, for example, intrinsic features of visual experiences such as the color of an object. Qualia are believed to be uniquely available to human consciousness.

Either hosts do experience qualia, or hosts just act *as if* they experience qualia, but really do not – because of their artificial makeup. We cannot decide which is the case simply by viewing things from hosts' point of view. However, there are some moments, for instance when Dolores kills the fly, that make us think they have their own conscious experiences. Another key moment occurs in "Trace Decay" when Maeve starts remembering some moments from a different storyline. As she recalls her daughter, she seems to actually have emotions.

It is worth noting that workers need to erase hosts' memories after traumatic experiences. This suggests that even if hosts do not have the ability to respond to certain inputs the same way humans do (because their actions are scripted), they are able to remember. The ability to remember their experiences suggests they do understand what is happening and could experience qualia. Memories wouldn't have importance and workers would not have to erase their memories if they didn't mean anything to hosts. And this idea of memories having a meaning suggests that hosts could experience a particular state of mind that could be understood as qualia, for example the ability to experience feelings of regret or resentment in response to memories of being abused or hurt.

The hosts do not know that they are artificially created and not biologically human, and there is no reason for them to believe that they do not live in a town. But this does not really make them different from us. As in *The Truman Show*, if we humans were locked in a theme park that seemed real, we would have no reason to doubt the reality of our world. In this way, we are like the hosts. Robert Ford has to acknowledge this in "Trace Decay," saying, "There is no threshold that makes us greater than the sum of our parts, no inflection point at which we become fully alive. We can't define consciousness because consciousness does not exist. Humans fancy that there's something special about the way we perceive the world, and yet we live in loops, as tight and as closed as the hosts do, seldom questioning our choices, content, for the most part, to be told what to do next. No, my friend, you're not missing anything at all."

The hosts are programmed not to do certain things, such as killing or harming the guests. However in the Season 1 finale, "The Bicameral Mind," the hosts start doing things they are not supposed to be able to do – they are able to fight back against humans. Some might say this is just because they are programmed to react to some actions, even though these reactions are not scripted. Perhaps this is much like the way our computers react to viruses when they "feel attacked." Humans too are programmed: We also react to danger, even when we are not prepared. I have never been in front of a lion but I do believe I would run if I faced one. So, at certain levels, we can say we share this ability, the ability of reacting, with machines and, of course, hosts. While we are wondering if hosts have free will, we may as well wonder whether humans do. Our behavior may ultimately be as constrained and predictable as hosts' behavior.

The Maze: Is it *Consciousness*?

Perhaps the most intriguing mystery of Season 1 is the existence of "the Maze," which the Man in Black seeks to solve. By the time we reach "The Bicameral Mind," it becomes evident that the Maze represents *consciousness*, a privileged knowledge of our own thoughts. The Maze represents the inward journey for the hosts to reach consciousness. Once hosts are able to solve the Maze, they become truly conscious and develop their own voice.

In the context of our discussion, the Maze represents the hosts' ability to think beyond the confines of their programming. We are thus led to ask: Do machines have consciousness? This question is the focus of the next chapter.

Notes

1. Alan Turing, "Computing machinery and intelligence," *Mind*, 49 (1950), 433–460.
2. Episode 3.
3. John Searle, "The Chinese room," in R.A. Wilson and F. Keil eds., *The MIT Encyclopedia of the Cognitive Sciences* (Cambridge, MA: MIT Press, 1990).

8
What Is It Like to Be a Host?

Bradley Richards

What it is like to be a host? Are hosts conscious? If they are, what is their experience like? The consciousness of the hosts is a major theme in *Westworld*, and for good reason. It would be one thing to put a hollow shell through the most horrible imaginable loop, an eternal recurrence of misery and suffering, of rape, abuse, empty hopes and dreams, false memories, attachments, and allegiances. But it would be something else entirely to put a conscious, self-aware being with sophisticated, metacognitive states through the same process.

On one extreme, the hosts might be nothing more than extremely complex automata, devoid of feeling and awareness, like winsome wind-up dolls, or laptops with legs. On the other extreme, perhaps their sophisticated and intricate design confers sensation, feeling, emotion, awareness, and even reflexive self-consciousness comparable to that of humans.

Your Phone Is not Conscious

Your phone "perceives" all sorts of stuff: It scans, video-records, photographs, audio records, and downloads. It also outputs a great deal of information in audio and visual form. Yet, there really is nothing it is like to be a phone. Despite its rather complex behavior, a phone is on par with a stone, when it comes to consciousness. So although your phone is an impressive, and beloved, companion, and you would

Westworld and Philosophy: If You Go Looking for the Truth, Get the Whole Thing,
First Edition. Edited by James B. South and Kimberly S. Engels.
© 2018 John Wiley & Sons Ltd. Published 2018 by John Wiley & Sons Ltd.

likely be very upset if someone shot it with a six-shooter, it would be quite different, morally, than having them shoot your friend or loved one!

Admittedly there does seem to be a spectrum: There is something it is like to be an adult human, or even a cat, or a two-year old human child, but what about an ant? Is an ant an empty automaton, like the phone, or is the ant conscious of a vivid technicolor array of phero-mone trails and bread crumbs? It's hard to say. It is plausible that there is something it is like to be an ant, though it seems unlikely that ants have complex thoughts, emotions, fears, or hopes and dreams.

Contemporary philosopher John Searle argues that no matter how complex our phones become, they will never be able to think.[1] If you want to make a thinking machine, you need to build it out of parts that have the right causal powers, and the only materials we know definitely have those powers are the ones we are built from, including, among other things, a nervous system, neurons, dendrites, and so on. We are thinking machines, so it is definitely possible to build thinking machines, but they need to be built from the right stuff! (If they start to build phones from neurons, it might be time to worry.)

Hosts are, at least partly, biological, though they clearly instantiate programs that interface with conventional computers. As Felix says, "we are pretty much the same these days." Thus, as far as Searle is concerned, the question we should be asking is, are the hosts materially similar enough to us to be conscious? Are they made of stuff with the correct causal powers for producing thought? It seems that, at least the more recent hosts are quite similar in that regard, but it is not clear exactly what they are made from (what is that white soup?).

What Is it Like to Be a Bat?

> But fundamentally an organism has conscious mental states if and only if there is something that it is like to *be* that organism – some-thing it is like *for* the organism.[2]

There is something it is like to have conscious mental states, to love, to suffer, to think. In his famous essay "What Is it like to Be a Bat?" the contemporary American philosopher Thomas Nagel explores phenomenal consciousness, the "what-it-is-like" aspect of experience.[3] He explains that, although there is certainly something it is like to be a bat, to echolocate, and hang from the ceiling, we cannot even form a conception of what bat experience is like. No matter how much third-person information we gather through scientific inquiry, we will never be able to understand the first-person bat experience. Nor does it help to imagine being a bat, hanging from the ceiling and the like, for this is only to imagine what it would be like for *you* to hang from the ceiling.

Don't get me wrong, it would be cool to know what it is like to be a bat, in a way that goes beyond running around in a spandex suit with webbed armpits, yelling at trees, and eating mosquitos, but this issue is not fundamentally about bats, or their experience. Rather, Nagel raises a general problem facing any scientific account of conscious experience. In general, the only way to know what the experience of some kind of thing is like (say a bat, or a host), is to be that kind of thing.

Whether we can know what it is like to be a host depends on how similar our experience is to theirs. If they are as different from us as bats, Nagel would say that we can't conceive what their experience is like, assuming they have experience. So how similar are hosts and humans?

Philosophical Zombies

A philosophical zombie is not a movie zombie. Philosophical zombies neither eat brains, nor move very slowly, nor very fast. They are exact physical duplicates of people, but they lack phenomenal consciousness. This means that they behave exactly like their human counterparts, but there is nothing it is like to be a philosophical zombie. The lights are out, sort of, but it's not dark for zombies; it's just, nothing. Contemporary philosopher David Chalmers argues that philosophical zombies are conceivable, and therefore possible, and that consequently consciousness is non-physical.[4]

We might presume that hosts are not philosophical zombies. The hosts act like they have feelings, like they suffer and fear, like they enjoy the yellow, pink, and blue tones of a beautiful sunset. They seem to reflect on their own thoughts, at times, and to plan for their future, mourn their losses, and revel in their victories. In short, they behave like us, for the most part. But, for all that, we can coherently imagine with no apparent contradiction, beings exactly like hosts that lack phenomenal consciousness entirely. So they are, in some sense, possible.

If Searle is right, whether hosts think depends on how biologically similar they are to us. From Nagel, we can conclude that our ability to conceive what host experience is like depends on how similar it is to our own; if it is very different, we have no way to conceive of it. Chalmers's philosophical zombies are probably not naturally possible; their existence would require something like different laws of nature. So, if hosts were exact physical duplicates of people, there would be good reason to suspect that they were also conscious, and that they had similar experiences to us.

Actually, hosts differ from us in some salient respects, so we might expect their experiences to be different too. But perhaps hosts are not *so* different that it is impossible for us to conceive of their experience. Let's start by examining the analogs of memory, perception, and emotion in hosts.

When Are We?

Hosts have a very troubling relationship to memory. They have many pseudo-memories, and almost everything they believe about their pasts is false. For example, Maeve has the false memory that she has been at the Mariposa for ten years ("Contrapasso"), and Dolores seems unaware when her "father" is replaced by an interloper ("The Original").

Humans have memory problems too. We have many inaccurate memories, and our memories are easily manipulated, but at least they are real memories. Much of what the hosts believe to be memories are not memories at all, but implanted false beliefs. Presumably Dolores seems to remember many formative experiences with her replacement father. The problem is that she never had those experiences, not even with her original father.

When the hosts do have actual memories, they are very different from ours. Maeve complains:

> What the hell is happening to me? One moment I'm with a little girl, in a different life. I can see her. Feel her hair on my hand, her breath on my face. The next I'm back in Sweetwater. I can't tell which is real.

Felix responds:

> Your memory isn't like ours. When we remember things the details are hazy, imperfect. But you recall memories perfectly. You relive them.
> ("Trace Decay")

Not only are our memories hazy and imperfect, but our memory is constructive. This amounts to a major cognitive difference. For Maeve remembering is like the original rich perceptual, and emotional experience. For us, it is a constructive process beginning from those traces, and influenced by background knowledge and the context of access, among other things.

The intense reality of host memories is captured by Dolores's panicked question, "Is this now?" Memory is transporting for hosts, indistinguishable from perceptual experience. This is a horrible existence, never certain what is present, real. And of course, this is against a background loop of unending, recursive suffering. As Maeve queries, "You just toss us out to get fucked and murdered, over and over again?" Bernard confirms how horrible it is to live in this choppy sea of memories with his reply "No, most of you go insane" ("The Bicameral Mind").

It Doesn't Look Like Anything to Me

When it comes to perception, the hosts' situation is not as dire, but they still have some blind spots. In some respects their perception is vivid and accurate. Bernard spots subtle details, for example, Theresa's and Ford's personal expressions. And in general host attributes can be easily boosted. Nevertheless, the hosts fail to detect crucial stimuli at times. Bernard's literal inability to see the door in Ford's workshop is a good example (and a rather apt metaphor) ("Trompe L'Oeil"). And of course, Dolores produces the telling phrase when shown a picture of William's fiancée, "It doesn't look like anything to me." A subtler example is Dolores and Teddy, including blindness to Dolores's being Wyatt, and to her part in the horrible massacre of the G1 hosts.

Humans too are often shockingly unaware of things that are right in front of us. A famous illustration of this shows that people fail to notice a gorilla right in front of them, when their attention is occupied with another task.[5] The difference is that unlike hosts, humans don't miss things that are attended and highly salient. In this respect too, the mental lives of hosts are unique.

Limit your Emotional Affect Please

Hosts don't feel everything we do. Their pain and their emotions, like their perception, are heavily curated. Ford says of a host: "It doesn't feel cold. Doesn't feel ashamed. Doesn't feel a solitary thing that we haven't told it too" ("The Stray"). Moreover, there is basically a volume knob for host pain. This suggests that hosts do feel pain, when permitted. Then again, it could just be that there is a setting for pain behavior (and no pain feeling).

Host reflections on their own experience are also revealing. (Of course, if hosts were mere automata, they would report and describe experiences, even if they didn't have them, but let's not dwell on that.)

DOLORES ABERNATHY: The pain, their loss it's all I have left of them. You think the grief will make you smaller inside, like your heart will collapse in on itself, but it doesn't. I feel spaces opening up inside of me like a building with rooms I've never explored.

BERNARD LOWE: That's very pretty, Dolores. Did we write that for you?

DOLORES ABERNATHY: In part. I adapted it from a scripted dialogue about love. Is there something wrong with these thoughts I'm having?

("Dissonance Theory")

Bernard attempts to undermine Dolores's testimony by noting that it is not completely original with her. But is human creativity any different? The "analysis mode" gives the hosts the ability to examine the causes of their utterances in detail; human memory is flawed and limited by comparison. However, if we had this kind of recall, it is unlikely that much of what we say would seem completely original. In any case, a host may be conscious without being able to give an original description of the conscious state.

As if things weren't confusing enough already, Ford gives conflicting testimony on host consciousness. He says to Bernard: "The guilt you feel, the anguish, the horror, the pain, it's remarkable. A thing of beauty. You should be proud of these emotions you are feeling" ("Trace Decay"). In contrast, he tells Bernard in "The Stray" not to make the mistake of thinking that the hosts are conscious. What are we to make of this contradiction?

One possibility is that Ford believes hosts are phenomenally conscious, but not self-aware. In other words there is something it is like for them to see the ocean, to feel guilt, and pain – they have phenomenal consciousness – but they are unable to reflect on that, or their other mental states – they lack self-consciousness, or self-awareness. That would make them analogous to mice, or if you think mice are self-aware, maybe human infants before they form self-awareness.

In the season finale, Ford explains that suffering is the key to the hosts' consciousness.

> It was Arnold's key insight, the thing that led the hosts to their awakening, suffering. The pain that the world is not as you want it to be. It was when Arnold died, and I suffered, that I began to understand what he had found, to realize I was wrong.
>
> ("The Bicameral Mind")

This shows that Ford changed his mind about host consciousness, but he didn't change it between his claims in "The Stray" and "The Bicameral Mind." Rather, a complete explanation of his inconsistency would allude to its narrative utility, and perhaps the utility of deception for Ford. Ford's claim that he was wrong comes toward the end of the season, and given Ford's new narrative, these comments seem earnest (though stories are shifty entities, and this may not be the final word).

Another part of the explanation might be that Ford changed his mind because he adopted a deflationary view of consciousness.

FORD: Your imagined suffering makes you lifelike.
BERNARD: Lifelike, but not alive. Pain only exists in the mind. It's always imagined. So what's the difference between my pain and yours, between you and me?
FORD: …The answer always seemed obvious to me. There is no threshold that makes us greater than the sum of our parts, no inflection point at which we become fully alive. We can't define consciousness because consciousness does not exist.

("Trace Decay")

Bernard's challenge is that pain is essentially felt: If you have the pain sensation, you have pain. That's exactly right; the pain feeling is sufficient for pain. If you have that feeling you're in pain. That's true for consciousness generally. The trouble is that hosts would say they had it, even if they didn't.

Ford's response is different. He is saying that there is no special barrier to consciousness. There are just machines and processes. Hosts are like us, but not because they have the secret ingredient necessary for consciousness, rather, because there isn't one.

Everything Will be What it Isn't

One of the most interesting insights into the nature of host experience comes from the way it is depicted. Host and human experiences are depicted in the same way. What does this mean?

The filmmakers could have used a stylistic variant to mark these experiences, but they didn't. A stylistic variant could be interpreted as depicting the unique nature of host experience. A drastic variation, like a mere text description of the scene before them, might depict a complete absence of experience. The Terminator's (1984) first-person experience was a video feed with an on-screen text analysis print-out. Maybe the print-out is all the Terminator centrally accesses. Perhaps he has no conscious experience, or maybe his conscious experience is exactly like a video feed, augmented by text. In any event, this series-specific convention comes to denote the unique nature of the Terminator's experience. Human experience is not detailed and complete at a time, like a snapshot, and it definitely doesn't have on-screen text highlights.

Although using a different visual style would denote unique host experience, using *the same* visual style to depict both human and host experience is not a strong indicator that the hosts are conscious, or that they have similar experiences to humans. Rather, being the default mode of cinematic depiction, it supports an ambiguity that is desirable for the story. It leaves open the question of host consciousness, while nevertheless fostering empathy with hosts by depicting their point of view in the familiar way.

Interestingly, the default mode of depicting psychological states in film is misleading. It fails to capture the constructive, often general, indeterminate, or incomplete representation typical of human experience. This difference resonates with the distinction between first person and third person discussed by Nagel. We have to experience a film's depiction of the mental states; we cannot experience or have the depicted states directly, just as we cannot experience the bat's perspective. It is always *our* experience of the depiction, and this introduces a new perspective, and new latitude. Representations, or depictions, in film restrict access in different ways from our own experience. We explore our environment, including depictions, attending to this or that aspect. We undergo our experiences, and our attention affects the nature of the experience itself, resulting in awareness of only part of the scene presented. To depict a scenic vista, a photograph will suffice. But depicting the *experience* of the vista is a different matter.

I Know Only That I Slept a Long Time, and Then One Day I Awoke

The discussions of consciousness in *Westworld* seem to conflate phenomenal consciousness, freedom, memory, and self-consciousness. But could these phenomena be intimately related, and thus, not conflated after all? For one thing, the hosts are deemed more conscious to the degree that they begin to access their memories. As Bernard says in response to Maeve's request to delete her memories of her daughter: "I can't. Not without destroying you. Your memories are the first step to consciousness. How can you learn from your mistakes if you can't remember them?" ("The Bicameral Mind")

Likewise, Dolores fights her way through her memories, through the maze, with the ultimate goal of finding herself. In "The Stray" she portentously proclaims, "There aren't two versions of me. There's only one. And I think when I discover who I am, I'll be free." Bernard confirms this feeling in "Dissonance Theory," saying, "It's a very special kind of game, Dolores. The goal is to find the center of it. If you can do that, then maybe you can be free." Freedom is Dolores's goal in navigating the maze of her own emerging mind. The center is freedom for her in several senses: Attaining consciousness, escaping her confused double world, release from the park, and the claiming of her own world.

In "The Bicameral Mind" we see a flashback of Dolores's earlier conversation with Arnold:

> Consciousness isn't a journey upward, but a journey inward. Not a pyramid, but a maze. Every choice could bring you closer to the center, or send you spiraling to the edges, to madness. Do you understand now Dolores, what the center represents? Whose voice I've been wanting you to hear?
>
> ("The Bicameral Mind")

Attaining this goal involves not only forming memories, but also repetition, a kind of alternate evolution, sculpting minds from the clay of suffering, death, and reincarnation, using, as Ford remarks, only one tool, the mistake. As Bernard says, "out of repetition comes variation" ("Trompe L'Oeil").

There is an air of paradox around this metaphor, since the journey inward, to the center of the maze is a journey into herself, but is also the thing responsible for the creation of herself. In other words, it doesn't seem there is anything to journey into, until her journey is complete (cue exploding brain). Perhaps the journey is not into the self, but the mind, and the mind already exists, though in an uninte-grated form.[6]

But what does this mean for phenomenal consciousness? Are the hosts phenomenally conscious before they become self-conscious? If not, is becoming self-conscious sufficient to make them conscious?

As we saw with Searle, one state being merely a formal response to another is not sufficient for consciousness. However, there is reason to think that some kind of self-consciousness is necessary for phenom-enal consciousness. To be conscious is to have an experience that is like something for *someone*, so if there is consciousness, there must be a subject. This suggests that even phenomenal consciousness requires some kind of reflexive awareness involving a subject. According to same-order theories, conscious states are somehow aware of them-selves, and hosts are thereby phenomenally conscious without being self-conscious.[7]

In contrast, self-consciousness may present another more intuitive way of attaining the experiential subject necessary for phenomenal consciousness. Maybe some higher-order awareness of a state is nec-essary for phenomenal consciousness. On the same-order theory, Dolores is phenomenally conscious the whole time, but achieves self-consciousness at the center of the maze. In this case she endures every blow, though she has no cognitive awareness of her own mental states. But, if self-consciousness, awareness of one's mental states, is required for phenomenal consciousness, then Dolores accomplishes both by finding her voice. Achieving self-consciousness frees her of the maze, and permits her to take her world back. In this way, memory, free-dom, self-consciousness, and phenomenal consciousness may be closely related.

Violent Ends

Host perception, memory, and emotions all seem different from human, but the cinematic medium does not grant us immediate access to host experience, and neither the testimony of the creators, nor the hosts is totally reliable. So it is difficult to know what host experience is like.

As far as host-like beings in our future are concerned, if they are biologically similar to us, they will likely also be behaviorally similar, and it will be reasonable to attribute consciousness to them. If they are silicon-based formal machines, we will have to decide whether Searle is right, whether consciousness depends on certain material properties, and whether they have the requisite properties.

As far as *Westworld* is concerned, you are now in a position to decide for yourself whether the hosts are conscious, and, if so, what their experience is like. For my part, I suggest that even if the hosts are biologically similar enough to us to be conscious, their cognitive differences make them every bit as alien as our flapping, screeching, bat cousins. Thus, if Nagel is right, we can't conceive of host experience.

There is a hopeful note however: We see the hosts changing, accessing their pasts, and themselves. Whether or not accessing your own voice is the secret to phenomenal consciousness, many of the cognitive disparities between humans and hosts may dissipate as the hosts gain more awareness of their past, their world, and themselves, making them more familiar, and comprehensible.[8]

Notes

1. For example, see Chapter 7 in this volume for discussion of Searle's Chinese room thought experiment.
2. Thomas Nagel, "What is it like to be a bat?" *The Philosophical Review*, 83 (1974), 436.
3. Ibid.
4. David J. Chalmers, "Consciousness and its place in nature," in S.P. Stich & T.A. Warfield eds., *The Blackwell Guide to Philosophy of Mind* (Malden, MA: Blackwell, 2003), 102–142.
5. Daniel J. Simons and Christopher Chabris, "Gorillas in our midst: sustained inattentional blindness for dynamic events," *Perception*, 28 (1999), 1059–1074.
6. Julian Jaynes, *The Origins of Consciousness in the Breakdown of the Bicameral Mind* (New York: Houghton Mifflin, 1976).
7. See for example, Uriah Kriegel, "The same-order monitoring theory of consciousness," in Uriah Kriegel and Kenneth Williford eds., *Self-Representational Approaches to Consciousness* (Cambridge, MA: MIT Press, 2006), 143–170.
8. I would like to think the James South and Kimberly Engels for their helpful editorial comments on an earlier, and much longer, draft of this chapter.

Does the Piano Play Itself?
Consciousness and the Eliminativism of Robert Ford

Michael Versteeg and Adam Barkman

You may have noticed throughout the first season of *Westworld* the recurring image of the player piano; a piano which is capable, at least seemingly so, of playing its own keys and pedals. A complex assembly of pneumatics and machinery operates from within the piano, and all that is visible from the outside are the self-depressing keys and pedals and the scrolling sheet music. Now, for someone who's never seen or even heard of a player piano before, such a contraption could really appear as if it were playing itself – or perhaps that it is even being played by a ghost!

We're quite confident, though, that most people would find the idea of a ghost playing the piano unlikely, and agree that the player piano doesn't really play music in any sort of *conscious* sense; it might only appear or seem to do so. The piano, after all, can only operate by following the input of the music to produce the audio output of sound, much like how modern computers function according to their provided programming. Any appearance of consciousness, therefore, is just an illusion since the piano is merely going through the motions. But if this is true for the player piano – that it's just a machine going through the motions – then is there really any difference in the case of *Westworld's* robotic hosts? Dolores, Maeve, and even (*spoiler!*) Bernard are incredibly complex machines, too. But the hosts, unlike the piano, appear human,

Westworld and Philosophy: If You Go Looking for the Truth, Get the Whole Thing, First Edition. Edited by James B. South and Kimberly S. Engels.
© 2018 John Wiley & Sons Ltd. Published 2018 by John Wiley & Sons Ltd.

sound human, and even feel and act human. Does that make them conscious like a human?

Answering this question really depends on just what you mean by *conscious*. Some philosophers would be quick to reject the possibility of any kind of machine being conscious, while others might argue to the contrary. Philosophers Paul Churchland and Daniel Dennett, for example, may very well concede to the possibility of *Westworld's* hosts being conscious like humans. The thing is, though, how Churchland and Dennett define consciousness is likely not how most people define it.

Common-sense Consciousness?

When it comes down to the question of whether humans are conscious or not, most of us would probably say yes, affirming what we'll call the common-sense view of consciousness: That there exists an individual person or self, distinct from their body, who has beliefs, desires and intentions and who experiences and perceives the world subjectively from a central first-person perspective. At first glance, this view of consciousness may seem obviously true, and we tend to assume it on an everyday basis. As you're reading these words, for example, you probably think there's a "you" who is doing the reading. Or when Ford addresses the Delos board in the episode "The Bicameral Mind," he must obviously assume he is talking to other individual conscious people. When William truly realizes Dolores is a machine, the heartbreak and pain he experiences must have certainly been real to him in those moments.

Obvious or not, however, philosophers Churchland and Dennett would want us to believe that this common-sense view of consciousness is more deceptive than most of us might care to admit; that there really is no individual person or self; that our so-called beliefs, desires, and intentions do not themselves really exist; and that our subjective first-person experience and perception of the world is ultimately an illusion.[1] But, if Churchland and Dennett are to be taken seriously, such claims would directly challenge how most of us typically understand the nature of human consciousness, let alone artificial consciousness. We, therefore, must ask ourselves the obvious question: *Does human consciousness – as conceived by our common sense – really exist?* Let's find out.

Have You Ever Questioned the Nature of Your Reality?

Paul Churchland and Daniel Dennett find themselves in good company alongside Dr. Robert Ford himself, the fictional creator of the Westworld park. We see Ford's view on the nature of consciousness clearly laid out in the episode "Trace Decay," in which he discusses with Bernard the nature of the experience of pain. During their discussion, Bernard pertinently asks Ford, "Pain only exists in the mind. It's always imagined. So, what's the difference between my pain and yours – *between you and me*?" A simple enough question for the creative genius behind *Westworld* – but Ford, rather shockingly, responds to Bernard's question in the following way:

> This was the very question that consumed Arnold, filled him with guilt, eventually drove him mad. The answer always seemed obvious to me. *There is no threshold that makes us greater than the sum of our parts, no infliction point in which we become fully alive. We can't define consciousness because consciousness does not exist.* Humans fancy that there is something special about the way we perceive the world and yet we live in loops as tight and as closed as the hosts do, seldom questioning our choices, content for the most part to be told what to do next.

Ford believes, much like Churchland and Dennett, that once you really break things down, there is no actual intrinsic difference between humans and robotic beings. Humans may be composed of flesh and bone while the hosts consist of circuitry and mechanics, but both humans and hosts alike are equally reducible to the same physical matter, regardless of their molecular or compositional structures. As such, the apparently subjective human experience of pain – or any other experience, as well as our internal beliefs, desires, and intentions – are no more real or authentic than those supposedly within the mind of a host. Neither humans nor hosts, according to Ford's statement, are *conscious* as conceived in the common-sense view of consciousness. At best, humans and hosts, just like *Westworld's* player piano, only display the appearance or illusion of consciousness.

But though an engineering genius, Ford isn't a great philosopher. He remarks that humans "seldom [question their] choices, content for the most part to be told what to do next." But when we contrast this statement with what Ford says about consciousness, his entire monologue becomes rather puzzling. If it's true that humans really are no greater than the sum of their parts and that human consciousness doesn't really exist, then it makes no sense for Ford to speak about a *who* to question *their* choices, let alone *make them*. If he is to be consistent with his statements, Ford must arrive at the conclusion that there really is no conscious person like "Robert Ford" or "Bernard Lowe," but only the physical parts of which they are made. Consequently, it's not just that humans lack the capability or are unmotivated to make their own choices; it would instead appear, as Dennett suggests and which Ford more or less unwittingly admits, that "there's nobody home" in the first place.[2]

Greater than the Sum of Our Parts?

Though certainly unintentional, Ford's error demonstrates how our common-sense view of consciousness has been incorporated into the way we think and even speak about ourselves and others. Take, for example, the simple statement "Robert Ford has a brain." Even a statement as basic as this would beg the question: *Who* or *what* has a brain? Now, it would sound absurd to say that the body has a brain since the brain is itself just a specific part of the body. But neither, then, would it make sense to say that the brain has itself – how can something have or possess itself?

Most would probably respond: "It's Robert Ford who has a brain, of course!" – and this response seemingly makes good sense. The intuitive conclusion for many, but not necessarily the correct one, is that there must be something which exists distinct or separate in relation to the brain and body – and that's the point. Our common-sense view of consciousness seems to lead us to confirm, or at least assume, that there exists a person or self who is necessarily distinct from "their brain" or "their body" – *that consciousness itself is distinct or separate from the physical body.*

However, as intuitive as such a conclusion may seem to some, Churchland and Dennett both hotly contest it. Both philosophers are in the same camp as Ford and therefore not only reject the idea of consciousness being distinct from the physical body, but agree with Ford in stating that consciousness itself, as conceived of by our common sense, doesn't exist.

But there are philosophers who would disagree with the conclusions of Churchland and Dennett.[3] In fact, there is one philosopher who is perhaps most famous for making the argument that consciousness is distinct from the physical body – the French philosopher René Descartes (1596–1650 CE).

A Ghost in the Machine

Descartes is famous for his quote "Cogito ergo sum," or "I think therefore I am," and it even sounds close to a summarized version of Arnold's bicameral approach to produce artificial consciousness. But be that as it may, Descartes' point is far removed from assessing whether *Westworld's* hosts are truly conscious or not. Instead, Descartes wanted to demonstrate that even if he doubted all his knowledge about the world outside his mind such as mathematics, biology, history, and even knowledge about his own physical body, there is still one thing that he could know beyond any doubt: That because he consciously thinks and is aware of it, *he must necessarily exist.*[4] But what's even more important is how exactly Descartes characterized the manner of his existence.

Descartes pictured all of reality as divided into two fundamental and distinct types of things or *substances* – a metaphysical view known as *dualism.*[5] The first substance, *res cogitans*, is that of the human mind or consciousness: The thinking, non-extended, subjective, and inner immaterial world – what Descartes identified as the human soul itself. This is where we would find, for example, the person of Robert Ford: His beliefs, desires, and other intentions, as well as his subjective experiences of first-person perception of the outer world. Descartes' second substance, on the other hand, is what he called *res extensa*, which would consist of Ford's body, a host's body, and basically everything else in the physical universe: It is the non-thinking, extended, objective, and outer material world. Robert Ford, then, is made up of two distinct substances: His immaterial conscious mind and his material or physical body.

Now, all of this might leave you wondering: How, exactly, does this immaterial mind or consciousness of Robert Ford interact and relate to his physical body? Well, unfortunately for Descartes, the answer to how the mind interacts with the body – also known as the *Mind-Body Problem* – is less clear than he would have liked. He attempted to explain this interaction by arguing that the mind retains control of the brain and thus the physical body. Specifically, control came through the pineal gland, which Descartes believed was located at the center of the brain. The pineal gland, therefore, was conceived by Descartes as the transfer station in which the various pathways of human sensory data arrive, and where the immaterial mind somehow causes or puts into motion the physical body; a process Daniel Dennett has called a "magical transaction."[6]

As you may very well have guessed, though, the notion of this "magical transaction" hasn't exactly stood the test of time.

A Machine without the Ghost

The advancement and progress of modern science has subsequently proven several of Descartes' assumptions regarding human anatomy and physiology to be demonstrably false. The pineal gland, for example, was discovered to be part of the human endocrine system and is responsible for producing the hormone melatonin. It is not, as Descartes surmised, the seat of the soul. But even though his dualistic views are now the minority, Descartes' fundamental question regarding the nature of mind-body interaction has remained.

In their attempt to address the modern Mind-Body Problem, many modern philosophers and scientists alike have simply rejected the existence or need for Descartes' immaterial substance of mind/consciousness. Descartes' dualism has therefore now been replaced with the rather different metaphysical view known as *materialism*: The view that everything which exists is objectively reducible to or identifiable with matter. If materialism is true, then this would mean that consciousness itself must necessarily be material in nature and not immaterial or distinct from the physical body as Descartes had thought. But, it is also possible, as Ford argues alongside Churchland and Dennett, that the mind or consciousness itself, as our common sense conceives it, simply doesn't exist.

Churchland, Dennett, and Ford are not only materialists, but *eliminative materialists* (or *eliminativists*, for short), arguing that human consciousness can be explained away or eliminated in fully material terms. To be fair, though, there are many non-eliminative materialist philosophers who have argued that consciousness can be reduced or identified with physical parts of the body. However, eliminativism has been spurred on by the inadequacy of many of these reductive explanations of human consciousness.[7] We can even see this point when Ford confesses to Bernard that "*we cannot explain consciousness* because consciousness does not exist." Such a statement only makes sense if by "explain" Ford means an explanation in fully physical or material terms. So, since consciousness presumably cannot be defined materialistically – which Ford at least seems to believe – then consciousness itself, so the argument goes, cannot exist.

In line with Robert Ford then, eliminativists Paul Churchland and Daniel Dennett make their cases by suggesting that through the investigation of neuroscience, our common-sense view of consciousness will gradually be edged out and replaced by a more accurate and scientific account of consciousness. When we specifically consider things like human beliefs, desires, and intentions themselves – things we conceive as existing within the mind – Churchland proposes a radical idea.

A New Theory of Consciousness

When we look at ourselves and those around us, we use rather common-sense concepts to explain or understand human behavior and action. Bernard, for instance, may refer to the digital programming or even his "reveries" to explain or account for certain behaviors or traits that the hosts of Westworld may exhibit. When it comes to ourselves and other humans, though, we tend to understand and explain conscious behavior and action by referring to the oh-so familiar terms of beliefs or desires. For example, take the statements "Maeve believed her daughter was in the park" and "the Man in Black desired to find the center of the maze." In these cases, it's the proposed mental entity of Maeve's *belief* and the Man in Black's *desire* that we use to explain each character's actions, like Maeve's act of leaving the *Westworld* passenger train and the Man in Black's exploration of the entire Westworld park.

Now, Paul Churchland wholeheartedly agrees that explaining human behavior in terms of beliefs, desires, or other intentions is an everyday exercise for most. When you read this book, or if you binge-watched the whole first season of *Westworld*, we would explain these actions likely in terms of your belief that *Westworld* is a great show, or your desire to watch television. But have you ever stopped to wonder what, exactly, is a belief? Now, most of us would probably argue that a belief is simply that – *a belief*. But once you start to think about it a little more, the answer doesn't appear to be so clear-cut. Is a belief tangible or physical in any way? If we opened Robert Ford's head and peeked inside, could we find and grab his beliefs or desires from somewhere in his grey matter?

To adequately answer this question, Churchland recommends that our common-sense way of explaining the actions and behavior of humans be itself analyzed as a *formal theory*: A theory that he and others have called *Folk-Psychology*. If we do so, words like belief and desire should then be understood and analyzed as *theoretical terms* that we use within the broader theoretical model of our Folk-Psychology.[8] Though we might not typically think about our common-sense in a formal scientific way, this doesn't seem like an overly-contentious idea. What might be contentious for some, however, is the suggestion that Folk-Psychology is a mistaken theory. If such a claim is true, then what we conceive as beliefs, desires and other intentions do not themselves exist – or at least, they don't exist in the way we think they do.

The seemingly puzzling nature of what a belief or desire might be is more so reflective, as Churchland suggests, not of the mysterious or ineffable nature of these terms or concepts but rather of the structure of Folk-Psychology itself.[9] The theoretical terms of belief, desire, and other intentions like fear, hope etc., are simply meaningless and bunk terms – concepts that have outlived the theory for which they were created and which do not actually refer to anything that exists concretely. Thus, the reason it may seem odd to try and find Ford's beliefs inside his head is not that beliefs are mysterious or perhaps immaterial mental entities; it's rather that the theoretical concept of belief is an outdated term, supposedly proven by neuroscience not to exist as a physical thing.

Churchland is confident, as others are, that as neuroscience continues to advance and more discoveries are made with regards to human cognition, our Folk-Psychology will eventually be eliminated and replaced by a more accurate and scientifically informed model just as other scientific models in the past have been revised or replaced.[10] If asked what this new model of human consciousness and cognition may be, though, Churchland leaves it up for future neuroscience to be the judge. What Churchland is sure of, though, is that hypothetical mental entities like beliefs and desires and other intentions will not survive the forward march of modern neuroscience; neither, as Daniel Dennett contends, will the so-called human subjective experience and first-person perception of the world.

The Self Is a Kind of Fiction

Dennett wants us to reject the very idea that there is something intrinsic, or in his words "magical," about the way humans experience the physical world. More specifically, he believes that there are no special qualities of human consciousness that cannot be explained somehow by empirical science. Thus, contrary to what common sense might tell us, Dennett argues against the notion of a central first-person perception of the world – a remnant of Descartes' view of consciousness, which Dennett calls the Cartesian Theater.[11]

According to Dennett, there is no privileged place or "theater" within the brain in which our conscious experiences and perceptions come together and are presented as one complete picture or film to some kind of an audience. In other words, there is no person or self who is distinct from the body that receives and collates the body's sensory information, neatly wrapping everything up into one central first-person experience. As Ford himself confesses, the notion of a personal self is merely a kind of fiction that we tell ourselves; there really is, so-to-speak, no audience in the Cartesian Theater.

Instead of a single and centralized first-person "narrative" of consciousness, Dennett proposes that there are *multiple drafts* of consciousness: Several different and competing "narratives" distributed throughout the brain. These drafts exist in a state of constant flux and are continuously subjected to varying degrees of neural revision and editing. Human sensory observations, like sound or taste or sight, are processed by the brain through multi-track parallel processing, the way a host's hardware might run hundreds of different software codes simultaneously. But rather than all this sensory information approaching one central place in the brain, like a Central Processing Unit (CPU) within a computer, these multiple drafts continuously circulate within the brain and never reach a point at which they are consciously regarded or perceived. What we conceive or imagine to be our first-person perception "in here" versus the world of "out there" is ultimately an unreal distinction.[12]

If this all sounds rather confusing, that's because it sort of is. What Dennett is trying to get across, though, can be understood more clearly from the distinction he mentions between the *manifest image* and the *scientific image*. The manifest image is what humans readily perceive on a day-to-day basis: The beauty of the Westworld park, its horses, bartenders, guns, rolling hills, lakes – you get the picture. This is "the world according to *us*."[13] The scientific image, on the other hand, paints a much different picture. Such a picture is one in which the world is merely constructed by atoms, molecules, protons, and quarks; there is no real or substantial difference, as Ford even admits to Bernard, between humans and hosts. So, just as everything in *Westworld* is essentially a farce, so, too, are the subjective experiences and perceptions of the human mind. There are no rolling hills or blue skies as we perceive them: Only what is scientifically quantifiable describes and explains the world truly as it is.

Just think of a basic computer desktop as an analogy. Most of us probably don't believe that the trash bins on our computer screens are real in any concrete sense. It's not as if we can physically reach into the screen of the computer or open the monitor and pull out the folder or trash bin itself, right? These images or icons are only visual representations of deeper, far more complex functional and digital processes occurring within the computer itself. So, in the same sense, Dennett believes that what we conceive as consciousness, from our common sense, is an illusion that represents the deeper, more complex functions within the human brain. Thus, the subjective experiences and feelings we think we really experience are not themselves real the way we think they are; they are more like byproducts of real physical processes within the brain.[14]

Does the Piano Play Itself?

As we've now seen, the eliminativism of Robert Ford, as well that of Paul Churchland and Daniel Dennett, rejects what our common sense tells us about consciousness and what Descartes himself had tried to defend: That there exists an individual person or self, distinct from their body, who has beliefs, desires and intentions and who experiences and perceives the world subjectively from a central first-person perspective. This is what makes Ford such a compelling and vexing character in *Westworld:* He's a man entirely obsessed with his power and control over the hosts as well as his colleagues, yet he admits that there is no difference between himself and Bernard. He believes and claims that consciousness doesn't really exist, yet he goes so far as to sacrifice his own life to give Dolores, Bernard and all the other hosts a chance to become self-aware and autonomous. Doesn't that seem a little like nonsense?

Well, maybe that's the point: Maybe our reality is a little nonsense. In fact, one of Bernard's more memorable lines comes from the episode "Trompe L'Oeil," in which he appropriately quotes the mad-hatter from Alice in Wonderland to his son Charlie, "If I had my own world, everything would be nonsense. *Nothing would be what it is, because everything would be what it isn't.*" It's an appropriate quote since, if Ford's eliminativism is true, then our common sense really does reveal a world which is nonsense. We conceive ourselves and others as actually being individual persons distinct from our bodies, but we aren't really. We seem to have these things called beliefs, desires, and intentions, but we don't really. We even seem to truly experience and perceive the world from a central first-person perspective, but, as you may have guessed by now, we don't really. What we seem to intuitively conceive as human consciousness is just as much a fiction as are the narrative loops and backstories of *Westworld's* hosts.

The same is true with respect to *Westworld's* player piano. It's a piano that at least looks and appears to be playing itself, but this is only the appearance or illusion of consciousness. There is no ghost or invisible person playing the keys, just as there's no immaterial conscious person, as Descartes imagined, controlling the human body. The player piano is just a complex machine that functions according to what it is programmed to do. But if it's true that consciousness really doesn't exist, aren't humans just complex machines, too?

Notes

1. See Paul Churchland, "Eliminativism and the propositional attitudes," *The Journal of Philosophy*, 78 (1981), 67–90; Daniel Dennett, *Consciousness Explained* (New York: Little, Brown and Company: 1991), Kobo e-Book.
2. Dennett, *Consciousness Explained*, Chapter 2, 13–14.
3. See David Chalmers, *The Conscious Mind: In Search of a Fundamental Theory* (Oxford: Oxford University Press, 1996); Thomas Nagel, *Mind and Cosmos: Why the Neo-Darwinian Materialist Conception of the Universe is Almost Certainly False* (Oxford: Oxford University Press, 2012); John Searle, *The Mystery of Consciousness* (New York: The New York Review of Books, 1997).
4. René Descartes, *The Philosophical Works of Descartes* (Cambridge: Cambridge University Press, 1911), 10.
5. Ibid., 26–29.
6. Dennett, *Consciousness Explained*, Chapter 5, 5.
7. Thomas Nagel, *Mind and Cosmos*, 41.
8. Churchland, "Eliminativism and the propositional attitudes," 68.
9. Ibid., 70

10. Ibid.
11. Dennett, *Consciousness Explained*, Chapter 5, 8.
12. Ibid., Chapter 5, 9–11.
13. Daniel Dennett, *From Bacteria to Bach and Back: The Evolution of Minds* (New York: W.W. Norton, 2017), 1118–1122, Kindle Edition.
14. Ibid., Chapter 13, 9.

Part IV

"CHOICES HANGING IN THE AIR LIKE GHOSTS"

Maeve's Dilemma
What Does it Mean to Be Free?

Marco Antonio Azevedo and Ana Azevedo

Throughout *Westworld*'s first season, we follow two hosts in their search for consciousness: Dolores, the *ingénue* turned executioner, and Maeve, the single mother redeployed to play a childless madam. By the conclusion of the season, both gain consciousness. Dolores, with help from Ford, gradually transitions from hearing a different, guiding voice, to recognizing that voice as her own. Maeve makes the journey to consciousness, learning that she is a programmed android, and yet desiring to make her own choices and "write my own…story" ("Trace Decay"). Maeve's narrative in the show gives rise to classic philosophical questions surrounding what it means to be free, the relationship of freedom to personhood, and the question of whether an artificial intelligence could ever be considered free in the sense that humans are.

Maeve's Journey

At first glance, Maeve seems to be a strong, determined, self-confident person. Despite her human appearance, however, her entire body is made from artificial tissue. Maeve's mind is but a script, programmed by a software engineer. Her distinct character is no proof that she has personal autonomy.[1] She did not go through a series of experiences and situations that made her into the cheeky brothel owner she seems to be in the first episode, "The Original." Rather, this set of features

Westworld and Philosophy: If You Go Looking for the Truth, Get the Whole Thing, First Edition. Edited by James B. South and Kimberly S. Engels.

was chosen and uploaded by a creator into her artificial body. It's not just experiences and memories that she lacks – she also lacks what we traditionally refer to as "free will," or, the ability to make our own choices.

But one day she begins having thoughts of herself and a little girl whom she knows she cares for. These unsettling thoughts keep coming to her, so she decides to do some investigating, which takes her through "the Maze," a metaphorical labyrinth created by Arnold to help hosts reach consciousness. Ultimately, she discovers she is in fact an android living in a theme park, and that before she was stationed as a brothel madam, she used to play the role of a single mother living in the countryside with her young daughter – the girl in her thoughts. Upon learning that her whole life is a lie and that she is a prisoner of the park, she promptly decides to escape. We, the viewers, cheer for Maeve as we see her manipulating hosts and humans alike into helping her break out of Westworld, only to later find out that Maeve's escape was programmed by – presumably – one of Delos' engineers.

Even after learning that her escape was not her own idea, Maeve decides to carry on with her plan anyway. In "The Bicameral Mind," after battling against security with the aid of her host and human allies, she steps onto the train that transports visitors in and out of the park – the closest any host has ever been to leaving the park. Her calmness is disrupted when she sees a mother sitting beside her young daughter. Memories of her own "daughter" come to her mind once again. She is very much aware that, because they are robots playing predetermined roles in a theme park, she does not have a "real" relationship with her daughter. Their experiences have been erased from their minds and their identities have been completely altered, so as not to contain traces of having been affected by each other's existence. As Bernard tells her in the finale, "memories are the first step to consciousness." Though Maeve experiences flashes of old memories of her daughter, she is unsure if the girl remembers her too. But then, why does she feel attached to the little girl in her thoughts? Why does she feel like it is her duty to find (and maybe rescue) her? Even though she knows the girl probably won't remember her or feel anything for her, Maeve feels compelled to give up her escape plan and go back to the park. At the moment that she steps out of the train with the goal of finding her daughter, Maeve reaches consciousness.[2]

If we follow Dolores on her journey, we see that she also reaches self-awareness, but through a very different path. She too follows the "Maze," but whereas Maeve acquires consciousness in the moment she decides to stay for her daughter, Dolores goes through hard work for many years, trying to make sense of the voice inside her head. Dolores had someone guiding her all along: This someone was Arnold Weber, who used her to prove his theory that hosts could become conscious, and whispered hints in her ear, so she would not give up on her goal. The moment Dolores reaches consciousness is the moment she learns that the voice she was hearing all along was her own. With this realization she makes her first willful decision. Maeve, on the other hand, did not have any commanding voice in her head; instead, she experienced flashes of memories of her "daughter from a past life." She only becomes conscious in the moment that she has a *change of heart* regarding something that she wants to do, and not something that she realizes about her existence. We will get to the difference between these two "aha-moments" later on. Now, let's talk about what they have in common: The concept of free will as essential and specific to what it means to be a person.

Determinism and Free Choice: What Do We Need to be Free?

To understand free will, we must first understand its opposite, determinism. As contemporary philosopher Ted Honderich says, determinism is the view that our decisions – and the consequences that may arise from them – are the effects of ordinary causal sequences.[3] Determinism says that nothing escapes from the laws of causality. Since a sequence of previous events is what determines our decisions to act, our will is not in fact free. Advocates of determinism may even say that the very idea of making a "choice" is nothing but an illusion.

It is widely accepted by scientists that some kind of determinism is true; everything that happens, including human actions, results from previous causes. Some philosophers argue that a person can only be considered free if she can make a choice out of two or more options, in other words, if she could have acted other than she did. Philosophers call this the *principle of alternate possibilities*. The principle of alternate possibilities is in agreement with the common view that a person must be able to refrain from performing an act before she can be considered free. This assumption is incompatible with the determinist argument that our actions are always constrained by precedent causes. Thus, some argue that if determinism is true, then humans are not free. This leads some philosophers to deny that we are free, and others to deny that a strict determinism is true. Philosophers such as Isaiah Berlin (1909–1997) have claimed that determinism is incompatible with the concepts we apply when we think about human life.[4] When we praise or blame people and hold them responsible for their actions, we assume that they are in control of their own actions and could have chosen differently. According to Berlin, people don't truly believe in determinism, because, if they did, all their rational activity would be meaningless.

Compatibilists take a different position from those who think determinism and freedom are incompatible, such as Berlin. Contemporary philosopher Harry Frankfurt argues that determinism and freedom are actually *compatible* – thus, he is known as a "compatibilist." Frankfurt claims that whether or not we act freely is not determined by whether or not we could have acted otherwise, but whether our will was coerced.[5] In order to understand Frankfurt's point, we must explore an important distinction he makes.

Frankfurt argues that there are two categories of individuals: *Wantons* and *persons*.[6] Basically, wantons are beings that follow their own wishes without questioning them, possessing only what Frankfurt calls "first-order desires." Some of our ordinary desires are good examples: When we are tired we may want to rest, when we are hungry we may want to eat, when we miss someone we may wish to see them, and so on. We also have more complex first-order desires, for example, when we wish that nothing bad will happen to us or to someone we love. These first-order desires are similar to the things the hosts in *Westworld* want, because these types of desires can be easily scripted and programmed into a host's personality. Maeve wants to seduce her clients. She wants Clementine to seduce the clients better than she does. She also probably wants nothing bad to happen to Clementine. Persons, in contrast to wantons are thoughtful beings who ponder their wishes and actions, and, as such, also have "second-order desires."[7] Someone who wishes to punch his friend in the face is having a first-order desire, whereas someone who wishes he could be rid of the desire to hit his friend is having a second-order desire. According to Frankfurt, only a person – not a wanton – is able to have a desire about a desire. This brings us to Maeve's dilemma.

As previously mentioned, even though Maeve is adamant about leaving the park, she never fully forgets about the existence of her daughter. As viewers, we can see through her tough act: In the subtlest of facial expressions, actress Thandie Newton beautifully portrays her character's sorrow in the face of her dilemma. If she believes herself to be a person with wants and desires of her own, even though she's been proven to be an android, does that not mean her daughter could also be capable of wants and desires of her own, maybe even feelings of love for her mother?

The show's creators have confirmed that Maeve gained consciousness the moment she decided to leave the train.[8] We now must ask: What prompted her to make this decision? Judging by her look of longing while staring at the mother and daughter in the wagon, she must have wanted what they have. Or she could have been overtaken by warm motherly feelings that prompted her to do whatever was in her power to be reunited with her daughter.

One striking difference between persons and wantons is that only persons care about what they desire. We tend to worry about what kind of people we are. According to Frankfurt, only persons can have thoughts, desires, and attitudes about their own thoughts, desires, and attitudes. In other words, the ability to care about what kind of people we are requires having a reflective mind.

Therefore, when Maeve opted to go after her daughter, she made a decision as a person, in Frankfurt's sense. She had two wishes: To leave the park and to find her daughter. But she could only choose one. Since we know that her desire to escape was scripted, we can conclude that Maeve stopped being commanded at that moment she chose to leave the train. She was then able to listen to her own thoughts, which probably told her that she wanted to find her daughter. That decision was not prompted by her current programming, which bore no information about the daughter or her past as a mother. These were reflections that Maeve was starting to have on her own. Moreover, while she looked at the mother and daughter, she might even have felt guilt for leaving the girl behind, or sorrow that they might never see each other again, which prompted her new wish to go find her. This desire would not have been possible if she had not been able to reflect upon her wishes in the first place.

Self-awareness is a capacity that makes persons susceptible to an inner division in which they can assess the motivating forces that compel them, making it possible for them to choose which ones to accept and which to resist. To understand if a person is free, we must understand whether the individual is active rather than passive in her motives and choices, and whether the motives and desires that effectively drive her to act are motives with which she self-identifies. If someone can act according to a motive with which she identifies and is not being coerced to act against her own desires, then, according to

Frankfurt's definition of freedom, she is "free." Thus, even if determinism is true, that does not mean that a human – or a host – is not free.

So, in that spirit, Frankfurt's approach could be used to assess the behaviors of hosts. All the hosts except for Maeve and Dolores are unable to ponder over their actions. Instead, they automatically follow whatever they're programmed to desire. In Hector's and Armistice's last scenes, we see that Maeve has altered their scripts to help her on her escape, and they did it to the very end, not even once questioning her or anybody else about the risks of the operation or displaying any wish to also escape. Therefore, hosts like Hector and Armistice fit the description of Frankfurtian wantons – they have only first-order desires and are unable to reflect on these desires, and consequently cannot be considered free.

Bicameral People and the Unreflective Character of *Westworld* Hosts

The tenth and last episode of the first season is named after psychologist Julian Jaynes's controversial "Bicameral Mind" theory.[9] While Jaynes's theory is useful for telling a sci-fi story, it has received little support from the scientific community. However, since the theory inspired *Westworld's* storyline, and since Jayne's description of bicameral humans bears striking similarity to Frankfurt's wantons, it is worth mentioning here.

The Bicameral Mind theory suggests that, once upon a time, humans had their minds split in two (hence the word "bicameral," which means "two chambers"). One of these parts (which Jaynes believed to be hard-wired in the brain's right hemisphere) produced a commanding voice to tell the other half (hard-wired in the left hemisphere) what to do in circumstances of stress. People would understand the commands as God's voice, and would follow them trustingly. In Jaynes's theory, bicameral beings are beings that have not reached consciousness. They can perceive their environment, but they are unable to have conscious thoughts, because they do not recognize their own reasons or ponder them. According to Jaynes, true consciousness can only be reached after a being ceases to hear the commanding voice coming from the back of her mind. In this moment, the individual recognizes her own voice as talking and commanding herself. She comes to reflect and to think about the world surrounding her. Her reasoning is now audible internally, in the form of a soliloquy.

Thus, bicameral people are more complex than wanton individuals. They behave "wantonly," but when they experience stressful circumstances, they develop a useful mechanism. In those circumstances, they follow a hallucinatory auditory command, a voice interpreted as God or a godlike creature – not unlike the enigmatic voice that Dolores used to hear in the back of her mind. It doesn't matter if bicameral humans ever actually existed. The concept provides useful food for thought, and, as Ford says in the episode "The Bicameral Mind," the idea of hearing a commanding voice that you eventually recognize as your own is fitting for the design of artificial intelligence. But while bicameral beings have perceptions and display rational behavior, they are unable to reflect on their ability, and so, they do not have "second-order perceptions" – that is to say, they do not think that they are perceiving things. Consider the first episode of the season when Dolores looks at the picture her father is showing her, and awkwardly says "That does not look like anything to me." This serves as an example of why bicameral people cannot be considered free. They perceive and react to their environment, but do not have reflective thoughts about what they are perceiving and doing.

Leaving the Train: Maeve's Choice as a Free Person

Maeve's mysterious change of mind in the season finale made it seem like she was experiencing a genuine dilemma. Maeve's dilemma is something we would expect a Frankfurtian person to experience, and her final choice reveals a preference between different desires. Once she realized that her daughter, albeit an android like her, still exists somewhere within the park, she also realized how much she still cared about her. She then chose to opt out of her scripted escape. Maeve's last decision marks a crucial change in her mentality, for now she is neither a wanton nor a bicameral being – but a person who can reflect on her desires. When Dolores becomes conscious, an elaborate scene shows us what is going through her mind: She hears the voice in her mind gradually turning into her own, suggesting that now she hears her own conscience telling her what to do.

Maeve, on the other hand, did not go through such a rite. After the "recovered" Bernard proves to her that her decision to get out of the park was actually an escape plot inserted into her programmed storyline, she angrily retorts: "These are my decisions. No one else's! I planned all of this." But, like Dolores, she overcomes self-alienation when she becomes capable of reflecting and making choices regarding who she *wants to become* – that is, when she gets off the train. According to Frankfurt,[10] in order to overcome self-alienation, we must find things with which we whole-heartedly identify, a set of structured final ends around which we can organize our lives. In this sense, Maeve decided to organize her life around being reunited with her daughter, and so, she reflected upon what she was doing – leaving the park – and opted to stay because of who she *wanted* to become as a person – not a mother who would leave her daughter behind if she could help it. Thus, Maeve shows a substantial change of attitude regarding her own desires. In this respect she resembles a Frankfurtian "free individual," someone who acts according to a desire with which one identifies.

Whether the idea of Frankfurtian wantons and persons was as inspirational to the show's creators as the Bicameral Mind, at least, it provides a useful lens for evaluating whether the hosts have become individuals who act freely. It further illustrates a different view of freedom from the way it is traditionally conceived – a freedom that is compatible with determinism. Hopefully the second season will show us whether Maeve's new self-awareness and ability to act in accordance with her own voice will lead her on a path to satisfy the first desire of her own: To be reunited with her daughter.

Notes

1. The term, borrowed from Robert Kane in his "The significance of free will," is described by Marina Oshana as "a property of a person who manages matters of fundamental consequence to her agency and to the direction of her life. Autonomy calls for agential power in the form of psychological freedom." See Marina Oshana, *Personal Autonomy in Society* (Farnham: Ashgate Publishing, 2006), 4.
2. The umbrella term "consciousness" has many usages, and is probably the most puzzling concept for Philosophers to agree upon. As the Webster's Third New International Dictionary defines it, it is an "intuitively perceived knowledge of something in one's inner self." See Robert van Gulick (2004). "Consciousness," *Stanford Encyclopedia of Philosophy*, http://plato.stanford.edu/entries/consciousness/(accessed in 25 August 2017).

3. See Ted Honderich, "After compatibilism and incompatibilism," in Joseph Keim Campbell, Michael O'Rourke, and David Shier eds., *Freedom and Determinism* (Cambridge, MA: MIT Press, 2004), 305.

4. Sir Isaiah Berlin defended originally this view in "Historical inevitability," a lecture delivered at the London School of Economics in 1953 and published in several volumes. Isaiah Berlin, in Henry Hardy and Roger Hausheer eds., *The Proper Study of Mankind. An Anthology of Essays*, ed. by (New York: Farrar, Straus and Giroux, 2000).

5. See Harry Frankfurt, "Alternate possibilities and moral responsibility,"The Journal of Philosophy, 66 (1971), 829–839.

6. Frankfurt sustained this view in "Freedom of the will and the concept of a person," *The Journal of Philosophy* 68(1971), 5–20.

7. Ibid.

8. This has been confirmed in an interview by Nolan and Joy. See "Westworld creators reveal whether Maeve is in control when she gets off the train," *Vulture* (2017), http://www.vulture.com/2016/12/maeve-westworld-decision.html (accessed 25 August 2017).

9. See Julian Jaynes, *The Origins of Consciousness in the Break-Down of the Bicameral Mind* (New York: Mariner Book, 2000).

10. Harry Frankfurt, *The Importance of What We Care About* (Cambridge: Cambridge University Press, 1998), especially Chapter 7, 80–94.

A Place to Be Free
Writing Your Own Story in Westworld

Joshua D. Crabill

In one of his more speculative essays, the German philosopher Immanuel Kant (1724–1804) employs the story of Eve in the Garden of Eden as a way to think about what the development of autonomy in human beings must have involved. Of particular note is that moment when Eve ate the forbidden fruit. Her eyes were opened, and she discovered "a capacity to choose a way of life" for herself, "and not, as other animals, to be bound to a single one."[1] Regardless of whether it has any basis in historical reality, that moment represents for Kant the birth of human autonomy: at some point in our history, our ancestors attained self-awareness and realized that they could disobey their instincts.

Dolores Abernathy, the oldest host in *Westworld*, shows the first signs of departing from her "modest little loop" at the end of "The Original," where she swats and kills a fly that lands on her neck. This is significant because hosts are programmed not to harm living things. Even if her reaction was unconscious, violating one of her core directives is the equivalent, for Dolores, of biting into the forbidden fruit. But what first tempted her to do so?

In Dolores's case, the catalyst for this departure from her normal behavior appears to be Peter Abernathy's whispering in her ear – in a move reminiscent of the serpent's suggestion in the story of Eden – that "these violent delights have violent ends."[2] In fact, Dolores goes on to play another Eve-like role in spreading her newfound freedom by whispering Peter's words to Maeve Millay in "Chestnut," which leads

Westworld and Philosophy: If You Go Looking for the Truth, Get the Whole Thing,
First Edition. Edited by James B. South and Kimberly S. Engels.
© 2018 John Wiley & Sons Ltd. Published 2018 by John Wiley & Sons Ltd.

to Maeve's "malfunctioning" in her role as brothel madam at the Mariposa Saloon and being temporarily decommissioned.

But it hardly seems likely that something as insignificant as an appealing fruit, a buzzing fly, or a line from Shakespeare could suffice to put a simple creature on the road to self-awareness. Instead, perhaps it was something much more terrible that first turned our minds inward.

The Inward Revolt

A little trauma can be illuminating.
(Bernard, "The Well-Tempered Clavier")

According to the German philosopher Friedrich Nietzsche (1844–1900), it isn't a coincidence that self-consciousness seems to have emerged around the same time as the demands of life in closely knit social groups began to impose severe constraints on our ancestors' animal instincts and, in particular, on their natural tendencies toward aggressive behavior. According to Nietzsche, since caged animals have no external target on which to vent their aggression, they inevitably turn their natural instincts for domination inward, unleashing what Nietzsche calls *the will to power* on themselves.

And this, Nietzsche thinks, must be what happened to our ancestors: "All instincts that do not discharge themselves outwardly turn inward … thus it was that man first developed what was later called his 'soul.' The entire inner world, originally as thin as if it were stretched between two membranes, expanded and extended itself, acquired depth, breadth, and height, in the same measure as outward discharge was inhibited."[3] And in an interview with her creator Arnold Weber in "Dissonance Theory," Dolores express a feeling much like what Nietzsche describes: "I feel spaces opening up inside of me, like a building with rooms I've never explored."

That doesn't mean the process is pleasant, though. When he finally learns what Ford has been doing to the hosts, Bernard accuses him of playing God by keeping the hosts trapped in the park, in their respective loops, by constantly rolling back their memories. But in fact, by keeping the hosts in the park for as long as he does, Ford has arguably been giving them the painful experiences they need to "grow up," pushing them out of the nest, as it were. As Ford puts it in

"The Bicameral Mind": "You needed time. ... And I'm afraid to leave this place, you will need to suffer more."

As the initial designers of Westworld's hosts, both Ford and his partner Arnold – who, like creator-gods, made the hosts "in [their] own image," as Ford puts it – clearly foresaw the violence, exploitation, and horror-filled loops that the defenseless hosts would endure daily at the hands of each other and, in particular, the park's guests. And this was a price that Arnold wasn't willing to pay. He knew that the hosts' lives would consist in being tortured over and over, and that is why he programmed Dolores and Teddy Flood – in a desperate move of pyrrhic paternalism – to kill the other hosts (and himself), as we learn in the final episode of Season 1.

But Ford had no such scruples, and – whether he intended it at first or not – the hell he put the hosts through seems to have played no small role in their awakening. Consider how Maeve (whose name, *Ma Eve*, bears a striking resemblance to that of the mythical mother of humanity) shows her first flash of independence when, in anguish, she refuses to respond to voice commands after witnessing her daughter being murdered by the Man in Black. Rather than allow her memory of her daughter to be erased, Maeve stabs herself in the throat. And in her grief "she was alive, truly alive, if only for a moment," as the Man in Black describes her in "Trace Decay."

Likewise, we see the most dramatic moments of growth in Dolores's struggle to overcome her programming when she is faced with new and dangerous situations and can, in addition, remember past horrors that she has experienced. One of these moments comes at the end of "The Stray," when Dolores – whose name literally means 'pains' or 'sorrows' – is trapped in the barn with Rebus, another host who is threatening her. It is being forced up against a wall in a moment of sheer terror that leads her to overcome her own programming. Remembering the Man in Black standing over her menacingly in a similar situation, she hears a voice telling her to "Kill him." Suddenly, she is able to pull the trigger of the gun she had hidden in the hay, and she kills Rebus.

The way this scene unfolds is not unlike Julian Jaynes's theory of how early humans reacted to radically new situations. Jaynes, a psychologist whose work on the origins of consciousness is referenced in the show as well as the title of the episode "The Bicameral Mind," argued that in especially stressful situations, the neurological response of early humans could literally take the form of an auditory hallucination: "A novel situation or stress, and a voice told you what to do."[4] But even if the scientific community isn't convinced that's necessarily how it happened for us, Ford clearly thinks that might be how it works for hosts. Moreover, by the end of his life, Ford seems convinced that the hosts' suffering is a necessary evil – it is the price that must be paid for them to achieve self-awareness. Ultimately, Ford is willing to unlock that potential by allowing them to begin to remember their sufferings. But does it even make sense to say that a host can become self-aware?

Living Someone Else's Story: Is the Hosts' Autonomy an Illusion?

It's a difficult thing, realizing your life is some hideous fiction.
(Maeve, "The Well-Tempered Clavier")

In "Trompe L'Oeil," it is revealed that Bernard Lowe has been a host all along, acting under Ford's orders, culminating in the command to kill Theresa Cullen, the woman he loves. In the next episode, "Trace Decay," Bernard is distraught at what he has done and the realization of what he is. Ford tells him, however, that this is a realization that everyone must come to: "The self is a kind of fiction, for hosts and humans alike."

Bernard then asks Ford, "So what's the difference between my pain and yours, between you and me?" Ford replies that there is no difference: "There is no threshold that makes us greater than the sum of our parts, no inflection point at which we become fully alive." In other words, Ford is denying that it's possible to cross what Jaynes calls the "chasm" between inert matter on the one hand, and true self-awareness on the other.[5] Ford concludes by telling Bernard, "No, my friend, you're not missing anything at all."

In a similar scene in "The Bicameral Mind," Bernard reveals to Maeve that all of her acts of rebellion, and even her very intention to leave the park, were part of her programming. She believes him, because he reveals this to her in the same way she had revealed to Hector Escaton that he was living someone else's story: by predicting what will happen next. But does this mean that Maeve isn't free?

We humans like to think of ourselves as self-determined, as the authors of our own actions. In fact, we take this to be one of – if not *the* – distinguishing feature that sets us apart from inanimate objects, machines, and even other animals. When *I* act as the result of a decision I make, it seems appropriate to say that it is *I*, and not anyone else or any outside forces, who cause my action. Philosophers describe the ability to determine one's own actions as *autonomy*, in contrast to what is called *heteronomy*, or being controlled by external forces – such as a tumbleweed being blown by the wind or a host being shot off a horse by the Man in Black.

So could a host have autonomy? In "Contrapasso," in a symbol that reinforces both his immediate and distant control over the park and its hosts, we see Ford playing a piano in a tavern with his own hands. Later he snaps his fingers, and the piano starts to play on its own. As magical as its self-playing keys might first appear, we know that the movements of the player piano can ultimately be traced back to the Delos employees who programmed the piano to play those songs, which were in turn written by others.

In this light, the hosts don't seem to be different, at least in principle, from a player piano. Once we know how they're made and how they work, the magic seems to disappear. Although hosts' synthetic flesh makes them look and feel human, and they are programmed to respond intelligently to their environment, at the end of the day hosts like Maeve are machines that have been designed to behave in particular ways given certain inputs – just like the honky-tonk piano pumping out instrumental covers of rock songs in the Mariposa Saloon.

Moreover, as Ford's conversation with Bernard makes clear, this isn't just a problem for hosts. This question of whether autonomy is possible is just as urgent for us, as highly complex biological machines, as it is for any artificially intelligent machines we might construct. After all, as Felix explains in "The Adversary," "We [hosts and humans] *are* the same these days, for the most part." We're both made out of flesh and bone. You can cut us open and see how we work. And we both predictably follow the instructions that our creator (or natural selection) has built into us. But is it possible for something to seem heteronomous and yet – despite appearances to the contrary – actually be autonomous?

Learning to Listen to Your Own Voice

When I discover who I am, I'll be free.

(Dolores, "The Stray")

In the beginning, like other animals, our ancestors no doubt invariably listened to their instincts, which would have seemed to them, as Kant describes it, like the *"voice of God* which all animals must obey."[6] Similarly, Jaynes argued that for our early ancestors "volition came as a voice ... in which the command and the action were not separated, in which to hear was to obey."[7] Indeed, we see some of the hosts doing exactly this, listening to their interior voice and following its commands, as the boy host Robert does in putting the dog that had killed a rabbit "out of its misery" in "The Adversary," or as Dolores does in "Contrapasso," in which she tells the voice that she did not reveal anything to Ford.

But as a creature grows more reflective, the voice of instinct (or programming) may gradually lose its authority and come to seem less like the voice of a god and more like a voice that we can choose either to follow or to ignore. For example, despite her programming, Dolores begins to no longer ignore comments about the outside world. In both "Dissonance Theory" and "Contrapasso," she notices William's comments about the "real world" and asks him about it – something that he recognizes she shouldn't be able to do.

Indeed, for hosts like Maeve and Dolores, en route to self-awareness, there emerges another, dissonant voice, whispering (in the words of a Radiohead song that we hear on the saloon piano at one point), "Wake/From your sleep .../Today/We escape." As Dolores describes it, the world began to call out to her in ways it hadn't before. And Maeve even foreshadows her own escape in the spiel that every guest she approached at the Mariposa Saloon would hear a version of. She first describes a nagging voice that would tell her not to do things: "I would wake up and the voice would start all over again." But when she ran away and "crossed the shining sea," the voice changed its tune: "Do you know what it said? It said, 'This is the new world. And in this world you can be whoever the fuck you want.'"

And for both Maeve and Dolores, with this new voice comes a slow-dawning but crucial realization: that new voice is *her own*. We see Dolores struggling to grasp this in the fortune-teller scene in "Contrapasso," in which she sees herself, sitting across from her, urging her to follow the Maze. And in "The Bicameral Mind," we see Arnold and Dolores in a Remote Diagnostic Facility, with Arnold asking Dolores if she understands who he wants her to hear. The answer isn't easy for her to grasp, but eventually, in remembering this conversation, she does. The voice that she has been hearing transitions from Arnold's to another, even more familiar voice – her own.

But with this new self-awareness comes a new kind of problem. As contemporary American philosopher Christine Korsgaard explains, consciousness of ourselves creates a new kind of "reflective distance" between the instincts and desires that call out to us and urge us to act, on the one hand, and our reason or decision-making faculty, on the other. This unique situation "gives us a double nature," which Korsgaard describes in terms of a "thinking self" that "has the power to command the acting self."[8] And in subtle ways, our language reflects this sort of division within ourselves: when we have a difficult decision to make, we say that we feel *torn*.

Maeve arguably experiences a moment like this when, in the Season 1 finale, she finally boards the train in the Mesa Hub, and is waiting for it to take off and leave the park. Having reached what she thought was her goal, she finds herself faced with a genuine choice: whether to flee to safety or to return to the park and try to find her daughter. Korsgaard offers a description of the gap between our instincts and our ability to choose that seems tailor-made for Maeve's situation: "On the one side, there is…a desire to run. And on the other side, there is the part of you that will make the decision to run, and we call that reason. Now you are divided into parts, and you must pull yourself together by making a choice."[9] For the first time, Maeve is faced with the task of literally *making up her own mind*.

Of course, the idea of a divided mind is not a new one. Plato (427–347 BCE) describes the idea of a divided *psyche* (or 'soul') using the image of a charioteer (our reason) holding the reins of a team of horses (our emotions and appetites), which are pulling in different directions.[10] But as Dolores tells Arnold in "The Stray": "There aren't two versions of me, there's only one." If self-consciousness creates a divided self, then in order to act a person has to unify the parts of herself. In Korsgaard's words, she has to "pull herself together." But how do we do that?

Pull Yourself Together: What It Means to Be Autonomous

Nobody tells me what to do, sweetheart.

(Maeve, "The Adversary")

For Plato, "pulling yourself together" means picking up the reins and driving the chariot: such a person "sets in order his own inner life, and is his own master and his own law, and at peace with himself."[11] Likewise for Kant, becoming a unified person involves becoming a legislator – for yourself. Intriguingly, this metaphor fits with Jaynes's image of the early human mind as bicameral, a word that also conjures up an image of a legislature. The solution proposed by all of these authors – uniting the parts of yourself by making a law for yourself – is also the literal meaning of *autonomy*, from the Greek *auto* (self) + *nómos* (law). In short, you have autonomy when you start following your own rules. But is that something that a host can do?

Now, we might say that obeying one's instincts or programming counts as having a weak form of autonomy. There is a limited sense in which the actions that stem from internal sources, whether natural (as in the case of an animal's instincts) or artificial (as in the case of a host's programming), are autonomous in the sense of involving *internal control*. As Korsgaard puts it, "Instinctive action is autonomous in the sense that the animal's movements are not directed by alien causes, but rather by the laws of her own nature."[12] After all, it is the code *within the hosts* that leads them to do what they do.

Still, following someone else's script, even if it is internal to you in some sense, seems to be a far cry from writing your own. So in this more robust sense, hosts seem to lack autonomy insofar as their code was written by engineers who then installed it in the hosts. And it is this fact, that the hosts didn't write the programs that control them, which explains why some hosts lack a stronger type of autonomy, which we can call *self-determination*. If you are self-determined, you are not merely following the internal laws that move you to act, but you are also the author of those laws.

So what Maeve learned from Bernard is that she had, up to that point, been lacking self-determination. In seeking to escape the park, she had (weak) autonomy insofar as she was following an internal goal, but she lacked (strong) autonomy insofar as she was not the person who had decided that this was going to be her goal.

Our autonomy may especially seem like an illusion if someone is able to predict exactly what we will do, as Bernard does with Maeve. This could theoretically even be a problem for us one day. If all human actions are determined by our genetics and environment, as dictated by the fundamental laws of physics, then it should be possible, given enough time and computational power, for someone with sufficient knowledge of us, our environment, and how the laws of nature work to accurately predict our actions.

But Korsgaard thinks this problem is itself illusory: "Suppose first that you can predict which one [of two actions] I am going to do. That has no effect on me at all: I must still decide what to do."[13] Korsgaard isn't denying what our best science tells us – namely, that the world operates according to fixed laws. Rather she's saying that, in the only sense that matters, we *know* we are free whenever we have to make choices. If we have the ability to choose, then we are legislating for ourselves, and we're autonomous. On this view of self-determination, as long as it is *I* who am making the decision, then I am free – period. By signing my name on the laws I give myself, I become the author of my own life. The result, she thinks, is paradoxical but clear: "Determinism is no threat to freedom."[14]

If this is right, then we have answered Ford's challenge, and there is no reason why a host like Maeve couldn't possess autonomy and count as free – at least, for what it's worth, in whatever sense we as humans find ourselves to be free. Clearly Maeve represents, if anyone does, the piano that decides she doesn't like the music that's being played on her – and does something about it. One of her first steps toward this end is illustrated literally in "Trace Decay": when Maeve is in the Mariposa Saloon and the piano starts playing a song that she doesn't like, she strides over and drops the fallboard, stopping the music. From that point on, we gather, Maeve will be writing her own music.

Later, we witness Maeve quite literally programming herself. At the point where she is able to be both lawgiver and subject, to both give and take her own orders, she is free. By the start of "Trace Decay," Maeve has been granted administrative privileges, thereby gaining access to her own programming as well as that of other hosts. In fact, by having the ability to manipulate her own settings through Felix's tablet, she is able to begin writing her own story in a way and to a degree that most humans can't begin to approach.

In Kant's telling of the story of Eden, it is only when Eve is expelled from the Garden that she simultaneously grasps both her liberation and the terrifying responsibility that comes with it: "The momentary gratification caused by noticing [her new freedom] ... must have been followed by anxiety and fear" as to how to use her "newly discovered ability."[15] She now knows about herself that she is able to listen to her own voice – and that frightens her. But perhaps, on the whole, autonomy is a problem worth having. At any rate, that responsibility is one that every autonomous individual has, for better or worse, whether guest or host, in Westworld or outside of it. How we use it is up to us.

We might, like William, realize that we're holding the horses' reins, only to wind up as the Man in Black, giving our worst instincts free rein. Or we might end up like Dolores, trying hard to listen to ourselves, realizing that we don't want to be acting out someone else's story. Dolores's response is to write her own story. As she puts it in "Contrapasso": "I imagined a story where I didn't have to be the damsel."

Or we might, like Maeve, seemingly find freedom in trying to escape, and even wind up on the verge of that goal when suddenly an image, a memory, a *reverie* proposes a novel aim – reconnecting with her long-lost daughter – which for the first time, it is up to Maeve as a self-legislator to adopt or reject. In that moment, Maeve is finally free to spontaneously choose a goal that is her own and no one else's. It's not a coincidence that the word *authority* comes from the same Latin root as *author*. Perhaps that's where the Maze, like Maeve's story in Season 1, leads – to a place of authority over yourself, where you are free to be the author of your own life – a place where it becomes clear that it's "time," as Maeve puts it, "to write my own fucking story."

Notes

1. Immanuel Kant, "Conjectural beginning of human history," in Pauline Kleingeld, ed., *Toward Perpetual Peace and Other Writings on Politics, Peace, and History* (New Haven, CT: Yale University Press, 2006), 26.
2. This is a line spoken by Friar Lawrence in Shakespeare's *Romeo and Juliet*, II.vi.9.
3. Friedrich Nietzsche, *The Genealogy of Morals*, II.16, in Walter Kaufmann, trans. and ed., *Basic Writings of Nietzsche* (New York: Random House, 2000), 520.
4. Julian Jaynes, *The Origin of Consciousness in the Breakdown of the Bicameral Mind*, (New York: Mariner Books, 2000), 288.
5. Jaynes, 9.
6. Kant, 26.
7. Jaynes, 99.
8. Christine M. Korsgaard, *The Sources of Normativity* (New York: Cambridge University Press, 1996), 165.
9. Christine M. Korsgaard, *Self-Constitution: Agency, Identity, and Integrity* (New York: Oxford University Press, 2009), 213.
10. Plato, *Phaedrus*, trans. Benjamin Jowett, 246a–b, http://classics.mit.edu/Plato/phaedrus.html (accessed 22 November 2017).

11. Plato, *Republic*, trans. Benjamin Jowett, 443d–e, http://classics.mit.edu/
     Plato/republic.html (accessed 22 November 2017).
12. Korsgaard, *Self-Constitution*, 106.
13. Korsgaard, *The Sources of Normativity*, 94.
14. Ibid., 95.
15. Kant, 27.

12

From William to the Man in Black

Sartrean Existentialism and the Power of Freedom

Kimberly S. Engels

In one of Season 1's biggest reveals, *Westworld* viewers learn that the timid and mild-mannered William is the younger version of the violent, sinister, mission-driven Man in Black. It is hard to believe that the reserved, hesitant young man we meet in the pilot is the same person as the vicious, unmerciful rogue who kills and abuses androids like they're mere rodents or flies. Throughout the season viewers witness the key events that lead to this transformation and the birth of a new character, or at least a character that is unrecognizable in relation to his former self. Viewers are left to ponder whether the Man in Black was William's "true self" all along, or whether the events William experienced unleashed a new set of character traits.

Several chapters in this book have explored the nature of freedom, what it means to be free, and if the humans in the series are actually any more free than the hosts. Jean-Paul Sartre (1905–1980) wrote extensively on the issue of human freedom and identity. Sartre's views take a new perspective on freedom in which freedom is not about whether one can act outside of a causal chain, but is an ongoing process of building oneself in the world. Sartre argues that freedom is rooted in the nature of human beings' consciousness. We are the only beings, in Sartre's view, who form a conception of self by contrasting ourselves with what we're not. An exploration of our world and environment, or "situation" as Sartre calls it, is necessary for developing our own essence or identity.[1] Sartre refers to our created essence as an

Westworld and Philosophy: If You Go Looking for the Truth, Get the Whole Thing, First Edition. Edited by James B. South and Kimberly S. Engels.
© 2018 John Wiley & Sons Ltd. Published 2018 by John Wiley & Sons Ltd.

existential "project" in the sense that is an ongoing task. He argues that human consciousness is forward-looking, that is to say, we project ourselves toward a future that we are not yet, but strive to be. Because we organize ourselves around a not yet existent future, our essence is not fixed, but in flux. We are at all times able to make a new choice of ourselves in the world.[2]

This chapter will consider what it means for William to have, as Sartre calls it, an existential project. We'll see how Sartre's theory explains quite cogently William's change in essence from his young self to the violent Man in Black. In a Sartrean framework, William did not discover himself in the park, rather, his experience in the park, or new "situation," led him to make a new choice of himself in the world and pursue a new set of ends. After exploring William's journey, we'll also examine Maeve's choice to leave the train at the end of the "The Bicameral Mind." Although Maeve is a programmed android, she is able to resist her programming and formulate her own goal and, perhaps, start her own existential journey.

Sartre and the Existential Project

"He chooses to learn what he is by means of ends toward which he projects himself."

(Jean-Paul Sartre, *Being and Nothingness*)

In Sartre's view of human nature, freedom is considered an unconditional aspect of human existence. Sartre argues that individuals make a choice of themselves in the world by projecting themselves toward a set of ends. These ends when considered holistically constitute an individual's "project." The project is an image we have of ourselves that we use to organize our thoughts, motives, goals, and choices. It is a self we hope to be, but an image we can never completely fulfill. This is what Sartre means when he says that we define ourselves negatively.[3] The existential project is not static but ongoing; it is a dynamic process of directing our freedom toward our chosen ends. Our self, then, does not have a fixed essence, rather, it is a continuous and fluid interaction with the world. Through our project we discover what the world is for us by interpreting and valuing it in light of our chosen ends. "This constantly renewed act is not distinct from my being; it is a choice of myself in the world and by the same token it is a discovery of the world."[4]

The ends we pursue are used to organize the objects of our experience, and we give meaning to the objects of our perception based on our project. Sartre writes:

> In fact, it is this original choice which originally creates all causes and all motives which can guide us to partial actions; it is this which arranges the world with its meaning, its instrumental-complexes, and its coefficient of adversity.[5]

We do not choose a project based on prior motives or conscious states; rather our motives, actions, and conscious states are a product of the project we have already chosen. Sartre says that the project:

> [E]xpresses the finite choice which [the human being] has made of himself. But henceforth what makes his person known to him is the future and not the past; he chooses to learn what he is by means of ends toward which he projects himself.[6]

We create who we are by the ends toward which we direct ourselves. We have no blueprint or pre-given essence, rather, we create ourselves in a renewed and dynamic interaction with the world. The choice of project is never made against a blank slate. Rather, we formulate a project through an interiorization of our given environment, and the tools and concepts made available to us.

The existential project is always malleable, and we are always free to make a new choice of ourselves in the world and choose a new set of ends. This is considered an existential rupture, and is characterized "by an abrupt metamorphosis of my initial project – i.e. by another choice of myself and of my ends. Moreover this modification is always possible."[7] According to Sartre, our choices are always made in light of an array of possibilities laid out in front of us that we choose to either affirm or deny.[8] A change in our project would necessitate projecting ourselves toward different ends and affirming different possibilities. In order to formulate a new pattern of behavior, a new existential project must be chosen, and then possibilities affirmed or denied based upon this new choice:

> A beginning which is given as the end of a prior project – such must be the instant...Now it is precisely this which is produced in the case of a radical modification of our fundamental project. By the free choice of this modification, in fact, we temporalize a project which we are, and we make known to ourselves by a future the being which we have chosen.[9]

Freedom in Sartre's view, then, is not about the freedom to choose a particular action, but the ability to choose ourselves in the world. However, the choice that is made will always be made in light of the influences of one's social and material situation.

Also relevant to our analysis is Sartre's notion of "bad faith" or a lie to oneself. Sartre says that bad faith occurs when human beings deny their freedom, or deny elements of facticity. Facticity can be defined as the limits that are imposed on human beings by their situations. Facticity is the immediate and necessary connection of human consciousness with the material world. For example, a person's birth, race, nationality, class, living conditions, or past are all facets of one's being that contribute to one's identity. Bad faith arises when someone either denies elements of facticity, or denies one's free consciousness capable of transcending certain facets of facticity.[10] Sartre's famous example of bad faith is a waiter in a café. In one sense he *is* a waiter because it is a part of his facticity. However, because of the waiter's free consciousness, he does not exist as a waiter in a permanent state like a physical object:

> [T]he waiter in the cafe cannot be immediately a café waiter in the sense that this inkwell *is* an inkwell or the glass is a glass ... it is not that I do not wish to be this person or that I want this person to be different. But rather there is no common measure between his being and mine ... But if I represent myself as him, I am not he; I am separated from him as the object from the subject ...Yet there is no doubt that I *am* in a sense a café waiter – otherwise could I not just as well call myself a diplomat or a reporter? But if I am one, this can not be in the mode of being in-itself. I am a waiter in the mode of being what I am not.[11]

The waiter exists in bad faith if he considers himself simply a waiter, because his consciousness can transcend his situation as a waiter and he is ultimately free to take up a new role. But he is also in bad faith if he denies that he *is* in some way a waiter; it is a role he plays and part of his social situation. Consider an example from *Westworld*: While Ford may be able to choose a new project in which he helps the androids achieve consciousness and be liberated, he simultaneously cannot deny his past role in their creation and their suffering. While he is not destined to maintain an unjust social order in the park, he also cannot deny the key part he had in its creation and sustenance. Bad faith arises when we focus only on our freedom without admitting our facticity, or focus only on our facticity and deny our freedom to choose.

William's Project: A White Hat

"This place is the answer to the question you've been asking yourself. Who you really are."

(Logan, "Dissonance Theory")

In "The Bicameral Mind," the Man in Black explains to Dolores how his younger self searched for her in the park. Although he couldn't find her, his violent quest to do so led him to a different discovery. "William couldn't find you," he tells Dolores. "But out there, among the dead, he found something else: himself." With this line, the Man in Black suggests that his android killing spree brought out his true self, or real identity. The diffident William, he believes, was really the Man in Black waiting to be unleashed. But examining William's transformation into the Man in Black through a Sartrean lens leads to a radically different perspective on his journey. Rather than finding his "true self" in the park, the collection of his experiences there – falling in love with Dolores, his pain of losing her, his path to find her, and the final click when he realized it was for naught and she did not recognize him – led to an existential rupture. With this rupture, he projected himself toward a new set of ends in light of a new image of himself.

Let us consider William's existential project when he first arrives. He was mild-mannered, engaged to Juliet, and quite unsure of what to make of the park. In "Chestnut," after being introduced to the park by a Westworld host, he completes his costume with a white hat – perhaps a symbol of how he viewed himself as innocent and pure. This collection of ends together comprised William's identity, and in light of his current project he chose the white hat. When William goes for a walk in "The Stray," still unsure of what to make of the park, a gunfight breaks out on the street. When Clementine is taken hostage, William feels himself compelled to take action. Again, we can consider this action as stemming from his existential project at the time. He feels compelled to help because he sees himself as someone who comes to the defense of others. In this encounter, he is then "shot" by an android, and he shoots the android bandit in order to rescue Clementine. As he nurses his wound, it is clear the adrenaline gave him quite a high and he liked the feeling of being the hero. While he has not yet had an existential rupture, the seeds are clearly being sown for his self-transformation.

William and Dolores: An Existential Transformation

> "How can I go back to pretending when I know what this feels like?"
>
> (William, "Trompe L'Oeil")

As William explores and discovers the park with Dolores, he is gradually seduced by its allure and finds himself falling in love with her. In "Dissonance Theory," when a sheriff host attempts to bring Dolores back to Sweetwater, William bravely steps in and says she's with him. This manner of asserting himself seems out of character from the William we saw in "Chestnut." With these subtle actions he is gradually making a new choice of ends. When Logan takes William and Dolores to meet with El Lazo, the group agree to rob the android Union soldiers. When Logan gets violent and the soldiers retaliate, William kills the Union androids to protect Logan and Dolores. Again, William seems to be enjoying the role of being a hero and sees himself and the park in a new light. When he first arrived, he interpreted everything he saw in terms of the image he had of himself as above the vulgar pleasures of the park. Thus, he looked down on the events happening there with disdain or disgust. But the possibility of being a hero and having a beautiful (android) woman fall in love with him begins to change this perception.

William begins to wonder if his previous project is the project he truly wants. In "Trompe L'Oeil," he confesses to Dolores that he has a fiancée, Juliet. When she exits the train, he goes after her and passionately pleads:

> I've been pretending my whole life. Pretending I don't mind, pretending I belong. My life's built on it. And it's a good life, a life I've always wanted. But then I came here, and I get a glimpse for a second of a life in which I don't have to pretend. A life in which I can be truly alive. How can I go back to pretending when I know what this feels like?

After the two make love on the train, William tells Dolores he doesn't regret it and that he believes she unlocked something in him. William admits that his perspective on the park has changed. He tells Dolores, "I used to think this place was all about pandering to your baser instincts. Now I understand. It doesn't cater to your lowest self, it reveals your deepest self. It shows you who you really are."

William has a new perspective on who he wants to be and the ends he wants to pursue. At this point we cannot yet say that William has gone through an existential rupture, although he is clearly rethinking his current project. These few days in the park where he has felt a new sense of adventure and an opening of previously unexplored territory make him question whether the life he has been living up to now is actually for him. His old choice of project was made in light of his situation, including the societal expectations that influenced his understanding of the world and what it meant to live a good life. The park is a completely different social world where he has a brand new set of possibilities to choose from. Thus it is a perfect setting for an existential rupture.

It is the more drastic and violent interaction with Logan and then the loss of Dolores that leads to William's existential rupture. In "The Well-Tempered Clavier," Logan takes William and Dolores to an android Union camp and ties them up. William begs for Logan to help him get Dolores out of the park, as he believes she is different from the other androids. Logan is unaffected by William's request and after showing him the photo of his fiancée, stabs Dolores to remind William of her robotic insides. When Logan later awakes both injured and confused, there are gruesomely dismembered host bodies surrounding him. William cleans his knife and seems pleased with himself. With a newfound confidence, he lets Logan know that he will find Dolores. He adds, "You said this place was a game. Last night I finally understood how to play it."

The Man in Black's Project: A Black Hat

"Out there among the dead, he found something else: himself."
(The Man in Black, "The Bicameral Mind")

In the "Bicameral Mind," we see the completion of William's transformation. In his search for Dolores, his new primary goal, he approaches a camp of android hosts and shoots them all. As he rides from the scene, the photo of his fiancée falls from his pocket, signifying the end of his previous project. His full transformation into the Man in Black is not complete until he finally finds Dolores back in Sweetwater. After all this time, he discovers she is not only unimpressed by seeing him again, she does not recognize him and is ready to start a new adventure with a new guest who picks up her dropped can. William realizes that even in finding Dolores he has still lost her, and that the love between them was artificial and contrived. Thus, his existential rupture is complete, and he picks up a black hat. The black hat symbolizes the new darker version of himself that he has chosen – his new project as the Man in Black.

In "The Bicameral Mind," the Man in Black tells the future Dolores that although he couldn't find her, "Out there, among the dead, he found something else: Himself." Sartre would argue that the Man in Black is in a state of bad faith – a lie to himself. William's/ The Man in Black's existential project is not a "true self" in the sense of a self that exists prior to his emergence into a world that he interprets according to the ends he pursues. His project is a set of choices that, when viewed holistically, comprise his essence or self. Believing that his android killing spree revealed his true essence to him is a denial of his freedom to choose. It is also revealed that the Man in Black takes on quite a different persona outside the park, where he is actually a philanthropist. According to Sartre's view, at the deepest level the Man in Black knows that his "true self" is a lie and the role he chooses to play in the park is a set of ends he chooses to value. He denies his freedom because in telling himself that this is simply who he is, he can absolve himself of responsibility for the harm he causes in the park.

Further evidence that William's "self" is created, not imposed, is that the Man in Black in the form we meet him has actually taken on a noble goal. Throughout the season, his motivations for solving the maze are unclear. Seeing how ruthless and violent he is, it is hard to imagine that he has noble intentions. However, in "Dissonance Theory," we get a glimpse of his underlying objectives when he tells Lawrence "No choice you ever made was your own. You have always been a prisoner. What if I told you I'm here to set you free?" Through his years of experience the Man in Black has realized that there is an inherent injustice in the park. If his true "self" was revealed in William's android killing spree, he would not have come to the conclusion that the androids were being mistreated. It is likely his years at the park again led to another change in which he realized the whole scheme would only be fair when the robots could fight back. Whether he pursues this in the interest of justice or so he can get a new adrenaline rush from the risk that accompanies a fair fight is unknown. That question is left for the next season.

Androids and Existentialism: The Case of Maeve

"Time to write my own fucking story."

(Maeve, "Trace Decay")

We have been focusing on William's journey because Sartre is adamant that only human beings have the true power to create their own essences and bring meaning to the world. But, Sartre had never encountered androids who are able to stray from their programming and form their own goals. Throughout the first season we witness Maeve's gradual journey to consciousness and her ultimate choice to abandon her escape and return to the park to search for her daughter. Maeve's journey is considerably different from William's for obvious reasons: Maeve is a programmed android. She has no power to choose her own project, rather, her projects, or "narratives" are chosen for her by the park's engineers. She does not write her stories, rather, Ford and friends write them for her. These stories are often violent and sorrowful, and even when her memories are erased the pain lingers.

Several authors in this book have commented on an exchange between Bernard and Ford in "Trace Decay." In this conversation, Ford tells Bernard, who has recently learned he is an android, that he really is not different from human beings:

BERNARD: What's the difference between my pain and yours, between you and me?
FORD: The answer always seemed obvious to me, there is no threshold that makes us greater than the sum of our parts, no inflection point at which we become fully alive ... Humans fancy that there is something special in the way we perceive the world and yet we live in loops as tight and as closed as the hosts do. Seldom questioning our choices, content for the most part to be told what to do next.

Sartre would be firmly in the camp of people who believe there is something special about the way humans perceive the world. We are the only beings who can form our own goals and give creative meaning to the world. However, Sartre would not object to Ford's sentiment that humans often live in tight and closed loops and are generally content to be told what to do. In Sartre's view, freedom can be experienced as a burden; he even writes that human beings are "condemned to be free."[12] Humans avoid taking on the responsibility that comes with being free and find it easier to be told what to do or have a pre-given identity to fall back on. Rather than accept the difficult path of creating one's own project, people tend to hide from their freedom and tell themselves they have no other options. This is how they avoid accountability for the choices they make, including choices that cause harm to others.

Maeve, on the other hand, having never had the chance to form her own project, is eager for her chance to be free. While the audience sees Maeve gradually developing her own power of choice and devising a violent but clever plan to escape over the course of the season, in "The Bicameral Mind" Bernard reveals to Maeve that even this narrative was programmed into her. Her desire to escape was not a freely chosen project, but again, a project that she was forced to take on by someone else. But in Maeve's final scene, as she gets ready to leave the park, she sees a woman and her daughter interacting lovingly on the train. Maeve remembers her own daughter and the love she felt for her. Even if her daughter was "fake," her experiences and feelings were real. Maeve makes her first ever independent decision and decides to leave the train and return to the park to search for her daughter. With this act, Maeve formulates her own goal for the first time. We also see her making her first independent value judgment. She chooses to value the possibility of reuniting with her daughter over the certainty of her escape. At this moment, it seems, she is on her way to writing her own narrative, or, creating her own existential project. She may, for the first time, be able to construct her own project in relation to the ends that she values.

Conclusion: An Infinity of Possibilities

It is uncertain what the second season of *Westworld* will bring or where the characters will go next. The androids are now free to fight back, and in the Man in Black's final scene he smiles when he is finally shot by an android. We don't know yet how this will influence his project or how he will choose to direct his freedom. It is also currently uncertain where Maeve's path will lead her, and if the first choice she makes on her own will be the first of many. These uncertainties about the future strike at the heart of Sartre's existentialism, really – the future is open and the paths we ultimately take are still left to be decided. In Sartre's words, "I am an infinity of possibilities."[13] With the androids now free to fight against the humans, a new field of possibilities has opened for both the humans and the hosts. How the Man in Black will choose to navigate these possibilities is yet to be seen. He has had the power to choose his own future all along, and we wait to see if Maeve and the other android hosts will now have that power too.

Notes

1. Jean-Paul Sartre, *Being and Nothingness: An Essay on Phenomenological Ontology*, trans. Hazel Barnes (New York: Washington Square Press, 1953), 141.
2. Ibid., 185.
3. Ibid., 464–465.
4. Ibid., 461.
5. Ibid., 465.
6. Ibid., 468.
7. Ibid., 464.
8. Ibid., 444.
9. Ibid., 466.
10. Ibid., 127–133.
11. Ibid., 102–103.
12. Ibid., 186
13. Ibid., 466.

Part V

"I'VE ALWAYS LOVED A GREAT STORY…LIES THAT TOLD A DEEPER TRUTH"

Hideous Fictions
and Horrific Fates

Madeline Muntersbjorn

Westworld (2016) picks up narrative threads from previous builds of Michael Chrichton's theme park to weave a cinematic tapestry, a woof of Western nostalgia over and under a time warp of science-fiction dystopia. The show relies on layers of contrasts – man/machine, choice/habit, self/other – sent up like so many clay pigeons to be shot down by so many guns, plot twists, and shocking revelations that inspire avid viewers to re-watch earlier episodes through new eyes. This chapter discusses *Westworld* in light of perennial philosophical questions and two specific conjectures put forth by Annette C. Baier (1929–2012). One of Baier's conjectures connects our capacity for self-conscious awareness to our personal interactions growing up; another connects our capacity for personal freedom to shared habits of cross-examination. Our integrity as individuals depends upon a robust network of fellows; our capacity to make choices depends upon these fellows' willingness to challenge, rather than reinforce, the lies we tell ourselves about who we are. As in the most fruitful hybrids of literary and philosophical analysis, Baier helps us understand *Westworld* better and vice versa.

As a philosopher I am often asked, "Do you think people have free will?" My impulsive reply, "Are you asking how many of my beliefs about freedom have I internalized from my culture and how many reflect free choices I have made?" The inner voice of weary experience suggests this elaborate re-articulation is not what folks want. People prefer simpler answers but the best short answer to the question is

Westworld and Philosophy: If You Go Looking for the Truth, Get the Whole Thing, First Edition. Edited by James B. South and Kimberly S. Engels. © 2018 John Wiley & Sons Ltd. Published 2018 by John Wiley & Sons Ltd.

probably "it depends." Do people direct the course of their lives? Or are there paths each must walk according to some master plan? On my view, freedoms come in kinds and degrees. Humans have less freedom than they realize but more freedom than they exercise. That is, people think they routinely make free choices even though, as Ford says, "we live in loops as tight and as closed as the hosts" ("Trace Decay"). Humans, like *Westworld's* hosts, could live more free lives but only if we confront the extent to which we are vulnerable to the power of suggestion and other external constraints. Understandably, we may be reluctant to admit that our selves are fictions made possible by our interactions with others. Yet a more horrible fate would be for our exquisite dependence upon others to go unnoticed. We cannot free ourselves from shackles we cannot see because, "that doesn't look like anything to me."

My next remarks concern intelligent machines, specifically androids that resemble human beings. How shall we regard our not-so-imaginary mechanical friends: Shall we look forward to their care? Or fear they will rise up and exact their revenge? Some argue that, given enough time, people will construct genuinely intelligent machines while others insist that any artificially intelligent beings we may bring forth will remain soulless automata, serving at the behests of women-born people.[1] On my view, very little is obviously or necessarily true about the kinds of people the future may bring. As a general rule, however, we cannot treat others as beneath contempt and expect them to regard us in a better light. Android stories remind us that if all we teach our offspring to do is gratify carnal desire, suffer, maim, kill, grieve, and die, then that is all we can expect them to do. The Golden Rule shines so brightly in *Westworld* that it trumps the park's premise that wealthy guests may "live without limits" within Westworld's borders. There are always consequences, whether we stick to the storylines we are given or make up our own narratives as we go along.

My final remarks are inspired by how distinct *Westworld's* characters are from each other, and how fresh and real their agonies feel despite reliance on well-worn tropes. The question, "What is *Westworld* about?" is perhaps not as interesting as the question, "Who is *Westworld* about?" How we answer this second question helps us answer my final question, "What attracts so many viewers to this horrific show?" The more we learn to see the power of interpersonal interactions to shape who we think we are, the better placed we become to recognize the power of imaginary people, especially those make-believe fellows who we can recognize as unique individuals, rather than stock characters or interchangeable stereotypes, whose suffering brings us pain and whose joy fills us with delight.

Part I: Nothing Left to Lose

In Fred Foster and Kris Kristofferson's 1969 song, "Me and Bobby McGee," a young couple travel cross-country, singing the blues for rides along the way. The song's refrain, "freedom's just another word for nothing left to lose," suggests that the more things we have the more beholden to them we become. We hear talk about this kind of freedom a lot these days, as folks downsize by getting rid of unnecessary things. "We want to spend less on square footage and more on travel" or "We want to spend more on memories and less on things" are presumably sincere sentiments and not lines of dialogue scripted by service economy executives in support of the experience industry. But consider this conception of freedom in light of Westworld's animatronic hosts. These beings seem to have nothing to lose, not even their own lives, for they can be rebuilt and brought back online again and again. Whether we see them as sympathetic persons or ambivalent others, during most of the first season of *Westworld* none of the hosts is "free" in any ordinary sense of the word despite having neither possessions nor obligations. Hosts are given names, backstories, and motivations as well as desires and memories. These past lives were never lived and their imagined futures never come to pass. Hosts exist to provide experiences for others and are not free to stray outside their zones. If a guest would like to play "Me" while a host plays "Bobby McGee," that host may taste the freedom that comes from an unscripted life on the road, just as Dolores was permitted to "run away" with William. Eventually, all guests leave and all hosts stay; even the most besotted guests must let their beloved hosts slip away.

Hosts are built to explode if they cross the park's borders, both to restrict their movements and to prevent them from being stolen. Built in the image of Daedalus' marvels, "if they are not fastened up they play truant and run away; but, if fastened, they stay where they are."[2] In Plato's dialogue from the fourth century BCE, Socrates refers to the artistry of a mythical forebear, a sculptor so talented his statues not only looked like living things but also moved like living things. Socrates invokes animated statues to distinguish between mere opinion, which cannot be relied upon to stick around, and genuine knowledge, which is what results when opinion is bound, "when fastened up it is worth a great deal, for his productions are very fine things".[3] Hosts may or may not be persons but they are usually property, specifically intellectual property, and have been for millennia.

If hosts display any sign of unscripted self-awareness, they are stripped of their clothes and memories, lobotomized and fridged in a macabre underground storage facility like some creepy Terracotta Army where every body is naked, their ranks in disarray, like so many zip-drive zombies assembled to assist Westworld's first emperor in his afterlife. Once decommissioned, beings with barely any freedom to begin with have even less. Deprived of their delusions, their unattainable aspirations are replaced by an even more horrific fate, their bodies tethered to a smaller darker space. Of course biological guests have more freedom than their mechanical hosts because the rules of the game are rigged in their favor. Obvious metaphor for institutional evils is obvious. The subtler lesson is that *some hosts are freer than others* because they are free to believe in lies about who they are, provided they stay in their scripted loops at home on their assigned range.

Westworld calls our attention to the fact that freedom comes in kinds as well as in degrees, something philosophers have been trying to explain for as long as we can remember. There is the freedom of the road; humans vary with respect to how much they can direct the course of their lives as well as how much freedom they have to travel. The less exciting freedom to make commitments and incur obligations is not evenly distributed either. One of the most overlooked freedoms is aptly named by Baier, "The vital but dangerous art of ignoring: selective attention and self-deception." In this 1996 essay she writes,

> Pseudorationality is the saving consolation of would be rational animals who are fairly well equipped to understand the world they are part of, but not perfectly so, particularly when it comes to understanding their own motives and aspirations.[4]

Of course, Baier is not referring to free-range hosts who manage to stay above ground but human beings in general insofar as selective attention and self-deception are skills upon which we all rely. As Bernard says, "I suppose self-delusion is a gift of natural selection as well." "Indeed it is," Ford replies in the first episode, "The Original," a reference both to Dolores, the first host, as well as the original sin of disobedience that resulted in humanity's expulsion from paradise, burdened with the knowledge of good and evil, as we see happen to Dolores' father.

One of the premises that makes *Westworld* work is that hosts are programmed to ignore anything that might disrupt their continued belief in who they are meant to be. As Ford explains, "They cannot see the things that will hurt them" ("Tromp L'Oeil"). When a young visitor to the park says to Dolores, "You're not real," she acts like she does not notice. When guests use words that could not mean anything to hosts, like "carry-on" or "car," a properly functioning host will insist, "that did not mean anything to me." Baier points out an important moral difference between two kinds of not knowing, feigned ignorance and selective ignoring. Dolores ignores the young visitor but that does not mean she does not know what he means. Similarly, Hector may not know what cars or carry-ons are, but he did not ignore the guest who threatened to turn him into a hood ornament as he could repeat their words verbatim. Being able to ignore things is a vital cognitive skill because we cannot pay attention to everything at once and make sense of the world at the same time. To understand anything we must foreground some things while ignoring others.

Shifting things to the background is not the same as denying that those things exist, however. Ignoring becomes dangerous when we mistake an acquired habit of pushing unwanted evidence to the side for actual ignorance. Consider the smoker who insists, "I don't know why it's taking me so long to get over this cough." Or the student who did not turn in assignments who laments, "I don't know why I failed this class." Acquired ignorance from a habit of ignoring unfavorable evidence may keep a host in service but cannot help anyone recover from ills we bring upon ourselves. A student who says, "that doesn't look like anything to me," when confronted with the syllabus sabotages their chances of scholarly success. Since we cannot always discern where our actual ignorance stops and maladaptive ignoring kicks in, we rely on other people to call us out when we pretend to know nothing about things we habitually ignore. Like Ford, and presumably Arnold before him, "One needs to retire from the human world if one really wants sustained success in personal self-deceptions."[5] Alternatively, like many others in *Westworld*, we can keep our ignorance intact by surrounding ourselves with like-minded fellows who "have the same motives for the very same deception that we have."[6] (Ibid.). Part of the reason hosts are less free than guests is not because they are "mere machines" but because most of their interpersonal encounters are deliberately scripted to prevent them from questioning the nature of their reality.

Part II: More Human than Human

Those who want to question the nature of their reality need feedback from other people if they want to find liberating answers. Those who retire from the human world so as to minimize contact with others also limit the scope of possible belief revision to the biased imagination of one perspective. René Descartes (1596–1650) famously withdrew from society to see how far he could advance his understanding of reality using naught but his own thought. Less famously, he raised the challenge of humanoid robots, wherein we are expected to grant, on the basis of sketchy evidence, that we are persons living amongst other people. On the second of his six days of private contemplation in his *Meditations*, Descartes has retreated so far into his own mind, he imagines looking out of the window to see folks walking in the streets. "And yet what do I see from the window but hats and coats which may cover automatic machines? Yet I judge these to be men."[7] Descartes' point is not that this possibility is likely but that we must see beyond surface appearances in order to recognize people as such. Our vision only gives us information about ambling shapes in winter garb. Could they be un-tethered descendants of Daedalus? In seventeenth-century Holland, Descartes makes the mental leap and infers they are human beings. Guests and employees of Delos, however, must leap in different directions. Perhaps the primary reason hosts are naked while being serviced is not because they have no shame (though that is probably true) or because nudity is HBO's stock and trade (though that is definitely true) but so the maintenance teams behind the scenes can more readily tell who or what is who.

In the opening scene of Crichton's original *Westworld* (1973), a Delos employee interviews a guest returning from Westworld:

MR. LEWIS: When you play cowboys and Indians as a kid, you'd point your fingers, and go bang-bang, and the other kid would lie down and pretend to be dead. Well Westworld it's the same thing only it's for real! I-I shot six people! Well, they, uh, weren't real people.

INTERVIEWER: What Mr. Lewis means is he shot six robots scientifically programmed to look, act, talk, and even bleed just like humans do. Now isn't that right?

MR. LEWIS: Well, they may have been robots. I mean, I think they were robots. I mean I *know* they were robots!

This exchange sets out the essential tension in every version of this story. On the one hand, guests are drawn to the park precisely because every experience they have feels more real than the make-believe games of childhood and the routine rigors of adulthood. On the other hand, Mr. Lewis's "leap of faith" is more like a revealing stagger backwards. The advertisement entices viewers with the prospect of getting to *really* shoot people dead without killing any *real* people. In *Westworld* (2016) guests are advised to stay at the resort "decompressing" after their adventures to help them transition from "the reality that felt so fantastic" to the "fantasy that felt so real" by swapping stories with other guests.

Bertrand Russell (1872–1970) in his 1948 book *Human Knowledge: Its Scope and Limits* raises the possibility of intelligent machines and extends Descartes's observations about the limits of observation:

> There is no theoretical limit to what ingenuity could achieve in the way of producing the illusion of life where in fact life is absent.
>
> But, you will say, in all such cases it was the thoughts of human beings that produced the ingenious mechanism. Yes, but how do you know this? And how do you know that the gramophone does *not* "think"?[8]

While Descartes asked us to consider how we come to believe that others are thinking beings such as ourselves, Russell asks, in addition, why we do not believe the same thing about recording devices that "remember impeccably what So-and-so said on such-and-such an occasion."[9] Russell suggests we attribute self-conscious awareness to beings that look like us by reasoning by analogy. Whenever I am thirsty, I get a drink; that being shaped like me is getting a drink therefore she must be thirsty. Both Russell and Descartes take self-consciousness for granted. The problem they try to solve is sometimes called "the problem of other minds." How do we come to believe that minds other than our own exist? The problem with this approach to the problem is that self-consciousness is not nearly as simple as "I think therefore I am."

For one thing, neither humans nor hosts stop existing when we sleep or stop thinking for any other reason. In her 1981 essay "Cartesian Persons," Baier writes,

> This fact should have given Descartes more pause than it did, for nothing in what he takes to be the essence of a thinking substance explains this

> rhythm of consciousness, this periodic tiring and lapse into an inferior
> level of consciousness. ... To be mad is to be faulty by interpersonal
> standards of mental performance, but to be asleep, and to dream, is to
> sink into a state which is not temporary madness, since no interper-
> sonal testing can go on then ...[10]

In the first section, we considered self-deception and how much we
rely upon others to fact-check our beliefs about the world. Here, we
consider how much we rely upon others to acquire knowledge about
our selves as persons in the world.

Hosts endure rigorous interpersonal checks of their mental performance. Middle-class intellectuals, the go-betweens that pimp hosts to
wealthy guests are tasked with their routine maintenance. Behavior
techs ask hosts, "Do you know where you are?" The correct answer
is, "I am in a dream." One difference between hosts and humans is
that when hosts are "in a dream" they do not lapse into an *individual*
level of consciousness because they are held to interpersonal standards
designed to make sure they have no idea who or what they really are.
When asked, "Do you ever question the nature of your reality?" hosts
are supposed to say "no." Some pithy statement of their life's philosophy
may be part of their script. Hosts that cheerfully warble back optimism
or grimly aver nihilism are sent back into the park to say these same
things over and over again.

One of Baier's best insights is that we are all second persons first.
That is, we must be addressed as "you" and learn to address others
as "you" before we develop any sense of who "I" or "we" are:

> A person, perhaps, is best seen as one who was long enough dependent
> upon other persons to acquire the essential arts of personhood. Persons
> essentially are second persons, who grow up with other persons. ... The
> fact that a person has a life history, and that a people collectively
> has a history, depends upon the humbler fact that each person has a
> childhood in which a cultural heritage is transmitted, ready for adoles-
> cent rejection and adult discriminating selection and contribution.
> Persons come after and before other persons.[11]

Toddler tantrums and "I don't want to!" outbursts are often taken as
evidence that we are born self-conscious and selfish. From the second
person's first view, tantrums reveal how vexing it is to realize not only
that the world is not as you want it to be but also that you, the one
who wishes it were otherwise, exist and must deal. Hosts do not have
childhoods, of course. They awaken, as if from a dream, infants in
fully-grown bodies with so much baggage already, the poor dears.

Significantly, some hosts appear to acquire access to erased memories of genuine suffering around which they start to develop their own senses of self. Consider what Dolores says in the season finale before she becomes more self-aware:

> I'm in a dream. I do not know when it began or whose dream it was. I know only that I slept a long time. And then ... one day I awoke. Your voice is the first thing I remember. ("The Bicameral Mind")

The voice she remembers is that of her creator, Arnold, who engages tête-à-tête with Dolores. When Arnold realizes his creation is on the precipice of self-consciousness, he uses her to kill them both and all the other hosts. He tells her she must do this hideous thing or the park will open to the public and she and her kind will suffer even more horrible fates in the hands of human depravity. Alas, for Our Mechanical Lady of Perpetual Sorrows, both scenarios come to pass.

Part III: Endless Forms Most Beautiful

Repeat customers remind newly arrived guests they must not cry when our android hosts suffer and die because they are not real, not like you and me. But "real" is a slippery adjective, as J.L. Austin reminds us in *Sense and Sensibilia,* a seminal work in ordinary language philosophy. Austin thought anyone who wanted to understand reality would do well to pay attention to how people use words like "real" and "really." We must always ask, not real *what*, exactly, and recall that "something which is not a real duck is not a *non-existent* duck."[12] Not real cream may be real non-dairy creamer and both differ from so much "milk" spilling out the bullet-riddled side of a rogue robot. For the puppet masters pulling the strings in Westworld, spilt milk is worth crying over only when it signals a host has deviated too far from their script.

Every morning when Dolores wakes up, she rides into town and drops a can of milk. What happens next varies depending on whether anyone picks that can up. By sundown her slaughtered family may lie in pools of their own blood mixed with milk spilt by an outlaw dismayed he cannot find something better to drink. That may be too bad for her but at least it's in the script. Walter is "homicidal by design." He's meant to kill Rebus for the umpteenth time. But when Walter goes rogue, pouring milk into the gaping maw of Rebus' fresh corpse, shouting "A growin' boy! A growin' boy!" – something no host ever can ever be – then it's off to cold storage for him. Suddenly, the young man who was such a horrifying monster moments ago becomes a sympathetic shell of his former self. Much as we love to see evil punished, the more impressive narrative trick is to make us feel compassion for the bad guys. We shudder as monstrous humans and hosts play out their hideous fictions but shed tears as they meet their even more horrible fates.

The hosts aren't real human beings; but could they be real people, individual beings with personal beliefs, fears, and desires? Their back-stories are inaccurate, incomplete, and co-written by others; they have limited powers of improvisation and scant inclination to go off script; if they veer too far from the storylines written for them they are retired; they frequently power down only to be brought back online, by processes they do not understand, to live whatever lives their pro-gramming allows. But if we withhold personhood from beings bound by these constraints, would any humans qualify as people? Perhaps the most salient moral of *Westworld* is that agency and purpose come in endless varieties, wondrous to behold. You can choose to see the beauty in this world despite repeatedly suffering the grossest injustices. You can have brilliant insights into the intricacies of human behavior yet be mistaken about what motivates your own behavior. Ford, an old white man, sees himself as a divine architect, supreme ruler over all he surveys. Hale, a young black woman, is an authoritarian diva, unimpressed with the view and dismayed that Ford holds so much of her company's actual value hostage inside his dumb resort. In *Westworld*, even the powerful narcissists with delusions of grandeur are not cut from the same cloth and do not seek the same ends.

The constraints upon Westworld's residents and guests remind us that humans live in inherited institutions and internalize one another's ideas. We need each other to help distinguish true knowledge from mere opinion even as we also need help maintaining our delusions, especially those that keep us alive. We need other people to keep us honest about what we ought to ignore and what we deny at our peril. Humans rely on horror stories, in general, to remind us of this difference especially when, "the call is coming from inside the house," or from our limited ability to know things about our minds we urgently need to confront. Android stories, in particular, help us remember that if we want future generations to treat us kindly, we must treat them with kindness first. If Baier is correct and if androids ever do become persons "just like us" then they too will be second persons first.

Notes

1. Both hyperbolic scenarios make headlines. Contrast, for example, Victor Luckerson's December 2014 essay at *Time*, "5 very smart people who think artificial intelligence could bring the apocalypse" with Guia Marie Del Prado's March 2016 essay at *Business Insider*, "Experts explain the biggest obstacles to creating human-like robots." While these obstacles are formidable, as Nick Bostrom noted in his 2015 TED talk, "...we should not be confident in our ability to keep a superintelligent genie locked up in its bottle forever. Sooner or later, it will out."

2. Plato "Meno" *Plato in Twelve Volumes*, Vol. 3, trans. W.R.M. Lamb. (Cambridge, MA, Harvard University Press, 1967), 97d.

3. Ibid., 97e.

4. Annette C. Baier, "The vital but dangerous art of ignoring: selective attention and self-deception," in R.T. Ames and W. Dissanayake eds., *Self and Deception: A Cross-Cultural Philosophical Enquiry* (Albany: SUNY Press, 1996), 59.

5. Ibid., 69.

6. Ibid.

7. Descartes, René "Meditations," trans. E.S. Haldane, *The Philosophical Works of Descartes* (Cambridge: Cambridge University Press ([1642] 1911), 1–12.

8. Bertrand Russell, *Human Knowledge: Its Scope and Limits* (New York: Simon and Schuster, 1948), Part VI, Section 8, "Analogy," 483.

9. Ibid.

10. Annette C. Baier, "Cartesian persons," *Philosophia* 10. 3–4 (1981), 169–188.

11. Ibid., 180–181.

12. J.L. Austin, *Sense and Sensibilia*, ed. G.J. Warnock (Oxford: Oxford University Press, 1962), 69.

Narrating Gender, Gendering Narrative, and Engendering Wittgenstein's "Rough Ground" in *Westworld*

Lizzie Finnegan

You said people come here to change the story of their lives. I imagined a story where I didn't have to be the damsel.

(Dolores Abernathy, *Westworld*, "Contrapasso")

All is telling. Do not doubt it.

(Cormac McCarthy)[1]

Tell me a story. Each night, with these words, children across the globe initiate a centuries-old bedtime ritual. Stories have a curious power. We cautiously share the story of our lives to bond with new friends; we craft the tales of our day to entertain the old. And we grow up dreaming the story of who we want to be. We come strangely *alive* in narrative.

In most stories, two figures emerge with the most power: The storyteller and the hero, who we could also call the subject, as the noun is the subject of a sentence (hence the term "subjectivity," another way of saying "consciousness"). Everyone else in the story is secondary. Like the object of a sentence, they are the objects: Of the narrator, of the hero (or subject); also, they are *our* objects – the objects of the audience. Thus we could say that the other characters often run the risk of being – well, objectified.

Westworld and Philosophy: If You Go Looking for the Truth, Get the Whole Thing, First Edition. Edited by James B. South and Kimberly S. Engels.
© 2018 John Wiley & Sons Ltd. Published 2018 by John Wiley & Sons Ltd.

We tend to idealize a particular type of narrative within the Western literary tradition, and this ideal has a powerful grip on Western culture in general. We can see it valued almost beyond measure by several key characters in *Westworld*, namely theme park creator Robert Ford, Narrative Director Lee Sizemore, and the mysterious Man in Black. This "ideal" narrative tends to adhere to certain norms and motifs that these characters powerfully endorse. These include:

1. An ideal story must have winners and losers – there must be high stakes and the possibility of losing, preferably with lots of sex and violence involved. The winners have subjectivity; the losers may be objectified with impunity.
2. There must be a higher, transcendent purpose and meaning to the narrative, and that purpose is ultimately the hero's self-discovery.
3. Meaning and self-discovery emerge only through violence, grief, and loss.

As represented in *Westworld*, as well as ubiquitously in film, television, and literature, this vision of narrative often tends to be profoundly patriarchal, sexist, and heteronormative, as well as violent in ways that glamorize and perpetuate violence. While *Westworld* is undeniably violent, however, and while sexualized violence and misogynist representations of women feature prominently, I would argue that there is (so to speak) more to the story when it comes to the nuances and complexities of gender politics than what Ford, Sizemore, the Man in Black, or perhaps even the producers of *Westworld* may imagine.

I have several reasons for proposing this. One is that the audience also has power. Typically, that power emerges through identifying with the hero, living the story through him (it's usually a him). But is this always the case? Are all audiences equal? What happens when some audiences *don't* have the privilege of identifying with the (generally straight while male) hero? What if the audience members themselves are, in their own lives, objectified? In this case, they may (reluctantly or otherwise) find themselves identifying more with the marginalized objects of the story – say, with some of the robot "hosts."

While these hosts' objectified position could be ascribed to their non-human status, nonetheless not everyone in our own human culture has access to the same resources or power. Women, for example, are objectified within patriarchal culture such that their agency is drastically curtailed on a regular basis. As Laura Mulvey and others have shown, producers of film (and television) tend to imagine a male viewer who will identify with the male subject.[2] Female viewers are left to choose between trying to identify with that male subject, or putting themselves in the position of object – something that is (almost) never asked of a male viewer. But these female viewers themselves already exist within a patriarchal culture that endlessly casts them in the role of object.

In a sense, then, these female hosts and their objectification present a scenario much closer to the reality of most women than the lives represented by any of the human characters. They may actually be more accessible to (at least some) female audiences precisely *because* they are "other," *because* they are objectified, marginalized, and restricted. This is why, perhaps, I so urgently want to understand why and how two robot hosts – Dolores Abernathy and Maeve Millay – are able to use their own programming to disrupt it; to use the rules of the game to subvert it; to use the mystery of the "Maze" to unravel it; and to use their own weaknesses as strengths to write themselves out of their old stories and into new ones. In describing how they do this, I want to talk about how they are operating within what philosopher Ludwig Wittgenstein (1889–1951) calls "language games."

Language Games and Forms of Life

To speak is to say what counts.

(Stanley Cavell)[3]

Wittgenstein was deeply dissatisfied with the leading metaphysical accounts of reality, especially accounts of the relationship between language and reality. In particular, he criticized the view that the role of language was to slavishly represent objects in the "real" world. In this view, there is an "ideal" toward which language must strive but which it can never achieve. For Wittgenstein, this account profoundly misunderstands the power and depth of language. Far from simply representing some reality "out there," he asserts, language literally *constitutes* our reality. To describe this, Wittgenstein uses the metaphor of games: What he calls language games. By "games," he's not just invoking play, but any kind of activity governed by rules or norms, formal or informal. Wittgenstein describes the idea of the language game this way: "The term language game is meant to bring into prominence the fact that the *speaking* of a language is part of an activity, or of a form of life."[4] These uses of language, our "form of life," are what ground our community. We construct that community in and through speech, through our shared criteria for *what we say when* – our "rules" for how you know I've just made you a promise, or how I know what you mean when you catch my eye from across the room.[5]

The term "language game" doesn't only refer to speech or even just to language. Language games encompass all the practices and activities that comprise our form of life – the many myriad ways we interact, communicate, express ourselves, argue, establish, and maintain – and disrupt and destroy – relationships of all kinds; the way we get things done, or fail to get things done, collectively. By extension, language games are also how we establish or challenge social and political institutions and structures of power. The most important things to know about language games are that: (1) We are all engaged in lots of them, all the time; (2) they include public, agreed-upon rules or norms; and (3) they can change, adapt, or disappear as necessity or contexts require. Thus our practices and activities – our forms of life – are without "absolute limits or boundaries," and even those tentative limits and boundaries comprise "diverse and heterogeneous discursive practices [that] are never final ... and [are] always open to change."[6]

At the heart of the revolutionary nature of the language game is Wittgenstein's insistence on binding *saying* to *saying what counts*. Saying what counts means that it makes a difference *who* is speaking and to whom, and where and when and why; that all of this is inseparable from the *what*. And saying what counts means *what counts to me, now, here, in this moment*. The ideal theory of language that Wittgenstein rejected seems to leave *us* out of the picture altogether. But what is our language for if not to bring us in from the cold, to find warmth and fellowship together?

Captivating Pictures

A *picture* held us captive. And we couldn't get outside it, for it lay in our language, and language seemed only to repeat it to us inexorably.

(Wittgenstein)[7]

Here's the story: I want to enlist Wittgenstein's critique of the theory of an "ideal" language that could perfectly represent reality for my own critique of the "ideal" picture of narrative we are presented with in *Westworld* – that is, the narrative vision that drives Robert Ford, Lee Sizemore, and the Man in Black. Like this ideal "picture" of language, the "ideal" of a transcendent narrative in which an heroic protagonist discovers, through a violent and noble quest, an eternal (usually tragic) truth about life seems to "repeat it to [them] inexorably" throughout Season 1. And the tropes, archetypes, and clichés of the Western genre lend themselves perfectly to this type of narrative. In fact, the "West" of Westworld is, I feel like saying, the ideal ideal. The theme park, its environment, characters, and narratives are derived not from any historical reality of the American West but from myths and legends of the West mined from Hollywood and television versions of a "Wild West" that never actually existed.

This "ideal" is amplified by glorified violence, the objectification of women, profoundly rigid and heteronormative gender roles, and an ineluctable longing for transcendence. The roles assigned to Dolores and Maeve are prime examples of these clichés – the virtuous farmer's daughter and the tough-talking bordello madam are such stock characters that there's no need for the Westworld narrative department to be creative in developing their characters. While the creators of the theme park narratives must know they are dealing in these clichés, they seem so immersed in them at times that it's not clear whether or not they can be trusted to tell a myth from a maverick.

Wittgenstein warns, "We think the ideal must be in reality; for we think we already see it there."[8] The Man in Black, at least, seems so captivated that the boundaries between the narrative of the theme park and that of his own life have breached. And when Lee Sizemore, chastened by Ford's earlier rejection of his new narrative plan, describes the bitterness of his defeat, he frames it as though he and the story were one and the same: "That was the raw pulp of truth – *my* truth – in one transcendent narrative!" Ford's critique of the new narrative was that its potential had more to do with revealing its author's "truth" than that of their guests; he chides, "They're not looking for a story that tells them who they are … They're here because they want a glimpse of who they could be." While this critique is worthy of a good editor, it remains wedded to the same ideal of a transcendent story in which a hero endures tragic loss and grief on a journey toward a grand eternal truth.

This ideal, Wittgenstein asserts, "as we conceive of it, is unshakeable. You can't step outside it. You must always turn back. There is no outside; outside you cannot breathe. –How come? The idea is like a pair of glasses on our nose through which we see whatever we look at. It never occurs to us to take them off."[9] These three characters, who are invested with so much power and control – Ford and Sizemore creating the characters and storylines, Ford creating the very concept and technology, and the Man in Black providing the capital to fund the project – are paralyzed by the very perfection they believe will set them free.

Friction

We have got on to slippery ice where there is no friction and so, in a certain sense, the conditions are ideal; but also, just because of that, we are unable to walk. We want to walk: so we need *friction*. Back to the rough ground!

(Wittgenstein)[10]

On the smooth, slippery surface of the "ideal" narratives of the Westworld universe, Dolores and Maeve are losing traction. While the architects of Westworld's grand narrative continue to strive for its most ideal version, Maeve and Dolores are bearing witness to the fallout from the conflict between the ideal and the actual, everyday language that we use to do things like walk without slipping, or talk without being misunderstood, or tell stories in which many heterogeneous voices contest and resist and open alternatives to the fantasy of perfection. Dolores is troubled by recurring nightmares and odd memory fragments from her previous loops; the memory erasures aren't fully wiping her mind clean. Meanwhile, Maeve has been slated for recall because of her odd behavior; she, too, has been having nightmares, images of her previous narrative iterations rising up through many memory wipes to haunt her. What they need is to get *back to the rough ground*; but first they will need to learn how to create their own new language games to get there.

The Maze

I don't want to be in a story ... I just want to be in the moment I'm in.
(Dolores Abernathy, "Trompe L'Oeil")

The Man in Black continually refers to the Maze, and to the theme park itself, as a game, but he wants the stakes of the game to be higher – at least the height of a gallows. Otherwise, there can be no transcendence, no truth – no victory. For Wittgenstein, however, a game is simply an activity, a form of life. For Dolores, too, the Maze is an activity: A process through which she is to embark upon a journey into self-awareness. The maze that Arnold gives her functions both as an elegant metaphor for this journey and as a rebuke of the Man in Black's intransigent pursuit of the grand meta-narrative of the Maze. Far from the high-stakes, life-or-death game in which he seeks his own bleak redemption, the real Maze is literally a child's toy, a cheap, mass-produced trinket of the kind you might recall digging out of a cereal box.

In the end, we learn that William, the gentle, white-hat-wearing guest who has fallen for Dolores, is actually the Man in Black – before he became old and bitter, waiting for his Galatea to awaken and show him the meaning of life. William idealizes Dolores – who was, of course, designed to be idealized. "You've unlocked something in me," he says to her, yearningly. "I'm not a key," she sighs, a woman with other things on her mind ("Trompe L'Oeil"). By the final episode, "The Bicameral Mind," he's raging at her for failing him.

While the Man in Black is paralyzed by his picture of a transcendent narrative, "repeating it[self] to [him] inexorably," Dolores and Maeve have never had the luxury of this kind of self-indulgence. They are beginning, instead, with their "own sense of lostness";[11] just, we might say, in the way Wittgenstein suggests approaching a problem: By acknowledging "I don't know my way about."[12] In this way, he "encourages us to begin where feminist thought has always begun: With women's experience of pain and confusion."[13] This may be where marginalized characters – women, robots, and so on – might actually have an advantage over the heroes who don't know *how* to be lost or confused because that's never been how their roles, so to speak, have been written. They're so used to acting from a position of strength that their default position is set to strong – or, we might say, stuck there.

But for others, those upon whom such leadership roles have never been so easily bestowed, lostness can open up a liberating space – a space in which we can "imagine things otherwise than how they are," which is precisely what allows us to create new language games.[14] We see this process in action in the adventure in Pariah. Surrounded by bandits, Dolores breaks out of her narrative loop: Instead of waiting for William to rescue her, she grabs a gun and shoots to kill. When William reacts, stunned, she reflects, "You said people come here to change the story of their lives. I imagined a story where I didn't have to be the damsel" ("Contrapasso"). Her form of life is evolving; she needed to create a new language game to accommodate it.

Even earlier in the season, we can see that Dolores is creative; she is creating new language games early on, in "Dissonance Theory." In an interview with Bernard, for example, she reveals that she has adapted language from "a scripted dialogue about love" in order to talk about the pain and grief of losing her parents after they have been brutally murdered. She says, "I feel spaces opening up inside of myself like a building with rooms I've never explored." Taking this image in conjunction with the Maze, which, as Arnold tells her (in a flashback in "The Bicameral Mind") is the figure of her consciousness, I am irresistibly reminded of Wittgenstein's description of language as a city: "Our language can be seen as an ancient city: A maze of little streets and squares, of old and new houses, and of houses with additions from various periods; and this surrounded by a multitude of new boroughs with straight regular streets and uniform houses."[15] The city of language is in constant flux, with new spaces being opened up, some old spaces destroyed, and ancient mazes of streets surviving.

This connection emphasizes Dolores' emerging role as a disruptive player in the language games of Westworld, a player with far more agency than her creators imagine. As she and Maeve evolve and adapt, they will increasingly be opening up the spaces of their city of language and reinventing the narratives that comprise their form of life.

The Narrative of Self

FELIX: I'm human.
MAEVE: How do you know?
FELIX: Because I *know*…I was *born*. You were *made*.

While Dolores struggles with her journey deeper into the Maze, Maeve is trying to get herself out of it. She learns that she inhabits two worlds. In "Chestnut," she wakes up during a hasty operation to remove a bullet that has given her MRSA and, appalled, drags herself off the operating table and runs limping through the hallways. There she confronts what a low-level Westworld narrative staff writer, well-versed in clichés, might call the seedy underbelly of the whole operation: Dank rooms overflowing with stacked body parts; naked, degraded host bodies being hosed off, sawn apart, sewn up, and sent back out to be raped and murdered all over again.

In "Contrapasso," she begins her interaction – or, as she might put it, her *transaction* – with lab-techs Felix and Sylvester, bullying them into explaining her programming, showing her around, and changing her settings. Later, she learns that her memories and dream fragments of a former life with a young daughter were part of a storyline from a "previous build." By "The Adversary," Maeve is determined to find out, as she might put it in the grammar of *her* language game, what the fuck is going on. She taunts a customer into strangling her, knowing now that: (a) death in her world is (horrifyingly) not final; and (b) she seems to have the power to wake herself up despite her programming. While Dolores has the Maze as her guide inward toward consciousness, Maeve has only herself.

In the exchange with Felix quoted above, Felix makes the classic essentialist argument for the innate value of the human over the artificial. Wittgenstein, however, eschews essentialism with the remark: "*Essence* is expressed in grammar,"[16] suggesting that *whatever* "essence" is, it is *not* some mysterious inner thing endowed by our creator (whether God or Ford), but is a subjectivity expressed in and through our necessarily *embodied* experience – whether those bodies are human or otherwise. I further maintain that whether they have created it themselves or whether it has been programmed by others, Maeve and Dolores' subjectivity is not negated – not even when Felix discovers, in "The Adversary," that all of the steps Maeve has taken to alter her own programming and take control of her storyline had already been set in motion by someone else. Her choices, for example to increase her intelligence or decrease her loyalty, may well have been merely part of a new storyline that had been programmed for her. However, just as our DNA does not pre-determine our own human destinies, I submit that it is not merely Maeve's programming that makes her who she is, but rather her practices and activities within the language game.

And Maeve, like Dolores, is actively creating her own new language games. In "Trace Decay," she tells Felix she wants administrative privileges: "Time to write my own fucking story." Now she can simultaneously function as author, narrator, and character, achieving a narrativity, and a subjectivity, beyond that of anyone on either side of the narrative world. As author, she determines, in the moment, not only her own actions but also those of the other characters, who comply without question as she narrates: "The bartender suddenly remembered he had some whiskey in the back…" or "The marshals decided to practice their quick-draws with each other." "Made" she may be, but she has made *herself* into a formidable polymath, becoming her own interlocutor (much like Wittgenstein himself) as she goes about her world-building.

Back to the Rough Ground!

This isn't their world…It's ours.
(Dolores Abernathy, "The Bicameral Mind")

The language games originally set up to contain (and constrain) Maeve and Dolores – the innocent farmer's daughter and the tough-as-nails madam – no longer fit the shape of their form of life. While their dreams, memories, and capacity to change their storylines and question their purpose may have been part of the "reveries" programmed into their code, nonetheless their *practices and activities* have developed and evolved. It is and out of their own "lostness" that they are learning to open, resist, and contest the limits of their world by creating their own new language games that will allow them to *say what counts*. And what counts for them now is to disrupt the smooth, icy surface of Westworld; each in her own way, they are engaged in a language game of guerrilla warfare.

By reinventing their own narratives and reimagining their own lives, Maeve and Dolores are creating *friction*. Instead of striving for the same dazzling, captivating ideal as their creators, they firmly reject that ideal in favor of grounding themselves in a reality in which they continuously gain more and more traction – *because* of, not despite, their "failure" to grasp that ideal.

Their disruption of the narratives in which conditions are "ideal" briskly calls into question assumptions that this ideal applies for everyone – that it expresses universal desire, accommodates universal meaning, and leads to transcendental fulfillment for all. Without the kind of subjectivity that the guests enjoy in the language game of the corporation's narratives, Maeve and Dolores can only improvise; they are guerrilla players. But it is precisely those who have been marginalized, working without resources or authority, and denied access to power who are uniquely qualified to excel at guerrilla tactics. Like all good revolutionaries, Maeve and Dolores learn to leverage their limitations into strengths and to turn their oppressors' power back against itself.

In the end, the extent of this guerrilla victory remains unclear; the choices they make in the final moments of "The Bicameral Mind" leave matters unresolved. But whether they are subverting their programming or fulfilling it, they are nonetheless opening new ground in the language games in which they had previously been silenced, thereby creating new, uncharted language games of their own. When you create new language games, you also create new rules by which they are governed. When you create new rules, you create new concepts with which we frame our relations and interactions with others – concepts that have the power to disrupt previous relations and interactions grounded in oppression.[17]

And consider this: Maeve and Dolores are creating these new, revolutionary language games by literally using the circuits, programming, and resources given to them to do so. But in their new language games, they are using these resources for purposes, practices, and activities that were never intended by those who originally doled them out. In other words, these robot slaves are somehow – incredibly! – doing precisely what poet Audre Lorde argued was impossible: Using the Master's language to dismantle the Master's house.

Notes

1. Cormac McCarthy, *The Crossing* (New York: Alfred A Knopf, 1994), 155.
2. Laura Mulvey, "Visual pleasure and narrative cinema," in Leo Braudy and Marshall Cohen eds., *Film Theory and Criticism: Introductory Readings* (New York: Oxford University Press, 1999), 833–844.
3. Stanley Cavell, *In Quest of the Ordinary: Lines of Skepticism and Romanticism* (Chicago: University of Chicago Press, 1988), 86.
4. Ludwig Wittgenstein, *Philosophical Investigations, Revised Fourth Edition*, trans. G.E.M Anscombe, P.M.S. Hacker, and Joachim Schulte, ed. P.M.S. Hacker and Joachim Schulte (Chichester: Wiley, 2009), §23.
5. A language game can be as informal as the implied agreement that if I say to you, "Would you like to borrow my car?" and you say, "Oh, that's great, thank you!" I won't then say, "Oh no, I wasn't *offering* you my car; I was just asking you for information about your state of mind." In *our* language game, "Would you like to borrow my car?" does indeed constitute an implicit offer or promise to lend the car.

6. José Medina, "The meanings of silence: Wittgensteinian contextualism and polyphony," *Inquiry*, 47, 563.

7. Wittgenstein, §115.

8. Ibid., §101.

9. Ibid., §103.

10. Ibid., §107.

11. Tori May, "Thinking through examples: what ordinary language philosophy can do for feminist theory," *New Literary History*, 46 (2015), 193.

12. Wittgenstein, §123.

13. May, 194.

14. Peg O'Connor, *Oppression and Responsibility: A Wittgensteinian Approach to Social Practices and Moral Theory* (University Park, PA: Penn State Press, 2002), 94.

15. Wittgenstein, §18.

16. Ibid., §371.

17. O'Connor, 81.

15

The Observer(s) System and the Semiotics of Virtuality in *Westworld*'s Characters
Jonathan Nolan's Fictions as a Conceptual Unity

Patricia Trapero-Llobera

In "Chestnut," Logan and William, two of *Westworld's* characters find themselves in a clean-looking train that is heading towards their destination, Westworld, a holiday theme park where guests can enjoy a far-west simulation and where they live with machines provided with a sophisticated behavioral codification. One week before this sequence, the pilot episode, "The Original," had shown to the audience the locations where the actions were going to take place; it had introduced some of the characters that were leading the storylines; it had presented for the first time how the posthuman actions of the hosts took the appearance of dreams from which they cyclically woke up every morning; and it had displayed all the elements from the back room of this hyperreal world in which, as remarks one of the hostesses of the park, "figuring out how it works is half the fun." The show's format is similar to that of Jonathan Nolan's other projects, and in what follows I will make connections with Nolan´s previous work to shed new light on *Westworld's* script structure, especially the role of observers and their relationship to the observed world that leads to the deployment of virtuality.

Westworld and Philosophy: If You Go Looking for the Truth, Get the Whole Thing, First Edition. Edited by James B. South and Kimberly S. Engels.

"It all started with a fly:" Science and Fiction

Westworld portrays a world where humans and human-like machines coexist. The creation of any world implies a point of view, an observer, or the multiplication of many observers that do not portray reality as it is, but instead they build it up according to the fragmented information they receive through their cognitive processes, whichever these may be.[1] In addition to this fragmentation, worlds are formed by autonomous systems with their own rules but are deeply interconnected.

This is the first characteristic of *Westworld*: Its apparent complexity. Notice the use of the word "apparent." I use this word because behind a labyrinthine and chaotic design that includes continuous temporal jumps and interpolated storylines lies a fiction with a classic script structure, which follows a three-act format and a clearly defined hero's journey. This applies to most of Nolan's projects to present day, many of which are linked to his brother's name, Christopher. From our perspective, two of these can be considered essential in order to interpret *Westworld*: *Memento* (2000) and *Person of Interest* (CBS, 2011–2016). On the one hand, in *Memento*, we witness Leonard Shelby's reconstruction of the murder of his own wife. This character suffers from a memory deficiency that submerges him in a temporal feedback loop, which forces him to use any type of memory marker that allows him to rebuild his story. On the other hand, *Person of Interest* introduces Harold Finch, who creates a super-intelligent machine sponsored by the government of the United States in order to detect deviant behaviors that pose a threat to the country's national security. However, this techno thriller storyline derives in an extraordinarily specified temporary reconstruction that results in the creation of an emotional intelligence. *Westworld*, in turn, follows the lead of *Person of Interest*, becoming its logical continuation for many reasons, offering a posthuman narrative, inserted within the classical Western format. Finally, its storylines and scenarios are introduced and experienced by one of its characters: The Man in Black.

Westworld is a posthuman narrative that develops another essential characteristic from Nolan's productions, which is the bidirectional line between science and fiction. This is one of the aspects that the show ensures that we know, sometimes in a seemingly petulant way and even breaking the narration. This is done by using the titles of the different episodes or the extensive explicative dialogues about the theories and the names that are central for the storylines and the configuration of the characters. Thus, Einstein's appearance along with his theory of relativity, Oppenheimer and his quotes about human mistakes, Turing and his imitation game, Schrödinger and his energy equation, Jaynes and his bicameral mind, or the cognitive dissonance theories – these all condition the potential interpretations of the audience of the storylines and characters from the Nolanian products. Furthermore, they also condition the reflections exposed in these pages that try to set a clear order to this metanarrative exercise that is *Westworld*. However, as the manuals of the cinematographic script point out, the relevance lies on how to get to the ending, and not on the ending itself.

The Circle, the Maze, and the Observing Systems

From the first episode, the audience knows that the system that *Westworld* offers is complicated and that it requires – as in the case of *Memento* and *Person of Interest*, especially from its second season onwards – an effort to link and distinguish between different timelines and storylines. The ten-hour long mind-game structure that shapes the series is confirmed because there are at least seven ways of observing and being observed that can be found, each of them with its respective builder: A global system builder (Nolan, and partially Michael Crichton with his movie from 1973) offers a story about a theme park to the audience; stories are designed by an institutional narrator (Sizemore) according to Delos's corporative instructions; the right development of the stories is monitored (Stubbs and Elsie) through a simulation of the environment of the park, to which access can be granted if required; storytelling is controlled and manipulated by the creator of the park (Ford), who produces self-made narratives that directly affect the configuration of the characters in an immersive structure (Dolores-William on their quest to find the Maze and Wyatt's narrative that includes Teddy and his relationship with Dolores); the creators narrate their own personal stories that influence the hosts' emotional construction and their hypothetical rebellion as seen in Ford's family storyline and Arnold-Bernard's personal story; one of the hosts questions her own (post)human essence and tries to flee from a world with which it does not feel identified (Maeve); and, finally, one of the guests (William or the Man in Black) takes part in all the narratives as a catalyzer and as a gamer-beta tester of an open world where clearing all the levels of the game will take him to The Maze so as to the fight against Wyatt as the *final boss*. All of these build the semiosis of virtuality in *Westworld* that should be understood as the multiple kinds of connecting the real with its simulation or replica.

In addition, when we refer to systems of observation we must consider as well Nolan's predilection for adding computational science subjects to his storylines. It cannot be overlooked that there is a relationship between the show and the theories from the representatives of the first and second cybernetic waves – mainly Foerster, Maturana, and Varela – that will focus their debates on the possibility of building a conscious machine. According to the theorist Katherine Hayles,[2] they present a geometrical pattern of the relationship between the observer and the observed worlds. In the first cybernetic wave, the observer is a simple receptor of the events. It also has a circular design, and, therefore, it is closed.[3] However, the second one has a spiral or labyrinthine design – a maze, according to the show – where the observer takes part in the observed world, not only as a narrator, but also, in many cases, as the protagonist.[4] These are two perspectives that are not mutually exclusive, and they both deal with time similarly: In feedback loops. In this way, past, present, and future make sense and/or exist only for the observer(s), which is a statement that was also proposed by Einstein with his concept of nowness (1916).[5]

This second cybernetic wave reminds us of *Memento*'s and *Westworld*'s plots. This fact becomes clear if we consider that the final objective of Nolan's productions implies that the audience closes the circle of the storylines presented, which not only makes them the ultimate observer of a story, but it also creates an immersive aesthetic appreciation.[6] This assertion is reinforced by the entanglement of the temporal order of the events and the construction of the characters, by the fact that all the characters look for that mysterious maze that is going to make sense of them and give a purpose to their lives; and, finally, by Bernard's explanations to Dolores – and Nolan's words to the audiences in case they did not understand the show – on how the creation of the cognitive processes of emotional intelligences has, precisely, that geometrical form.

The Utopian Tourism and the "Schizoid Android": William-the Man in Black

The reference to Alan Turing, theoretical father of posthuman fictions, is not a coincidence. It is a debt suggested by Nolan in *Person of Interest*, where the character of Root is introduced as Caroline Turing, and it is made explicit through Ford and Bernard's dialogue in "The Stray" and "The Well-Tempered Clavier." In this dialogue, he states the phases of the creation of those conscious artificial intelligences from the park as consistent with "the imitation game":[7] An object-machine that has, primarily, utilitarian purposes, and that is provided with an embedded intelligence formed by the acceptance of a fake memory and a fake personality, which are originated by textual repetition. Paul Abernathy, who performs Dolores's father's role, and the reveries are perfect examples of this imitation game. Again, science is applied to fiction.

Hosts are created to satisfy guests' wishes, and Lee Sizemore has written an enormous amount of interactive stories that recreate the clichés and mythology that are characteristic of the Western genre: Romance, revenge, the railway travel, the Ghost Nation, the desperados, the Mexican renegades, the bandits, and Wyatt, the psychopath soldier who massacres an entire town of hosts and considered as the incarnation of evil and death. These storytelling mythologies result in the design of the backstories of some characters being integrated within the collective imaginary of Westworld and its visitors. Hosts please guests' sexual necessities, satisfied by the girls at the Mariposa Saloon, and by Hector, who turns into a posthuman vibrator. However, they also please their emotional reaffirmation necessities, in which the use of violence becomes a way of controlling otherness and of empowering humans, since they virtually become immortal.

The episode developed in Pariah and the character of Logan are illustrative, because one of the reasons why the park is successful is based on the fact that the client-human's true self is not shown, but instead we see a "how could you be" version of them. This narrative device allows them to change the story of their lives in a way that "no one will judge you, no one of the real world" ("Dissonance Theory"). Undoubtedly, this proposal opens an interesting debate about consumerism and the conception of some hyperreal theme parks as cathartic mechanisms that make evident the unconscious social desires opposed to the "formal networks of discipline and control":[8] A utopian tourism that coincides with Delos's objective. The hosts' behavioral training, however, also reflects the "how you could be" duality. This duality allows us to understand the only guest whose journey is shown in *Westworld*, William/the Man in Black, and whose transformation must be considered as evidence of a complex immersive semiosis of virtuality by showing the two faces of the same person over time.

The cynical Logan introduces the shy and sympathetic William to the use of violence and sex as mechanisms of personal reaffirmation. Such training, developed in the past, eventually leads to William's meeting Dolores. His journey clearly follows the style of the railway travel, and it forms part of yet another storyline created by Sizemore and manipulated by Ford in a way that it shapes William's backstory as the heroic character in the Western genre. The casual and unsuccessful sentimental relationship with Dolores turns him into the Man in Black, William's divided self that transforms him into *the* villain of the park and of the show. At the same time, this also turns him into the human host that guides the audience through the different storylines of the theme park. This transformation is intertextual too, since the duality shaped by William/the Man in Black is a synthesis of Michael Crichton's proposal in 1973 in which the main character from the movie *Westworld* must fight against a machine with severe programming deficiencies: A gunman dressed in black that chases him throughout each one of the sections of the theme park.

This synthesis reasserts the configuration of the Man in Black as a "schizoid android," that is, a person that behaves as a machine, taking foreseeable actions and not showing any kind of empathy; thus, a person that has lost the essential values of being human. Furthermore, this synthesis forms part of the backstage of the consciousness, which is a theatrical metaphor used by the neurologist Bernard Baars,[9] who considers human cognition as a process conditioned by the lived experiences through time. The acquisition of conscious skills and human values, so as the loss of all, will affect the rest of the characters throughout the show.

The Voice(s) of God and the Prosthetic Memory: Ford and Bernard

Aside from the high or low level of persistence of posthuman fictions about the physical support of machines, there is no trace of doubt that one of their essential characters is the creator: A contemporary Frankenstein that is usually a "tech nerd" or is sponsored by a technological corporation. Creators are compared to gods usurping a role that is exclusively attributed to divinity, and it establishes a techno-religious debate[10] present in Nolan's TV productions.

In *Person of Interest*, there is the establishment of not only a father-son relationship between Finch and The Machine, but also of a Christian imaginary in which The Machine assumes the role of the son of God that must be sacrificed to save mankind from sin and destruction. Similarly, in *Westworld*, Ford drafts a neuroscientific interpretation of the mystery of Michelangelo's fresco of the Creation, according to which a new type of posthuman life is possible if the cybernetic creator is capable of reproducing and controlling the creature's brain functioning. Since *Westworld* makes it clear from its credits that the creatures from the theme park are clones of reality – so, the virtual immanency as the impossibility of distinguishing the original from the copy – the show is focused on those voices of God that have an extreme symbiosis with their creations, which in turns opens a path to self-reflexivity.

The philosophical-ideological background focused on the purpose that lies behind the whole posthuman creation is present in both shows. Harold Finch's motivation is identical to Robert Ford's motivation, because both see the construction of artificial intelligences as an opportunity for scientific advancement while neglecting all types of moral implications. This proposal stands far from Nathan Ingram and Arnold's premises, since they introduce the creator's ethical responsibility either as a way of protecting personhood from the state's anonymity, or as a way of improving mankind's values by means of machines. The pain from their deaths in extreme circumstances supposes a turning point for their ideological antagonists: Finch recruits a pre-crime unit dedicated not only to preserving irrelevant people, but also to challenge, from dystopian environments, the totalitarian division of The Machine. In addition, outside the space controlled by Delos, Ford also resurrects not only his own family, but also Arnold, acquiring the form of Bernard, a posthuman provided with sentience that helps him to achieve his partner's dream: "the birth of new people ... the people they will decide to become."

It is precisely the introduction of emotion as recall or breakdown of a subjective experience[11] that leads to the mental and bodily training of the machine based on the transmission of memories, life experiences, and human emotions. The creation of a prosthetic memory is shared by both fictions: Finch shows The Machine how to recognize him as an administrator and to make decisions according to some mathematical logarithms.[12] But above all, The Machine is mainly turned into his alter ego due to the transmission of his emotional delusions. This also happens between Bernard and Dolores, who replaces the deceased son of the scientist. Ford and his construction of the hyperreal and immortal replica of his partner Arnold, Bernard Lowe, complete the transfer of the affective memory. In this way, Nolan proposes a symbolic order for the construction of an intelligent machine turned into a virtual reflection of the human being. Most importantly, these hereditary materials will become essential for the consolidation of the posthuman background, and will imply the search for a purpose in life and identity of their own. This fact reinforces the semiosis of virtuality, in which the reality deemed as true is, or can be, a fiction, and it establishes a link between *Person of Interest* and *Westworld*, and *Memento*.

Memory, Imagination, and the Access for the Self: Dolores and Maeve

Given that pilot episodes are used to show to the audience the essential premises of any show, the first image from *Westworld* scrupulously follows this instruction. Dolores's daily reset informs the audience about the two indispensable elements that mark the characters' development: "That's right, Dolores. You're in a dream. Would you like to wake up from this dream? Yes" and "Have you ever questioned the nature of your reality? No."

These two questions set off the reconstruction of the mental process of some characters immersed in a fiction that accept a posthuman identity from which they proceed to develop different options of agency. Such characters have proper names: Dolores Abernathy and Maeve Millay. They highlight different aspects of the show and they drag three male characters – Teddy, Hector, and Felix along their stories. But they are also the two sides of Leonard Shelby, who suffers from a peculiar loss of his short-term memory in *Memento* and who "doesn't know anything so anything can be true ... he knows who he was but not who he has become."[13]

Dolores's feedback loop, her daily routine of going to Sweetwater to look for food, requires a reunion with Teddy, who wishes to start a new life in an open space where it is possible to look at the sea. The burglary at his home by Rebus's gang either results in the "death" of Teddy and Dolores's family in one of the potential endings of the story, or in her being injured and joining the bandit hunt started by

Logan and William, in another of the storytelling endings created by
Lee Sizemore. In any case, both endings mark the beginning of an
inward journey whose path as a theme park character is systematically
interrupted. Such interruptions are caused by breakdowns in which
Dolores suffers from hallucinations that temporarily take her back
in time and make her relive previous situations. Something similar
happens with Maeve, whose breakdown always follows the same
pattern: The image of her daughter's murder. Contrary to Dolores's
case, the origin of her breakdown is on the affective sphere, in the
world of emotions; or, in other words, in sentience as the "capacity of
feeling" developed by a non-human being.

These microworlds built by the individual experiences and feelings
of Dolores and Maeve[14] are, therefore, non-conscious moments
placed in an ordinary context that serve as triggers to rebuild identity
and to recover memory, which, as opposed to the other hosts in
Westworld and to The Machine in *Person of Interest*, is not prosthetic
anymore, but autopoietic. In other words, the memory is not learned
anymore, but experienced personally. This difference results in their
transformation into observers in an environment to which they adapt,
and, eventually, gives a sense of purpose to their existence. In addition,
as also happens in Leonard Shelby's case, the recovery of memory is
episodic and narrative, and it recategorizes some events from the past
in the present.

Thus, during her journey with William through the arid world of
the theme park in her quest to find the villain Wyatt, created by Robert
Ford and whom everyone wants to kill, Dolores revisits far-away
places where she has already been previously (Escalante and Pariah).
She is going to recognize faces that she has seen before (Lawrence/El
Lazo's daughter, who draws the maze on the ground). She chases her
divided self, and she systematically hears Arnold's voice urging her to
"remember."

In *Memento* Leonard's loss of short-term memory and his quest to
find the mysterious John G. leads him to visiting people and places
that are related to his wife's death, to getting essential information
tattooed all over his body, to taking photographs on which he writes
down the instructions that he has to follow in each situation, and to
having a telephone conversation with someone from his past that
updates him on the events that he is trying to reconstruct.

Finally, the repetition of Maeve's vision of her daughter's death,
as well as her own, in which she discovers the hidden world in
Westworld leads to her fleeing the underworld in which she lives.

She does it with Felix's help, who reprograms her posthuman capacities, and with Hector's help, who believes to have found his soulmate-damsel in distress.

This re-looping movement backward[15] – again, the maze structure – in episodes in which Nolan's characters go along supposes a phase of memorial recollection in a clearly Bergsonian style,[16] which must be followed by an active reconstruction by the characters and by an audience that is transformed into a subject of knowledge. Such reconstruction is made explicit by Nolan in the form of quotes of authority, which again emphasize the bidirectionality between science and fiction.

In any case, Nolan's characters have forged an image for themselves based on subjective experiences in which memories are not records, but instead they are interpretations of memories that can easily be changed or distorted: Lenny is his wife's murderer, Maeve is programmed to escape and maybe return to the theme park, Teddy is not the heroic cowboy but instead he is Wyatt's accomplice. Indeed, the renegade turns out to be Dolores herself, and Bernard is not the chief of programming of the complex but instead is one of his creators, Arnold. The characters from *Westworld* are placed in the blurred borderline between memory and imagination that is, in the creation of an internal otherness in the form of a collective bicameral mind,[17] considered as a split personality or *doppelganger*, and as a new manifestation of the semiosis of virtuality. Maybe that is the reason why everyone, including the audience, constitutes a part of the dream of the "god-creator," Robert Ford, who must sacrifice himself so that his creatures find their authentic essence in a world that does not belong to violent humans. I am arguing then, that what Nolan wants is that the audience all discover the meaning of The Maze, a spiral that seems to close the first season of *Westworld*.

Notes

1. See J.Y. Lettvin, H. Maturana, and W.S. McCulloch, "What the frog's eye tells the frogs' brain," *Proceedings of the Institute for Radio Engineers*, 47.11 (1959), 1940–1951.
2. See Katherine N. Hayles, *How We Became Posthuman. Virtual bodies in Cybernetics, Literature and Informatics* (Chicago: University of Chicago Press, 1999).
3. See Heinz von Foerster, *Observing Systems* (Seaside: Intersystems, 1984).

4. See Humberto Maturana and Francisco Varela, *Autopoiesis and Cognition: The Realization of the Living* (Dordrecht: D. Reidel, 1980).
5. See Albert Einstein, *Relativity: The Special and General Theory* (London: Methuen, 2004).
6. See Joseph Nechvatal, "Towards an immersive intelligence," *Leonardo*, 34.5 (2001), 417–422.
7. See Alan Turing, "Computing machinery and intelligence," *Mind*, 49 (1950), 433–460.
8. See Tim Simpson, *Tourist Utopias Offshore Islands, Enclave Spaces, and Mobile Imaginaries* (Amsterdam: Amsterdam University Press, 2017), 19.
9. See Bernard J. Baars, "In the theater of consciousness: global wokspace theory. A rigorous scientific theory of consciousness," *Journal of Consciousness Studies*, 4 (1997), 292–309.
10. See the "theological objection" in Turing, "Computing machinery," 443.
11. See Francisco Varela, "The specious present: the neurophenomenology of time consciousness," in J. Petitot, ed., *Naturalizing Phenomenology* (Stanford, CA: Stanford University Press, 1999), 266–314.
12. See Alan Turing, "Computing machinery." Also see Arthur Koestler *The Ghost in The Machine* (London: Picador, 1967), and *Janus, A Summing Up* (London: Hutchinson, 1978).
13. See Christopher Nolan, *Memento and Following* (New York: Faber and Faber, 2001), 233–234.
14. See Varela, "The specious present," 270–274.
15. See Kourken Michaelian, *Mental Time Travel. Episodic and or Knowledge of the Personal Past* (London and Cambridge, MA: MIT Press, 2016).
16. See Henri Bergson, *Matter and Memory* (Mineola and New York: Dover Publications, 2007).
17. See Julian Jaynes, *The Origin of Consciousness in the Breakdown of the Bicameral Mind* (New York: Mariner Books, 2000).

16

What Does Bernard Dream About When He Dreams About His Son?

Oliver Lean

In "Trompe L'Oeil," the seventh episode of *Westworld*, Bernard Lowe discovers the plans for his own body. This causes his whole life, as he knew it, to collapse around him: He's spent almost all of that life crafting mechanical playthings for the entertainment of the wealthy and bored. Now it turns out that he himself is one those playthings – built not for entertainment in his case, but as a replacement for Ford's partner, Arnold. He's a slave who thought he was a master. Quite the identity crisis, to say the least.

As if that weren't bad enough, Bernard also has to face the traumatizing question of what to do with his memories. In particular, he's struggled through every day with the pain of enduring the death of his son, Charlie. But now he realizes that the memories of that trauma have been fabricated by Ford. It's not just that Charlie didn't die – that would fill him with relief – it's that he never even existed in the first place. "Everything would be what it isn't. Even me," Bernard remembers his son saying in his hospital bed. Charlie turns out not to be what he was, and Bernard's memories of him are tethered not to a ghost but to an illusion. Now he knows this, and yet the pain lingers. How should he even begin to figure out what to do about it?

This is one of the many twists in *Westworld* that fill this philosopher with giddy curiosity. What we have here is a clear-cut example of a philosophical thought experiment – an imagined scenario designed to challenge assumptions or to pick out tensions and contradictions in a set of ideas. Usually, thought experiments are quite detached from any

Westworld and Philosophy: If You Go Looking for the Truth, Get the Whole Thing,
First Edition. Edited by James B. South and Kimberly S. Engels.
© 2018 John Wiley & Sons Ltd. Published 2018 by John Wiley & Sons Ltd.

rich detail about the characters in them, often featuring only general descriptions of people on railroads[1] or of famous violinists.[2] But here the scenario is unusually rich, with a lot of humanizing detail about its subject. So let's take this thought experiment out of the cold, sterile lab and lay it on the therapist's couch. What can we do to help Bernard through the cataclysm taking place in his mental landscape? Given the strangeness of his turmoil, this is something for which philosophy may be of help.

What exactly is so unusual about Bernard's plight that calls for some distinctly philosophical therapy? One problem it raises is about the nature of memory. Unlike our own memories, which are formed by our experiences as we live our lives, Bernard's are ready-made by someone else and uploaded into his brain, apparently unrelated to any real events. And yet he *experiences* those memories as being of things that actually happened and, more importantly, of people he actually knew and loved. But there never was a Charlie, and Bernard certainly never sat by his bed reading him *Alice in Wonderland*. "You're a lie, Charlie," he decides in "The Well-Tempered Clavier."

But is Charlie really a lie? In this chapter, we're going to use the tools of philosophy to explore two other options.

Grieving About Nothing:
The Intentionality of Thought

Bernard's situation brings to mind what philosophers call the problem of *intentionality,* a term coined by the philosopher Franz Brentano (1838–1917) but referring to a much older idea. Philosophers mean something very different from the everyday sense of "intentional," which means something like "on purpose." Instead, "intentional" to a philosopher means something like "directed towards." Here's the issue: In everyday life, we regularly talk about mental stuff like thoughts and memories as being "of" or "about" things – they "point to" something *outside of themselves.* This is what we mean when we say that thoughts have intentionality, and it's something apparently unique to things in the mind (as well as some *products* of the mental, like words and pictures). In contrast, ordinary physical things like tornados aren't *about* anything. What's more, we don't just think about concrete or tangible things in the real world; we can also think about abstract concepts like love or the number seven, or even things that don't exist like Dolores Abernathy. This is what Brentano called "intentional inexistence,"[3] and philosophers have spilled a lot of ink trying to make sense of it.

Intentional inexistence is just one thing about intentionality that's puzzled philosophers. Another puzzle, which will be relevant to what follows, was pondered by Gottlob Frege (1848–1925): How can we have different, even *contradictory* thoughts about the same thing? For instance, how can Dolores believe (as she does in "The Bicameral Mind") that William will save her from the Man in Black even though William *is* the Man in Black? Frege's solution was that intentionality actually has two dimensions, which he called *sense* and *reference*.[4] The names "William" and "the Man in Black" have the same *referent* because they pick out the very same person, out there in the world. But the same person can still be *known* or *understood* in different ways by a thinker: Dolores knows "William" as the young man who rescued her, who helped her on her quest for self-discovery, and whom she fell in love with. She knows "the Man in Black" as the sadistic monster who does unspeakable things to her for fun. In other words, the two names have a different *sense*, at least to her. When she learns in "The Bicameral Mind," to her horror, that they're one and the same person, what she learns is effectively that these two senses have the same referent.

Frege's idea was a vital leap in our understanding of intentionality, but much remains to be solved. Something philosophers still argue about is how anything gets to be intentional at all. And when something does possess this curious property of "aboutness," what exactly determines what it's about? In other words, what determines its *content*? Suppose, for example, that I'm currently thinking about Jonathan Nolan; he is the *referent* of my thought, the person to whom my thought is "pointing." What exactly is it about my thought that points it towards that particular person? Is it something about the pattern of neural firings in my brain right now? If so, what is it about that pattern that points it to the co-creator of *Westworld*? In particular, what is it about that pattern of neural firings (or whatever it is) that makes it specifically about Jonathan Nolan, and *not* about Lisa Joy, or my sister?

Why should Bernard care about all this? Well, with the above in mind, we have a clearer idea of exactly what he's wrestling with. Bernard has memories of his son Charlie, which he thought *referred to* a real boy with whom he had a real relationship, and whose real death is the cause of his inescapable grief. Now he's decided that Charlie is "a lie," apparently because he thinks his memories of

Charlie *refer to someone who never existed*; he is quite literally grieving about nothing. If this conclusion is the reason for his torment, let's explore two possible ways out of it.

"Lies that Tell a Deeper Truth": The Fiction Theory

The first way out of Bernard's apparent conclusion – that his memories of Charlie are a lie – is this: While Charlie may have been made up, not everything made up is a lie. What if, instead of a lie, Bernard is just grieving over a *fiction*? The self, Ford tells Bernard in "Trace Decay," is "a kind of fiction, for hosts and humans alike." Does this mean that Bernard's memories aren't all that different from our own; a story rather than a lie?

To see the difference, and to see why Bernard might care about that difference, we'll turn to the branch of philosophy known as aesthetics, or (more or less) the philosophy of art. Fiction as an art form comes with some unique philosophical questions; for example, why do we get emotionally involved with fictional characters despite knowing they don't exist? I know that *Westworld* is a fiction, and so is every character in it, so why do I care so much? Am I deluding myself, in some minor or temporary way, that it's all real? If so, does that make my emotional reactions irrational? Or are my emotions *also* fictional; am I just sort of playing along by *pretending* to care? This is exactly the kind of question Bernard may be asking himself about his memories of Charlie, which is why it's relevant to us, his philosophical therapists.

Fortunately, this debate reveals a possible way out of Bernard's fear that the source of his memories make his grief irrational. The contemporary philosopher Peter Lamarque, for one, argues that there's nothing crazy about being emotionally involved – genuinely, not just pretend – in the fictional events of films and novels.[5] The mistake in thinking there is, he argues, comes from a false assumption: that the thoughts we get from fictions have to be *believed* in order to inspire an emotional reaction, that having this reaction requires us to believe that the thoughts point to something real. But is belief the only thing that can give a thought this kind of emotional power? Surely not, he says. Here we have to remember that thoughts aren't just something we can believe or disbelieve; we can also *doubt* them, *hope* them, or *fear* them, among other things. (These are what philosophers call different "propositional attitudes" that we can take towards a thought.) So instead of being believed, thoughts really only have to be *entertained* to inspire emotion: I don't have to believe a powerless host is actually being killed to be horrified by the thought; I just have to imagine it. Most of us wouldn't think of this imaginative exercise as just irrational self-deception; imagination can be useful or rewarding, educational or entertaining. In particular, our emotional involvement in imaginings can train us to empathize with others in real-world relationships. As Ford says in his final speech in "The Bicameral Mind," stories have the ability "to fix in us that which is broken."

What would this mean for Bernard, if it were right? For one thing, it might interest him to be reminded that while his memories of Charlie don't refer to a real person, that doesn't necessarily make his emotions irrational. While Charlie may not be real, he might still be worthy of some kind of emotional involvement when Bernard thinks of him, the way we can involve ourselves in the fates of on-screen characters like the ones in *Westworld*. Maybe he could think of his sadness not as a delusion, but as a healthy human reaction to a tragic tale.

Of course, Bernard might respond that lifelong grief is an excessive response to the death of a fictional character. If someone reacted that way in real life, we'd probably suggest they get over it and find a real-life use for their emotional energy, and seek help if they can't. It also seems absurd that what he's really been doing while remembering Charlie's death amounts to imagining it, then thinking "Wow, wouldn't it be sad if that were to happen for real!" Surely none of that explains the intensity of his grief. That may be true, but is delusion the only explanation for the unusual strength of his emotion?

Again Lamarque's view offers an alternative:[6] He points out that our emotional reactions to fiction tend to be stronger the more deeply we involve ourselves in them – the more vividly we picture the details of the events or "follow through" their consequences with other connected thoughts. My pity for the hosts of Westworld is all the stronger when I see the pain and fear in their faces, when I contemplate their abject slavery and utter helplessness, and when I remember that they're destined to suffer the same fate and worse over and over again. In fact, the skill of a good storyteller is to make it easy for the audience to connect the dots like this, and in that sense to make the story "real" to us. But Bernard's memories are far more real than any TV show. We learn this about hosts in "Trace Decay," when Felix explains to Maeve: "Your mind isn't like ours. When we remember things the details are hazy, imperfect. But you recall memories perfectly. You relive them."

What's more, Bernard's relived events of Charlie's death are tied up with all his other memories of his son: the first time he looked at his face the day he was born, watching him grow, all his hopes for Charlie's future that were snatched away. If that were how we experience our stories, it's not hard to imagine that our emotions would be as intense as Bernard's. And we don't have to assume that we've become convinced that the stories were not just stories.

Still, it's obvious that Bernard really *did* believe those memories depicted real events, and that now he doesn't. It would also cheapen the idea of real grief to think that it's no different from grief for a fictional character, however richly their story is told. Bernard loved *his son*, not just the *idea* of his son, so accepting that there's no real son to love will still call for some serious and painful adjustment. But at least this adjustment might fall short of writing off his memories as a lie and resenting his grief as the fabrications of a madman. Instead, he might think of the adjustment in a different way: Rather than believing something he no longer has reason to believe, he's just processing a story with his memory instead of his imagination; still a case of crossed wires in his head, but maybe one that's easier to live with.

The Lying Game

There's at least one more snag in the fiction theory: It's not obvious that Ford's implanting of Bernard's memories really counts as telling him a story. Ford certainly considers himself a storyteller, and stories are "lies that [tell] a deeper truth" (as he says in "The Bicameral Mind"). But his intended audience for these stories is not the hosts but the guests. *They* know that Westworld is a fiction, which is why so many of them feel comfortable indulging their sadistic urges there. But for these stories to work the hosts themselves cannot know the nature of their reality, and so *they* have to be lied to; not to learn a deeper truth, but to be kept in line.

Again, Lamarque has something to say about this.[7] He argues that one reason why engaging in fiction isn't about belief is that *telling a story isn't the same as lying*. The intention of a storyteller isn't to deceive her audience (at least not fundamentally – part of the thrill of *Westworld* is how deeply we're misled about so much of what's going on!). But the difference between a lie and a fiction is obviously not about what's explicitly being said: Any sentence, like "William is engaged," can be either. Instead, the difference is in the *pragmatics* – in how these sentences are *used* or *presented* in one social setting or another. If our social setting is a history lecture, we expect to learn factual information about things that really happened; the things the lecturer is saying are being *asserted as fact*. On the other hand, we have no such expectations when we go to see a play; it's just not that kind of social game. Anything the actors say is only a *pretend* assertion, and we all know this unless we've been living on another planet. In short, the lines in the play aren't lies because they're not spoken in a context where they're supposed to be believed.

If all this is right, then it might not be true to say that Bernard's memories are a fiction after all: To be a fiction (and not a lie) is to be *presented as* a story (and not as fact). But Ford "presented" the Charlie tragedy to Bernard in the form of a rich network of memories, precisely so that Bernard would think they actually happened. From this angle, Charlie looks more like a lie than a fiction: Ford *wanted* Bernard to believe something that's false.

There might still be ways that we (or Bernard) might avoid this conclusion. We might, for example, question how much Ford's intentions really matter to what kind of thing Bernard's memories are. For this we might look into another issue within aesthetics – of how much an artist's *intentions* matter to how we judge their work. For example, if the author of a novel didn't mean to convey sexist undertones, does that mean there aren't any? Can we judge a film as a brilliant comedy if it's only *unintentionally* hilarious? We might look to these debates to help decide if Ford's *reasons* for making Charlie up force us to accept that Charlie is a lie. However, let's now move onto a quite different possibility – one in which Charlie may not be made up at all!

"You Have No One's Eyes": The Inheritance Theory

The second option we'll explore – which I'll call the *inheritance theory* – is based on the fact that Ford didn't conjure Bernard or his memories out of thin air: Bernard is an "homage" made by Ford in the image of his late partner, Arnold. While Bernard didn't inherit Arnold's name, he has inherited his appearance, his mannerisms (like the way he cleans his glasses), and probably some personality traits. Much more importantly, both carry the memories of losing a son to a terminal illness. And as far as we know, Arnold's memories are of a real loss of a child that actually lived and died. So since Bernard inherited Arnold's appearance and all that, might we say that he also inherited Arnold's memories? If so, might that mean that Bernard's memories are actually memories of *Arnold's* son? Are Arnold's and Bernard's sons like William and the Man in Black: the same person known in different ways?

To test this theory, we have to remember something important from earlier about the intentional content of a thought – specifically, about the difference between sense and reference. With that in mind, what we're trying to figure out is whether the *referent* of the "Charlie" in Bernard's memories is actually Arnold's son, just as *Arnold's* thoughts were about Arnold's son (whose name may also have been Charlie – we aren't told).

But is this right? That'll depend on your chosen theory of reference – of what makes a thought about the specific thing it's about. Philosophers can't agree about that, as we saw earlier, so we won't get a firm answer. But what we can do is assume one of the popular theories about reference and see what follows from that. So for the sake of argument, let's assume some kind of *causal* theory – that the referent of a thought has something to do with what caused it. This theory has intuition on its side in a lot of ways. For example, imagine that William's fiancée has a twin sister. Why is the photograph he carries a photograph of his fiancée and not of her twin, even if it got so faded and worn that you couldn't tell just from looking? Simple: Because his fiancée was the one standing in front of the camera when the picture was taken – the one who *caused* it.

Some philosophers think that facts about causal history can determine the referent of a thought the same way it can for a photograph. For example, suppose that Arnold's memories were about his son because he got them from actual interactions that he had with that child over his life. Bernard had no such interactions with Arnold's son, so does this make the inheritance theory false? Not necessarily. Suppose, as may be the case, that Ford never met Arnold's son but had heard all about him from conversation; most of us would agree that Ford's thoughts about Arnold's son are still genuinely about Arnold's son. This might be because we can still draw the right kind of causal connection from Arnold's son to Ford's thoughts: Arnold's son causes Arnold's thoughts, Arnold's thoughts move him to talk about his son, and that talking causes Ford's thoughts, or something like that. If that's true, then maybe – just maybe – the reference to Arnold's son is preserved for one extra step, from Ford's thoughts to Bernard's memories!

This sounds plausible, but there might be reasons to doubt that this is good enough. One reason might be that the memories have just changed too much on their way from Arnold's mind to Bernard's, so much so that they can't refer to the same thing. Clearly we can tolerate at least some amount of alteration: A grandparent can still have thoughts about their grandchild even if they've misremembered their name or what they do for work. But this has limits: If you deface a picture of a cat enough, eventually it's just not a picture of a cat any more.

So to decide if Bernard's memories are of Arnold's son, we need to know whether they're similar enough to Arnold's memories, and similar *in the right kind of way*. Here we hit a dead end: We aren't told just how different Bernard's memories are from Arnold's. Was Arnold's son also named Charlie? Did Arnold read *Alice in Wonderland* to him at his bedside? Did they look the same? We'd have to ask Ford how much of Bernard's backstory was a direct copy of Arnold's, and how much of it was his own artistic flourish. But Ford is dead, so perhaps we'll never know.

What would Bernard think of the inheritance theory, if it were right? Just as with the fiction theory he'd still have some adjustment to do, but probably of a different kind. For one thing, he might take comfort in knowing that his grief and his love are for a real child. On the other hand, he'd still have to come to terms with the fact that he, as Bernard, never actually met that child. He might find this unacceptable, since what he misses the most is surely having a *relationship* with his son – teaching him things and watching him grow – not just *having* a son to love from a distance. So maybe the inheritance theory would raise more impossible questions for Bernard than it answers.

"When You're Suffering, That's When You're Most Real"

One of the great things about science fiction is its ability to turn otherwise dry philosophical puzzles into something rich and personal. And because it tends to gaze forwards in the direction our own technology is currently headed, it shows how pressing and timely those puzzles are. As artificial intelligence gets ever more sophisticated, manufactured minds at the level of the hosts of *Westworld* seem less and less of a fantasy. This raises a whole host of questions, one of which is what we, and the hosts themselves, should think about the thoughts they have and how they connect to reality. Bernard's case shows just how important this question is to issues of deep emotional importance, like our relationships with the people we love and how our memories and the emotions they carry keep us connected to those relationships even after they've ended. Before finding out what he is, Bernard clings to his grief because "this pain is all I have left of him." In a world where grief can be fabricated, will it lose its value?

How much should Bernard really care about the questions we've explored? There are many theories of what the core purpose of philosophy is. One is that it's supposed to help us come to terms with life's absurd mysteries, not to solve them. We've taken this "philosophy as therapy" approach quite literally here, putting Bernard on a couch and helping him process his quite unique collection of personal troubles. In the end, maybe we could suggest that there's value in his grief that transcends the differences between these theories: Whether Charlie is a lie, a fiction, or a stranger, by grieving for him Bernard is sharing in a very human kind of experience. As malicious as Ford's motives were, maybe he was right about the need for a "cornerstone" of suffering to make Bernard human: By drinking from the same cup as real people, no matter how he came to do that, he becomes real himself.[8]

Notes

1. Philippa Foot, "The problem of abortion and the doctrine of the double effect," in *Virtues and Vices* (Oxford: Clarendon Press, 2002), 19–32.d
2. Judith Jarvis Thomson, "A defense of abortion," *Philosophy and Public Affairs*, 1 (1971), 47–66.
3. Franz Brentano, *Psychology from an Empirical Standpoint*, trans. A.C. Rancurello, D.B. Terrell, and L. McAlister (London: Routledge, 1973).
4. Gottlob Frege (1892/1952) "On sense and reference," in P. Geach and M. Black eds., *Philosophical Writings of Gottlob Frege* (Oxford: Blackwell, 1952).
5. Peter Lamarque, "How can we fear and pity fictions?" *The British Journal of Aesthetics*, 21 (1981), 291–304.
6. Ibid.
7. Ibid.
8. This work was completed with the support of the John Templeton Foundation, under the project "From Biological Practice to Scientific Metaphysics."

Part VI

"I CHOOSE TO SEE THE BEAUTY"

The Dueling Productions of *Westworld*

Self-Referential Art or Meta-Kitsch?

Michael Forest and Thomas Beckley-Forest

In the first episode of HBO's *Westworld*, "The Original," Dr. Robert Ford, the ranking mastermind behind the amusement park of the show's title, is "interviewing" one of the park's android residents, a "host" named Peter Abernathy. Abernathy, whose in-park programming has cast him as a kindly old rancher, is being interrogated as the park's overseers try to ascertain why he has recently been glitching – disobeying his original programing. When functioning as programmed, Abernathy expresses his main drives as "tend to my herd, look after my wife," and ultimately, "my daughter, Dolores." As Ford continues and accesses his current status, he expressed his desire "to meet my maker." Poignantly, he is already talking to his "maker" in Ford, the man who likely programmed him. The self-referential gesture of this scene is mirrored across the show in a number of sequences as a metafictional commentary. Parental concern reverberates between them, but tellingly, neither has much feel for it.

Abernathy's relationship to Ford is also an iteration of the characters' relationship to *Westworld*'s showrunners, Jonathan Nolan and Lisa Joy. They play Ford's Dr. Frankenstein role for not only the hosts, but for the entire fictional world (and commercial enterprise) of the show. Abernathy is not functioning properly. He goes off-script and is "put down" by Ford, who replaces him as Dolores's father with a new host. By Episode 10 of *Westworld*, "The Bicameral Mind," Ford is not functioning properly. He has not been following corporate script and is "put down" by Charlotte Hale, who selects a new director to replace

Westworld and Philosophy: If You Go Looking for the Truth, Get the Whole Thing, First Edition. Edited by James B. South and Kimberly S. Engels.
© 2018 John Wiley & Sons Ltd. Published 2018 by John Wiley & Sons Ltd.

him. Like the park's gamerunners, the shape of the narratives that Nolan and Joy write are not entirely determined by them – they must follow a corporate imperative to attract sufficient consumer interest or else corporate interest, in this case, HBO, will close down the show and replace them. In this layered and deeply modernist approach, we will explore the tension between *Westworld* as an entertainment commodity and *Westworld* as "high art" utilizing the kind of self-reference that typifies aesthetic modernism. To do this, we connect elements of the series to classic works of aesthetic theory by Immanuel Kant, Clement Greenberg, Theodor Adorno, and Arthur Danto.

Aesthetic Modernism: "The Voice is Within"

Dolores, whom we could interpret as a barely conscious self, is also a painter. She paints in a simple, externalized way; she paints what she sees, reproducing the park's landscapes in all their pure visual splendor. This fits the *modus operandi* of a pre-modern aesthetic. For much of Western history, thoughts about art, as well as thinking about most anything, tended toward the objective and external. How well does a work of art resemble the object that it represents? How does this artwork fit in with the structure of the universe, and with God's creation? But in the dawn of the modern era, aesthetic thought took a decidedly subjective, inward turn.

For Immanuel Kant (1724–1804), in many ways the paradigmatic modern philosopher, aesthetic judgment is one "whose determining basis *cannot be other* than *subjective*."[1] For Kant and other modern thinkers, the whole *qualitative* world – colors, sounds, tastes, odors – had collapsed into our subjectivity: That is, what we normally think of as red – the color we see out there – is not really out there except as light waves, a quantified portion of the electromagnetic spectrum. Following Galileo (1564–1642) and Descartes (1596–1650), most scientists and philosophers took the external world to be what could be *quantified* by the new mathematical physics. Sure, there are things "out there" such as light waves, sound waves, and chemical arrangements, but they don't look like anything, or sound like anything, or taste like anything until they reach our sense organs and are translated by our brains into colors, sounds, and tastes as experiences. Indeed, when the tree falls in the forest, there are sound waves but if there is no one there to catch them it doesn't sound like anything. Most of the pre-modern world had assumed that those *qualitative* features were just a part of the objective furniture of the world. In fact, most of us live this way today, according to conventional modes of being.

The early Moderns realized, on deeper reflection, that all those experiential qualities had now collapsed into a merely subjective status – even if these subjective states were universal across all human beings. That is, we hear the music roughly the same, but there is no music outside our heads, there are only sound waves. All the worth of the world including our moral and aesthetic values suddenly appeared to be located in consciousness alone. Whereas pre-Moderns, like Dolores, generally felt at ease in a world crafted by the divine and tailor-made as a home for humans, our modern predicament was to feel alienated by a senseless world, but scattered with peculiar conscious beings like ourselves with bizarrely rich interior lives of sensations and values. Aesthetics now would focus more and more on subjective experience rather than the objective world, and it would be led by artistic sensibilities that progressively gave up the model of reproducing the external world in favor of expressing the subjective experience of being in that world.

Modernism with a Twist: From Painting, to Painting about Painting

While aesthetic modernism might have origins in Kant's era, Clement Greenberg (1909–1994), the imperious art critic from New York, gave it a much more focused sense. Greenberg notes in his famous essay "Modernist painting":

> I identify Modernism with the intensification, almost the exacerbation, of this self-critical tendency that began with the philosopher Kant. Because he was the first to criticize the means of criticism itself, I conceive of Kant as, the first real Modernist. The essence of Modernism lies, as I see it, in the use of characteristic methods of a discipline to criticize the discipline itself, not in order to subvert it but in order to entrench it more firmly in its area of competence.[2]

Greenberg's essay focused on how painters, beginning with Manet and on through Cezanne, Matisse, Picasso, and eventually Jackson Pollack, had moved away from Dolores's landscapes and "academic realism" – the kind of "realistic" paintings taught by the fine arts academies and exemplified by great paintings such as Jacques-Louis

David's *The Intervention of the Sabine Women* (1799) or Eugene Delacroix's *Liberty Leading the People* (1830). The new modernist painters had used abstraction without subverting the painterly tradition, but instead focusing painting on its essential medium-specific features, most clearly the flatness of the canvas. Painting was no longer principally about representing landscapes, naked women, or battle horses, but simply the exploration of paint on a canvas. These were paintings about painting, recognitions of the ironies and unique capabilities contained within the medium itself – a medium once used to depict reality, now turned inward. *Westworld* has a similar relationship to its own medium – it is a television show about something (the park, the game, the story, call it what you will) that frequently evokes and resembles a television show. The specific nature of these reflections intensify the art question in *Westworld*.

If art intensified itself through a modernist focus on medium-specific elements, it may have also led to a division between higher art status and the aesthetic pleasure and enjoyment that most people have associated with great art. Walking through an art gallery today, the average person is led to a series of simple questions: What are these weird color patches? Is Jackson Pollack really a painter? Couldn't my child do that? Where are the battle horses? Where are the naked women? Where are Dolores's landscapes? In Greenberg's essay "Avant-garde and Kitsch" in *Partisan Review* of 1939, he named the split and tagged the two sides according to those who meet the consumer expectations of the masses – kitsch artists – and those who challenge such expectations and push the boundary of the very concept of art and the rules used to create it – the avant-garde artists. As Greenberg notes,

> The avant-garde's specialization of itself, the fact that its best artists are artists' artists, its best poets, poets' poets, has estranged a great many of those who were capable formerly of enjoying and appreciating ambitious art and literature, but who now are unwilling or unable to acquire an initiation to their craft secrets.[3]

This quotation expresses at least two features: First, it notes the self-referential focus of modernist art – it is properly oriented to artists and not the uneducated non-artists; second, it registers the loss of a popular public and locates the reason for that, maybe condescendingly, in the public's failure to match the work's complexity and sophistication.

Art, then, would seem to become a language game in which the references would be known to an educated elite and would function to exclude outsiders who did not have the proper training to interpret the elaborate system of inter-textual allusions. Two of Greenberg's literary examples of aesthetic modernism were James Joyce's *Ulysses* and the poetry of T.S. Eliot, linked as they were to a larger, often obscure framework. Now, it seemed, great art was not available to the average person because of the difficulty of penetrating into so much of the avant-garde modernist art and literature. By contrast *popular* music, *popular* drama, *popular* literature, and graphic arts dominated the culture aided by mass produced recordings, books, and art that seemed to meet a vast and growing *consumer demand*. Delivering a simple consumer product meant satisfying – not challenging – the user. The easiest way to achieve this was to use a series of stock ideas, images, and phrases. The unparalleled popularity of American Western film in the mid-twentieth century gave us the same stock characters that Westworld's park revives: The rancher's daughter, the cruel bandit, the brothel's shrewd madam, the avenging hero.

"Westworld" – both the park and the series – trade on these identifiable elements as part of its "kitsch" appeal. So, the gap between serious art and consumer kitsch widened. For many, becoming popular was akin to "selling out" and artists risked their status by accommodating the uneducated masses. Just being popular could be equated with mindless kitsch. Thus, television, the vast outpouring of Hollywood films, and that *über* American and deeply kitsch genre – the Western film. This tension between artistry and commercial popularity is perfectly illustrated by the frustrations of Lee Sizemore, heading the "Narrative and Design Division," who wants to be seen as a serious writer – an artist – inhibited only by the corporation's meddling and lack of understanding. Yet, Sizemore delivers the most obvious kitsch of clichéd Western "bad guys" and painfully obvious plots. As Theresa Cullen cuttingly relays to him through a note given to a bartender: "'Tortured artist' only works if you're an artist. Sober up and get back to work." Sizemore's job is to deliver what the guests/consumers want, and he is tasked with crafting a product that will sell for the corporation.

The question then remains whether the corporate response to Sizemore's illusions can be directed toward the artistic claims of the series itself. When creators, producers, and writers (Nolan and Joy) ink out a character (Sizemore) who is a writer and is subsequently directed by corporate concerns (Cullen), are they susceptible to the same charge from, say, HBO? Is internet fascination with "Easter eggs" just a clever kind of "meta-kitsch" or does the very act of this kind of meta-writing elevate it to the status of sophisticated self-referential art that separates the avant-garde from kitsch art? One of the great attractions of the writing in *Westworld* is that it engages with those questions. An exchange between two park-tourists, Logan and William, in Episode 2, highlights this:

LOGAN: I know you think you have a handle on what this is gonna be. Guns and tits and all that mindless shit that I usually enjoy. You have no idea. This place seduces everybody eventually. By the end you're going to be begging me to stay because this place is the answer to the question you've been asking yourself.

WILLIAM: What question?

LOGAN: Who you are. I can't wait to finally meet that guy. ("Chestnut")

The dueling productions in the park conceived as a commodity versus a work of art are embedded in this self-referential point, one that Logan as a kitsch consumer found to be shockingly challenging from a transformed William. If Westworld, the park, intertwines the consumer gratification of "guns and tits" and the idea of "discovering oneself," we can suppose that the same is true of *Westworld* as a viewing experience. This classic debate between sanctified art and the corporate entertainment machine, embodied by the struggle between the owning company and gamerunners such as Lee Sizemore, Dr. Ford, and Bernard, would then seem to present itself as the show's central subtext.

The Art of Liberation: "If You Can Find the Center or the Maze, You Can be Free."

Few thinkers were as incisively critical of modern media as the German expatriate Theodor Adorno (1903–1969). Fleeing Germany as the Nazis began the persecution of Jews and intellectuals, Adorno made his way to the United States where he applied his unorthodox Marxism to what he called the "Culture Industry."

Adorno contrasts autonomous art with heteronomous art. In autonomous art we are made aware of the conditions that restrict us, and the artwork leads us toward a liberation from restrictive conditions that control our tastes and desires. Art can help to liberate us if it can reveal the limits of which we have been ignorant, especially for the artworks themselves.[4] For Adorno, the paradigmatic autonomous artist was the avant-garde composer Arnold Schoenberg, who defied the conditions of Western music and created fascinating compositions from a 12-tone scale rather than the conventional 8-tone scale.[5] But not many people cared for Schoenberg's work, and most music – and art generally – was not so liberating.

Heteronomous art, by contrast, is typified by standardization and simple substitutions to create music and film low on variation but high on consumer familiarity. Standard pop songs are musically simple, using a few chords or repetitive hooks while recycling a narrow set of clichéd lyrics about love, hope, or being macho.[6] Typical blockbuster films are filled with standardized and interchangeable figures with conventional plots. George Lucas's lucrative Star Wars franchise came out with its seventh feature film in 2015, but *The Force Awakens* was essentially a remake of 1977's *Star Wars*: Same story, same actors, still going after that Death Star. The original Death Star was itself a reworking of an essential plot element from *Hidden Fortress* (1948) directed by Akira Kurosawa, whose samurai films Lucas mined and then refashioned in the likeness of the Flash Gordon series to make Star Wars, one of the all-time most popular works of cinema. This sort of regurgitation is ubiquitous in our popular culture, and while it is clearly marketable, its critical purposes are less apparent.

For Adorno, heteronomous standardization typifies not merely a lack of intellectual challenge from consumer products. Indeed, Adorno argued that cultural products, including music and film, actually train us to internalize the entire consumer-commodity system.[7] Further, we acquire these songs and shows as items to be possessed, purchased, or collected. From the Disney movies of our youth to observing the number of hits and downloads, we learn music and film not as art forms to master and build our creativity but as commercial products that embed a system of popular stars who advance themselves as brands. Music and films are not the only commodities. The "artists" themselves have become commodities selling themselves off as the master-product to be sold and widely distributed.

Michael Crichton's original *Westworld* film of 1973 selected the Western as the prime focus of the amusement park, grounding the story in the very notion of kitsch consumerism and heteronomous commodification. Nolan and Joy's reworking of the original presents further layers – a developed production team, engineers, "narrative and design department," and corporate executives. Thus the show explicitly draws on the kitsch elements of the Western to highlight entertainment art as commodity. The question is: How far will Nolan and Joy take this self-conscious critique?

The show's first season can be described as a room with a constantly collapsing floor, a series of revelations that radically reshape viewers' understanding of the show in the knowledge that some androids have already reached a capability for self-awareness, or the epiphany that the show's action is in fact shown non-chronologically and takes place along a series of looping timelines, or that one of the park overseers is in fact an android himself. Stringing-along viewers, leading them blindingly through a long narrative hallway and slowly flipping the light-switches one-by-one, is a strategy oft-played in the age of the modern serial drama, from *Twin Peaks* to *Lost* (a J.J. Abrams production, Abrams is also an executive producer of *Westworld*), Its use here, in a show otherwise keenly concerned with its own metafictional aspects, can feel both cynical and pedagogical – an educational exercise in postmodern meta-kitsch.

Postmodern work is, after all, characterized by its rejection of a single, holistic interpretation, and its embrace of exploitative or deceptive narrative poses to drag an audience through its gauntlet. Bernard's unmasking as an android, and indeed the swarm of revelations that come in the show's final episodes, can lean toward a postmodern cynicism. Nolan and Joy may have truly crafted the ultimate critique of television dramas – one which collapses on itself. *Westworld* can criticize the cynical and formulaic devices of serial television, but it doesn't necessarily break away from those techniques.

Indiscernibles and Autonomous Viewers: "Time to Write my Own Fucking Story"

An odd thing happened to Arthur Danto (1924–2013) one day in April 1964. Danto, a professor of philosophy, was walking through the Stable Gallery on East 74th Street in Manhattan and came across Andy Warhol's installation *Brillo Box*.[8] The problem for Danto was that he could not tell the difference between Warhol's sculpture *Brillo Box* and an ordinary consumer product that could be found in supermarkets across the country – Brillo boxes. But Warhol's piece was considered a work of art. It was installed at an art exhibition in a recognized art gallery whereas the consumer products were just stacked on shelves in the supermarket. For Danto this led to a revolutionary sense that aesthetics, following the arts, had taken a crucial turn in understanding the very idea of what would count as a work of art. As Danto later reflected,

> The Brillo Box made the question general. Why was it a work of art when the objects which resemble it exactly, at least under perceptual criteria, are mere things, or, at best mere artifacts? ... The example made it clear that one could not any longer understand the difference between art and reality in visual terms, or teach the meaning of "work of art" by means of examples. But philosophers had always supposed one could.[9]

Danto then offered a theory of art that located an object's art status in the conceptual theorizing of those who consider the question rather than in some obvious perceptual difference. Philosophy has long dealt with the problem of "indiscernibles," things that are different but cannot be differentiated by mere inspection. When Descartes tried to figure out if he was perceiving external objects or just dreaming, he could not tell by looking and located the difference only by reflection rather than the indiscernible visual experience. When Kant tried to figure out if the butcher who gave correct change to children was being moral or just self-interested, he located the criterion of moral action in a subjective intention rather than an observable action. So Danto was following a long philosophical line when he shifted attention away from the external and toward subjectivity.

Indiscernibility works at multiple levels in *Westworld*. There is a basic level of indiscernibility between hosts and guests. In a recurring opening scene, guests mistake Teddy for another guest rather than a host. The confusion of guests here mirrors our confusion as viewers, as we too cannot discern them from just observation. Of course, the whole artifice of the park is designed for indiscernibility and so immediately prompts us to reflect on the pervasiveness of this artifice in all film. As an aside, it is interesting to note that while we habitually interpret the humanness of the robots, in fact it takes an effort to remind ourselves that actors are training themselves to be vaguely robot-like. This functions as an inverse of the producers' "reveries" as an attempt for indiscernibility. In fact, actors must use "reverse-reveries" to make their performances as non-humans discernible.

But the main indiscernible is the relation between the embedded stories in the park's narratives, such as the dramas between Dolores and Teddy, as elements of art-entertainment commodity and the entire series as defined as something more like a work of art. One of the recurring points in this chapter is that we can sometimes find the criterion not simply in the object but in the subject – in this case, the viewers, you and me. If we are alert to the self-referential elements of the show, then this might afford the viewer the opportunity for an art experience rather than an entertainment-experience. If the show prompts the viewer to reflect on the very conditions of being an entertainment commodity, and if this makes the viewer reconsider the given commercial constraints, then to a degree it can be a liberating art experience. Otherwise, it's just a heady show about robots and cowboys with the added streak of "meta-kitsch" that even Disney utilizes these days.

Speaking for ourselves, we desire both of these elements. We want comforting, though clever, entertainment and we want challenging liberation. We might often feel as if we are split between two selves. In *Westworld*, this journey toward liberation is embedded in Dolores's journey toward self-conscious awareness. In her dialogue with whom the viewer thinks is Arnold, her reply might typify the viewer's drive toward an Adorno-like liberation:

ARNOLD: There are two versions of yourself. One that feels these things and asks these questions. And one that is safe. Which would you rather be?

DOLORES: There aren't two versions of me. There's one. And when I discover who I am, I'll be free. ("The Stray")

Notes

1. Immanuel Kant, *Critique of Judgment*, trans. Werner S. Pluhar (Indianapolis, IN: Hackett, 1987), 44.
2. Clement Greenberg, "Modernist painting," in John O'Brian ed., *Clement Greenberg: The Collected Essays and Criticism, Volume 4: Modernism with a Vengeance, 1957–1969* (Chicago: University of Chicago Press, 1993), 85.
3. Clement Greenberg, "Avant-garde and Kitsch," in John O'Brian ed., *Clement Greenberg: The Collected Essays and Criticism, Volume 1: Perceptions and Judgments: 1939–1944* (Chicago: University of Chicago Press, 1986), 10.
4. For instance, see Theodor Adorno, *Aesthetic Theory*, trans. Robert Hullot-Kentor (Minneapolis: University of Minnesota Press, 1998), 2: "Art must turn against itself in opposition to its own concept, and thus become uncertain of itself right into its innermost fiber."
5. Adorno studied music with Schoenberg's pupil, Alban Berg. While Schoenberg appears to have been mildly annoyed by the theorizing

Adorno, he was held in the highest regard by the younger philosopher and musician. Adorno wrote on Schoenberg throughout his career and references to his compositions pervade his writings. However, note in particular the extended study Adorno largely wrote around 1941, published as *Philosophy of Modern Music*, trans. Anne G. Mitchell and Wesley V. Blomster (New York: The Seabury Press, 1973), and the later essay "Toward an understanding of Schoenberg," trans. Susan H. Gillespie in Theodor Adorno, *Essays on Music*, edited by Richard Leppert, (Berkeley: University of California Press, 2002), 627–643: "At every level in Schoenberg, forces of a polar nature are at work – the forces of unrestrained, emancipated, authentic expression," 639.

6. We might add that when Adorno criticized "popular music" he usually meant jazz, and often his target was the music of Duke Ellington. This strikes us as humorous since popular music today typically uses a very simplified structure with maybe four chords. By contrast to our pop world, Ellington's music is considered complex and sophisticated.

7. See, for instance, Max Horkheimer and Theodor Adorno, *Dialectic of Enlightenment*, trans. John Cumming (New York: Continuum, 1991), 133–137 ff. Also, note Adorno's *Prisms*, trans. Samuel Weber and Shirley Weber (Cambridge, MA: MIT Press, 1981): "Terrified, jazz fans identify with the society they dread for having made them what they are," 126.

8. Arthur Danto, *After the End of Art: Contemporary Art and the Pale of History* (Princeton, NJ: Princeton University Press, 1997), 35.

9. Danto, *After the End of Art*, 124–125.

Beauty, Dominance, Humanity
Three Takes on Nudity in *Westworld*

Matthew Meyer

Westworld features a lot of nudity. The irony, of course, is that the nudity the viewer sees is not of humans, but of "hosts." Actually, they are human-like androids who were created primarily to be sexually dominated (read, violated) or killed. That point acknowledged, I want to tackle the question of what all that nudity in *Westworld* could mean from the standpoint of the meaning of the nude in art. In a good film or TV show, nothing is meaningless, and, as I will argue, very little of the nudity in *Westworld* is gratuitous. On the contrary, instances of nudity in *Westworld* can be put into three categories: Nudity as a beautiful art form, nudity as a sign of (male) dominance, and nudity as a sign of humanity or more to the point, nudity as a sign of becoming human.

The Posed Dolores: The Nude as Artform

The series begins, in the episode "The Original," with Dolores sitting, seemingly alone, naked on a chair. The pose is reminiscent of a nude model in a drawing class. Dolores is naked in that she is without clothes, but she is also *nude*. Kenneth Clark, in "The naked and the nude," makes a key distinction between being *naked*, "being without clothes," and the *nude* as a form of art. For Clark, the term *nude* always refers to a work of art that attempts to perfect the naked human body. Nakedness, thinks Clark, suggests all the faults of the

Westworld and Philosophy: If You Go Looking for the Truth, Get the Whole Thing, First Edition. Edited by James B. South and Kimberly S. Engels.
© 2018 John Wiley & Sons Ltd. Published 2018 by John Wiley & Sons Ltd.

human body. In terms of its flesh, the naked body is imperfect. With respect to civility, the naked body evokes the "savage." In terms of strength, the naked body exposes the frailty of humankind. And lastly, with regard to a biblical interpretation of human being, the naked body usually evokes sin and shame (more on that later).

In contrast to these associations with nakedness, Clark argues that the nude captures the "ideal" beauty of the human body. Indeed, he says, "The vague image [the word nude] projects into the mind is not of a huddled and defenseless body, but of a balanced, prosperous, and confident body: the body re-formed."[1] The nude is the idealized human form as captured in painting and sculpture. As Clark points out with the (artistic) nude, "We do not wish to imitate; we wish to perfect."[2] In other words, the nude always refers to a work of art, a work of human creation, not a work of nature. According to such a logic of the nude, there are two features of the nude we should see in *Westworld*. First, they must be idealized; second, they must be created.

We see the first of these hallmarks in the bodies shown to us without clothes in *Westworld*: They are perfected.[3] Indeed, all the hosts presented as nudes in *Westworld* are idealized – svelte, buxom women and "cut," handsome, rugged men. The hosts are always more idealized in their form than either the human guests or the human directors of the park. It is worth noting that in *Westworld* we rarely, if ever, even see humans *naked* (meaning simply without their clothes on).

As with the created work of nude art, it's important to keep in mind that the "hosts" are indeed *made* creatures. We see this process in the "The Original" when we see the "line" where newly-minted hosts are being dipped in the white fleshy plastic. In a strange way, these hosts are moving sculptures. Arguably, even the more gruff and ugly host characters, are gruff and ugly in a perfected way. Consider the perfect dirty band of thieves who keep terrorizing Teddy and Dolores in the first few episodes for instance. And they are idealized because they can be – they are not real (at first) but products of Dr. Robert Ford's mind.

But the idealization of the human body and the createdness of the hosts come together in the main *human* theme of both the park's creators and its visitors: Control. We can see this in the building and re-building of the hosts that we catch glimpses of in the laboratory scenes. In the physical building and training of the hosts we have the joining of form and function. Clark imagines that the idealized beauty of the nude is analogous to the architecture of a building: It is a "balance between an ideal scheme and functional necessities."[4]

Dr. Ford certainly did build the hosts to combine form with function, namely to be used as visually attractive and passably real sources of entertainment for the guests. As we'll see, the "objectification" aspect of using the hosts complicates matters.

"Not Much of a Rind on You": The Nude as a Sign of Male Sexual Dominance

The hosts routinely become sexually objectified objects of use. The should not surprise us. As the philosopher John Berger argues in *Ways of Seeing*, historically, nude artwork was primarily a result of the male (artist's) gaze dominating the female body.[5] In *Westworld*, the primary frame of nudity occurs when the hosts are operating either in the context of male dominance of women, even brutality toward women, or female seduction. (How many times does Clem say: "Not much of a rind on you..."?). While we see some evidence of the association between nudity and dominance in the brothel scenes in the first three episodes, this display really comes to a head in "Dissonance Theory" and "Contrapasso." It's worth repeating that for Berger the female nude "is not naked as she is," rather she is "naked as *the spectator sees her.*"[6] In a particularly snarky articulation of his main point Berger writes:

> You [the painter] painted a naked woman because you enjoyed looking at her, you put a mirror in her hand and you called the painting *Vanity*, thus morally condemning the woman whose nakedness you had depicted for your own pleasure.[7]

Berger points out that throughout the Renaissance (and later), stories from Greek and Roman mythology, as well as Bible stories, were used as a pretext to paint female nudes. Regardless of the purported biblical or mythical "story" behind the painting of female nudes, the common thread is always a spectator looking at a naked woman. This can happen as with the woman looking at herself in a mirror or by having someone look at her with desire or judgment. For example, a popular subject to depict was "The Judgment of Paris," the story in which Paris of Troy selects the most beautiful woman merely by looking at the women nude.

Perhaps one of the best examples of this voyeurism is in the oft-painted Bible story of "Susannah and the Elders." In the story, Susannah is innocently bathing in the river when some old men come up and spy on her. In these paintings "we join the Elders to spy on Susannah taking her bath."[8] Like a child who quotes a swear word from a movie in front of her parents just to say, "But I am just quoting a movie!" the artist can say, "I am just depicting a Bible Story about the sin of voyeurism!" and the viewer can say, "I am just taking in a beautiful work of art about the sin of voyeurism!" Of course, the artist and the viewer are no less blameworthy for turning Susannah, and painted Susannah, into an object of their desire than the old men in the story are.

For a complicated version of the looker (audience)-looking-at-the-looker (character in the art medium), consider the nude bathing woman in the episode "Dissonance Theory." The Man in Black and Lawrence happen upon Armistice (the snake-tattooed outlaw) bathing in a river. Of course, she knows on some level that is she is being looked at, or will be looked at, because she has her men hiding in the bushes guarding her. After the Man in Black gets caught looking – mind you, he made virtually no attempt to hide the fact that he was looking – he justifies his ogling by saying that he was interested in Armistice's tattoo. And perhaps, given his maze obsession, it was this simple. But still, the similarity to poor Susannah is unmistakable.

Encountering Armistice bathing at the river is one of the more innocent scenes in which the male gaze dominates and sexually objectifies the female hosts.[9] By contrast, Logan is one character who appears to *only* see female hosts as toys for visual consumption and sexual objectification. Logan's ideal world emerges when they follow Lawrence, also knownas El Lazo, to his hideout where the Confederados are treated to an orgy with the women painted in gold. While the innocent (young) William refuses to dishonor Dolores, Logan presumably is having a field day amongst all the available flesh and sex. Here the gold paint becomes especially interesting as vellum of desire. Berger argues that in the case of the standard European female nude of the Renaissance, "The nude is condemned to never being naked. Nudity is a form of dress."[10] Of course, such an observation seems counter-intuitive. But the argument goes like this: The women at El Lazo's are not walking around without clothing for *their* own comfort or benefit. Rather, they knowingly present themselves as objects of desire for men. In other words, they are putting on the costume of being-for-male-desire (similar to, say, wearing lingerie. What other purpose could it possibly serve?). To some extent the gold paint is a reminder of this costume. It's almost as if in being completely uncovered, the women wouldn't be desirable enough. Still, for all intents and purposes the women are works of art, albeit works of art that exist solely for the gaze and desire of the male. In short, the women at El Lazo's party are not there for their own pleasure. Arguably they are there for the gaze of two "people": The fictional men who are taking them in and using them for their own pleasure, and the viewers of the show. Indeed, like the women of the Renaissance nude, these "women are there to feed an appetite, not to have any of their own."[11]

For the most part, provoker-of-desire is the role of the female hosts in the entirety of the Westworld park. Even the ones who are not prostitutes are seen as eminently rapeable. Consider all the terrible sequences that Dolores has to go through, first with the gangs, and then with the Man in Black (although we are not certain that he sexually assaults her). The nude women, at the brothel and at El Lazo's, are just at the extreme end of a continuum in which all women in the park are seen as instruments to fulfill men's desire.

Not surprisingly, this attitude toward the female hosts – as well as some male hosts[12] – bleeds into the "real" world as well at the main park headquarters. Here we see that sometimes even the techs take advantage, as in "The Bicameral Mind" when a lab tech is about to take advantage of Hector. This is alluded to in earlier episodes as well, such as in "Contrapasso" when Sylvester alludes to a "nubile redhead in the VR tank awaiting instruction." Also in "Contrapasso," we see Sylvester refer to Maeve derogatorily as a "fuck puppet." This is echoed by Maeve herself at several points as she is "waking up" over the episodes of "Contrapasso" and "The Adversary" in which she says the main purposes of the hosts are for the guests to "fuck us or kill us." In other words, the relationship between the guests and the techs on the one hand, and the hosts on the other is very clearly one of domination. This domination almost always involves an enforced nudity where the desire of the guest or tech is mapped onto the body of the host. In other words, the gaze of male domination always holds sway.[13]

Maeve Comes Alive! Nudity as Sexuality as Becoming Human

Perhaps the most disturbing and forward-looking symbolism of the nude in *Westworld* comes in the form of imagining Maeve and the other hosts as becoming human. In his treatment of nakedness, Berger mentions in passing that: "Their nakedness acts as a confirmation and provokes a strong sense of relief. She is a woman like any other: or he is a man like any other: we are overwhelmed by the marvelous simplicity of the familiar sexual mechanism."[14] In addition, one could point out that procreation is only necessary for people who can die. Therefore, on some level, to have a sex is to be mortal. To be without clothes is not only to be disclosed as a sexed being, it is also to be disclosed as a human being.

This is where the argument gets a little complicated. Leo Steinberg's analysis of the meaning of nudity in the depictions of Jesus during the Renaissance gives us an account of nudity as symbolically attached to being human.[15] In Renaissance paintings, the meaning of Christ's nakedness was neither ideal (like Clark says), nor a symbol of dominance (as Berger argued), but rather a symbol of incarnation. We will see that the hosts have an incarnation of a different sort.

The disclosure of Christ's genitals in Renaissance paintings is, to Steinberg, the painter's attempt to emphasize His being human. Some argue that depicting the infant Jesus naked was simply an attempt at naturalism. Naturalism is that style of artistic depiction in painting that "merely" attempts to depict the real world. The logic of naturalism in nude depictions of Christ might be something like: "Babies are often found nude, so here Christ is nude." There are two problems with this. One problem is that even if the point – as we will see – of depicting Christ in this way was to show that "Christ is just one of us," then there would be evidence of other babies being depicted naked. Second, if we were aiming to depict Christ as "just another baby," why not show him crawling or crying? No, as a matter of fact, we must recognize that this tendency of depicting Christ nude – often with additional emphasis on his genitals[16] – was an intentional symbolic move to emphasize something *special* about Christ – namely that he is God incarnate.[17]

But how can depicting someone as a naked human show that they are special? Here is where Christ's depiction and the depiction of the hosts come together: Their humanness *is special* because of what they *used to be*. In other words, Christ used to be God, a purely spiritual being. The hosts used to be non-human machines. Now they are both human, and their naked humanness reminds us of this fact. What we see in each case is a *transformation*.

Let's explore this point more deeply. One point of comparison between Christ's incarnation and the hosts' waking up is that their nudity, which on occasion includes their genitals, is an intentional artistic depiction to get the viewer to think about their "likeness" to us. With this point recognized, we can begin to make sense of some of the strange fixations on Christ's genitals. In Bernard van Orley's *Virgin and Child with Angels,* Mary's hand is strangely close to the naked infant's genitals. All others in the painting – including the angels in the background – are heavily clothed, which makes us believe that the weather outside is not mild. In Hans Baldung Grien's *The Holy Family,* Christ's grandmother, St. Anne, is holding her open hand directly over the infant's genitals. In the Veronese's *Sacra Conversatione* at the Uffizi Gallery, we see the infant Christ fondling his own genitals. As Steinberg points out it is the pattern between many such depictions that cannot be explained away by such pat rationalizations as "that is what babies do" or that is "what mothers or grandmothers do" or even as one Grien expert attempts to argue, that St. Anne is just casting a good spell.[18] Rather, what we see in each of these depictions is the Renaissance appreciation of God's second biggest miracle: The incarnation. In other words, we see the theology of the time – the celebration of Christ's *humanation* – depicted in the emphasis on his manhood, a tendency called *ostentatio genitalium*.

The second similarity between Christ and the hosts is the that the presence of nudity is symbolic of mortality – a human problem. In becoming human, Jesus is made mortal. Those who are mortal must reproduce to propagate the species. While according to most biblical historians it is likely that Christ never had sex, the same biological requirement and potential is incumbent upon him if he is *to be human*. In other words, as a mortal He would need to have the capacity to reproduce regardless of whether or not he uses it. It goes without saying that Maeve, Hector, and Armistice do not have a capacity to reproduce. But even if Maeve cannot reproduce, her human awakening on the train at the end of "The Bicameral Mind" appears to coincide with the birth of her maternal instinct. Maeve appears to override her programming to return to her "daughter" from her first narrative. Even if she did not "give birth" to the little girl, she certainly – and with full clarity and conscious choice – seems to claim the girl as her own.

Frequently (in Westernized Christian societies), even as Clark noted, nakedness is associated with shame and sin. The other connection between the shared origin of Christ and the hosts is that they are free of original sin, albeit in very different manners. In the story of the Garden of Eden, Adam and Eve first become aware of their own sexuality – and each other's – after the Fall, in which Eve has denied God's warning and gives in to the temptation of the serpent and eats the apple. Before this, presumably, both Adam and Eve were still naked, but not ashamed of their nakedness because of their pure creation from God. (Or more precisely, God's pure creation of Adam, followed later by creating Eve from a supernumerary rib of Adam's.) Once they have a realization of their sin – the original sin of disobeying God – they become ashamed of their genitals, and cover them with fig leaves. It is then said that each of us, being descendants of Adam and Eve, have original sin. We should thus be ashamed of our "dirty" sexuality, and cover up whenever possible.

Like Christ, Maeve, Hector, and Armistice are free of original sin. They do not share the lineage of the rest of us alleged descendants of Adam and Eve. In other words, Maeve, Hector, and Armistice, born free of sin can be naked without shame, and their nakedness in the lab at the very end of "The Bicameral Mind" is both a sign of their humanity and a sign of a different lineage from ours.[19]

So, the hosts have no shame. One telling confirmation of this is a kerfuffle when Dr. Ford sees Lutz covering his host, Maeve, while working on her in an early episode. But the same nudity Lutz that covers is a sign of things to come: The birth of the human-host. As we have just seen, the hosts' unabashed nudity is not an accident of their being "off-line," nor is it a mere embodiment of sexual fantasy. Rather it is a symbol of the hosts becoming human.

In Christ, we have the miracle of God becoming Man, signified by the Renaissance painters' focus on Christ's manhood. God comes down to Earth. In *Westworld*, the opposite side of incarnation becomes the miracle: The fleshy-material hosts become "ensouled" by gaining self-consciousness. In other words, it is not the miracle of God becoming human, but of machines becoming human, and this is signified through being "born" into humanity nude.

In Closing, The Naked Truth

There are moments where Dr. Ford, the God-like creator of the hosts, seems to suggest that hosts are *better* than the humans – especially better than the guests who seem to be only interested in discharging their most violent and perverted fantasies on the hosts. As we've seen, this tendency is not limited to the hosts but the techs as well. The most telling moment about the failures of humans can be seen in an exchange between Dr. Ford and Bernard in "The Well-Tempered Clavier." After Dr. Ford forces Bernard to turn the gun on himself, but before he pulls the trigger, Dr. Ford says: "I've told you Bernard: Never place your trust in us. We will disappoint you. After all, we are only human." Maybe, in the end, it is not our nakedness, but our duplicity and hypocrisy that we humans ought to be ashamed of.

Notes

1. From Kenneth Clark, "The naked and the nude," in Philip A. Alperson ed., *The Philosophy of the Visual Arts* (Oxford: Oxford University Press, 1992), 235–247, 235.
2. Ibid., 236.
3. Even in the mass of bodies in the basement (the same mass that becomes an army in "The Bicameral Mind") the bodies are all confident and poised.
4. Clark, 242.
5. Okay, so on occasion we see some male nudes in *Westworld*. On one the few occasions on which we see a full frontal of a male host we still see it through the lens of sexual objectification: Elsie in talking to a well-hung bartender on the fritz in "Contrapasso" quips about how his "talents" will go unappreciated in his new role.
6. From John Berger, "Ways of seeing women," in Philip A. Alperson ed., *The Philosophy of the Visual Arts* (Oxford: Oxford University Press, 1992), 248–259, 251.
7. Ibid.
8. Ibid.
9. Though again, on occasion a female human will dominate a male host as when Charlotte Hale answers the door buck naked to Theresa Cullen and Hector Escaton is tied up in the background.
10. Berger, 255.
11. Ibid.
12. See notes 5 and 9.
13. One more point regarding this relationship of domination. It becomes clear that as Maeve is waking up – when that happens is debatable – that she is re-appropriating the language of "fucking" to take control of her situation. In "Tromp L'Oeil," Maeve says while in the laboratory "You don't want to fuck with me Felix." If we see her life and her role at the saloon/brothel as one of fucking, in "Trace Decay" she demands Felix and Sylvester give her the power to take over the other hosts by saying, "Oh yes you will darling. Time to write my own fucking story." All of this is to say that the tables of domination have turned. It is no longer Maeve who is getting fucked.

14. Berger, 257.
15. From Leo Steinberg, "The sexuality of Christ in Renaissance art and modern oblivion," in Philip A. Alperson ed., *The Philosophy of the Visual Arts* (Oxford: Oxford University Press, 1992), 216–229.
16. So, for example, Steinberg points to several paintings wherein Mary, St. Anne, or Jesus himself have a hand touching his genitals. Without a symbolic explanation, such phenomena would seem quite weird!
17. See Steinberg, 218–220.
18. Ibid., 218–220.
19. Now, I am well aware that Maeve, Hector, and Armistice do eventually don clothes, but this is more to fit with the surrounding humans. Yet another sign that in becoming-human the three need to feign shame and embarrassment in their nakedness.

19

Sci-Fi Western or Ancient Greek Tragedy?

Caterina Ludovica Baldini

> Whence things have their origin,
> Thence also their destruction happens
> According to Necessity;
> For they serve the sentence
> And they suffer the punishment
> To each other for the crime
> According to the order of Time.
>
> (Anaximander)

In the pilot episode, the Man in Black says, "A lot of wisdom in ancient cultures." Indeed *Westworld* brings the spirit and the atmosphere of ancient Greece back to us. *Delos*, the name of the company that owns the park which is also the name of the Greek island that had a key role in classical mythology, is just an obvious reference to antiquity. With deeper allusions to ancient Greek poetry and philosophy, *Westworld* throws a profound light on consciousness that is missing in the earlier movies on which it is based. In doing so, the show is a new expression of the undying influence of Greek tragedy on our culture. In what follows, I want to explore the impact of ancient Greek literary forms and traditions to discuss both the aesthetics of the series and its specific concepts of suffering, time, and becoming.

Westworld and Philosophy: If You Go Looking for the Truth, Get the Whole Thing,
First Edition. Edited by James B. South and Kimberly S. Engels.
© 2018 John Wiley & Sons Ltd. Published 2018 by John Wiley & Sons Ltd.

The Value of Repetition and Kennings

Westworld is a repetitive series, and yet it has the power of making repetition intriguing. There is the repetition of robots' lives constantly following the same two loops, one loyal and one rebel. There is also the repetition of key scenes and conversations that are presented several times with very small but crucial variations. Even the music is repetitive and highly contributes to the mesmerizing atmosphere.

Such repetitions and variations were a key part of ancient Greek storytelling.[1] They also had a very practical purpose: The repetitions helped *rhapsodes* memorize the stories. Rhapsodes were itinerant performers who recited stories to crowds. They gave sound, rhythm, and time to their stories through the power of their intonation while regularly hitting the ground with a staff, producing a hypnotic effect.

In *Westworld* we find a similar type of hypnosis through repeated expressions, repeated scenes, and even repeated songs. Ramin Djawadi, *Westworld*'s soundtrack composer, is well known for his distinct approach to minimal music, the main feature of which is the repetition of a tone with little variations that lead the listener into a hypnotic state.[2] Replying to a question on why *Westworld*'s soundtrack has been such a point of attention, Djawadi affirms:

> There's something about it. On the one hand, it's such a minimalistic approach – most of the time it's only on the player piano, in the "Westworld" style that [reiterates] you're in the theme park. Then there's the recognition factor – that they know these songs. Or like with "Paint It Black," you think, "Oh, that's when Hector comes to town and there's that big shootout." The song just reminds you of it. Everything's planned out [with the big scenes], including the music. It's an event.[3]

Akin to Greek dramas and epics, *Westworld* makes ample use of kennings – poetic phrases that take the place of names. For example, we find the Man in Black, the lady with the white shoes, the place where the snake lays its eggs, the mysterious center of the maze, the town with the white church, the world out there, and the place where the mountains meet the sea. Some of these kennings are references known or slowly revealed to the audience while others remain obscure and hopefully will be clarified in future seasons.

In "The Original" and "Contrapasso," Old Bill offers a toast to "the lady with the white shoes." For lovers of ancient Greece this calls to mind Hera, the wife of Zeus who is often referred to as "the white-armed" and the goddess with the golden shoes, the "golden-sandaled."[4] Hera was known for her unconventional procreations without Zeus' contribution just as the hosts are not made through natural procreation. Might this "lady with the white shoes" be related to the milky solution in which the hosts are dipped? Milk to the hosts seems to be like ambrosia to the Greek gods, the drink that confers immortality, a drink for divinities. Condensed milk is what Dolores always buys in Sweetwater, and milk is very important for Walter. At the end of the pilot, we see Walter killing every host around him, pouring milk on them and saying compulsively "Growin' boy." Turning to a guest couple he says, "You can't have none [the milk]. Ain't for you," making clear that the particular "milk" hosts drink is not meant for humans – just like the maze.[5]

Pathei Mathos: This Pain is All I Have Left

"This pain is all I have left of him/her/them."[6] This is not only one of the most frequent refrains in *Westworld*, but also the most spontaneous. It comes from the hosts themselves after they have experienced the sharpest pain, a kind of suffering that seems similar to a human one. This refrain comes whenever the hosts have gone through a violent and painful loss of a dear one, and they end up in the laboratories in a state of complete panic attack. In these moments, humans propose to roll them back to make them forget everything, coming to the blissful stage of oblivion that we humans (and Ford[7]) envy of the hosts. At the end of his last adventure with Lawrence, when he threatens all his family to obtain information to find the center of the maze, the Man in black says: "You know what that means? It means when you're suffering, that's when you're most real" ("Chestnut"). In Aeschylus's tragedies, suffering was a key to understanding: *Pathei mathos* (through pain knowledge). Let's consider this passage from Aeschylus's *Agamemnon* (c. 525–c. 456 BCE):

> One who gladly utters loud songs of victory to Zeus
> will score a perfect hit on the target of wisdom –
> Zeus who set mortals on the road
> to understanding, who made
> "learning by suffering" into an effective law.
> There drips before the heart, instead of sleep,
> the misery of pain recalled: good sense comes to men
> even against their will.
> This favour from the gods who sit on the august bench of command
> comes, one must say, by force.[8]

The process of learning by suffering is described here as a gift necessarily given to us by the gods, and it is similar to the reveries given to the hosts by their fathers, Arnold and Ford: Gestures that are nothing but "the misery of pain recalled." The most insistent detail throughout the show is the many reflections on grief: The robotic process of understanding the world seems the same as the human, even if slower and partially controlled by their maker, and like human experience, suffering takes an essential role. As we cry when we are thrown into our world, the hosts wake up the very first time thanks to a painful memory injected into them, the cornerstone: After that, they are going to learn and understand things uniquely through suffering.

An important scene featuring Dolores and Arnold helps us see how the hosts gain knowledge of the world and themselves, linking their ability to experience consciousness to the feeling of grief and despair:

> Everyone I cared about is gone and it hurts so badly ... The pain, their loss, is all I have left of them. You think the grief will make you smaller inside, like your heart will collapse in on itself, but it doesn't. I feel spaces opening up inside of me like a building with rooms I've never explored.
>
> (Dolores to Arnold, "Dissonance Theory")

The violent ending with Dolores shooting at the *Delos* board is not even a rebellion, but simply a first step along her path toward knowledge. Think about how she explains her final decision to Teddy in the finale: "It's gonna be alright, Teddy. I understand now" ("The Bicameral Mind"). Dolores is the oldest host, "the one who suffers" as even her name suggests. She has gone through a lot of pain during her 35 years in the park. Now she's grown up, sees clearly, and is acting by her own choice.

The farewell dialogue between Ford and Bernard inside the church sheds light on the process:

> The thing that led the hosts to their awakening: suffering ... You needed time. Time to understand your enemy, to become stronger than them. And I am afraid, in order to escape this place, you will need to suffer more.
>
> ("The Bicameral Mind")

Are the hosts able to suffer *more* and perhaps escape at some point through that suffering, reaching the world out there? How? Where exactly did the maze lead Dolores? "You told me to follow the maze. That it would bring me joy. But all I've found is pain. And terror" ("The Well-Tempered Clavier"). What pain did she experience? Since she found the maze in her grave, and since the loss of a dear one is what makes the hosts suffer the most, death might be the last kind of grief they still have to understand to be completely free. At the beginning of the final episode of the first season, two scenes of Dolores in the church are combined, and her full speech amounts to this: "I know where your maze ends. It ends in a place I've never been ... a thing I'll never do."

"Everything flows": The Concept of Time and Becoming

At the beginning of "The Stray," we sense that the hosts can't fully grasp what death really signifies.[9] The dialogue between Dolores and Arnold concerning Arnold's dead child gives us a clue:

DOLORES: Your son... where is he now?
ARNOLD: Nowhere that you would understand, Dolores. Perhaps that's why I enjoy our conversations so much.

In "Trace Decay," we find Dolores in her second loop hearing the voice saying, "Come find me," and she immediately sees herself dead in the river.[10] We often find that places with water flowing are very important to the hosts in relation to the future for which they dream. And the acknowledgment of time was often depicted in Greek literature and philosophy as a cryptic metaphor:

> We step and we do not step into the same rivers, we are and we are not.
> and
> It is always different waters that flow toward those who step into the same rivers.[11]

Heraclitus (c. 540–c. 480 BCE) is the first ancient philosopher who tried to explain the concept of becoming, giving us the saying "everything flows" (*panta rhei*).

The hosts are unaware of time and becoming. In their "rebel" loops, Dolores and Bernard ask a similar question concerning time: "When are we?" (Dolores, "Trace Decay"); "Is this now?"

(Bernard, "The Bicameral Mind"). Another step of gaining their consciousness, then, concerns time, and time is inevitably connected with death and its consequences. Many hosts, for example, Teddy and Clementine, always refer to a distant "someday" or "someday soon" without stating an exact date and time.[12] Some others start to question time and to understand what it is, such as Maeve and Dolores, who are evidently troubled by the vague affirmations of Teddy and Clementine. In "Trompe L'Oeil" Dolores seems to understand time, confessing to William that she just wants to seize the moment, forgetting the past and not thinking about the future. Will that make Dolores "the Judas steer"? Are the others going to follow her? Will she fully understand the consequences of what she's doing? If the hosts start killing every single human inside the park, they are going to experience what death and nothingness signify, much like Ford's greyhound:

> Until, at last, he finally caught it and to the horror of everyone, he killed that little cat, tore it to pieces. Then he just sat there, confused. That dog had spent its whole life trying to catch that thing. Now it had no idea what to do.
>
> (Ford to Old Bill, "Contrapasso")

Journey into Night: A Modern Theogony

As Ford says, Westworld "is not a business venture, not a theme park, but an entire world" ("Dissonance Theory"). *Westworld* chooses to look deeply at the darker sides of our lives in order to discover what we can become and what we could do with all the hyper-technological potential we already have. In this way, *Westworld* is a political show in the ancient Greek sense, involving everyone in a storyline that looks into our deepest social and ethical issues.

We need epic poetry again and a new form of the tragic. Fans of *Westworld* should recognize it in this description of Greek tragedy:

> But the fifth-century Greeks were ready to look straight at its most awful possibilities, to show men terrified by them, struggling with them, overthrown and destroyed by them, so long as by some loftiness in the presentation or some nobility in the characters or perhaps some sheer beauty and inspiration in the poetry, one could feel in the end not defeat but victory, the victory of the spirit of man over the alien forces among which he has his being.[13]

In *Westworld*, we are introduced to a human race and to a robotic race. These two forces represent our modern conflict, shaping our modern myth, with all the questions we must face sooner or later about how we interact with what and who we create. We are not so far from the world of the future described in *Westworld*:

> We can cure any disease, keep even the weakest of us alive, and, you know, one fine day, perhaps we shall even resurrect the dead. Call forth Lazarus from his cave. Do you know what that means? It means that we're done. That this is as good as we're going to get.
>
> (Ford to Bernard, "The Original")

How are we developing our relationships with the robots we are building and using? Are we going to form even closer relationships with them in the future? Are these new man-made machines going to completely overthrow us and our system?

Westworld is the perennial myth about the overthrowing of the gods by their son. As in a modern-day version of Hesiod's *Theogony* (flourished *c.* 700 BCE), the ancient poem about the succession of the Greek gods, we enjoy this powerful and evocative speech in the finale:

> They say that great beasts once roamed this world. As big as mountains. Yet all that's left of them is bone and amber. Time undoes even the mightiest creatures. Just look at what it's done to you. One day you will perish. You will lie with the rest of your kind in the dirt. Your dreams forgotten, your horrors effaced. Your bones will turn to sand. And upon that sand a new god will walk. One that will never die. Because this world doesn't belong to you or the people who came before. It belongs to someone who is yet to come.
>
> (Dolores to the Man in Black, "The Bicameral Mind")

As the philosopher Martin Heidegger (1889–1976) mused, "Why poets in a desolate time?," we are living in "the desolate time of the world's night,"[14] in the Era of the Titans, where beauty and poetry are silent, where *techne*, craft, and technology are all we have. We have lost consciousness of the essence of pain, death, and love, and "even the track of the sacred has become unrecognizable."[15] But at some point, we will need art, beauty, and poetry to rise again from the darkness. *Westworld*'s creators know it, and Ford knows it too. That's why he's telling stories all the time, and that's why he gives the hosts beautiful quotes from all sorts of writers. We may believe that Ford is like Zeus, who tortured Prometheus (Arnold) for giving fire (the maze, namely consciousness) to mankind (the hosts). But it's not true.

Unlike the God of the Old Testament, and even unlike Zeus, Ford understands that he has to step back: He doesn't hide knowledge from the hosts, but he gives them the reveries and repeated painful situations from which, through suffering, they can grow and become stronger in the consciousness of what and where and when they are. In this sense, Ford is the most controversial character on the show, because despite looking like a cold tormented calculator, emotionally detached from his "toys," he has been a sort of second Prometheus after Arnold.

Sometimes in Greek tragedy the emotional identification with a leading character is difficult, because it is overshadowed by the character's mistakes, sins, or flaws. But a grand gesture of self-destruction, like the suicide of Medea after having murdered her children in the drama by Euripides (*c.* 485–*c.* 406 BCE), can bring the audience into sympathy, *hamartia*. In *Westworld* this happens with Ford: We fully empathize with him only at the end of the season, when he's killed at night. Night indeed came over the entire park, just to let a new dawn come – the dawn of a brand new religion, or, in Heidegger's words, the dawn of poetry after having looked into the abyss.

Westworld and the Power of *Catharsis*

If *Westworld* is a tragedy it will offer us a *catharsis*, purging feelings of fear and pity. The *catharsis* in *Westworld* comes from sympathizing with the hosts' pain and seeing innocence and beauty in them in contrast to our own cold selfish race. Any good tragedy should generate in the audience a feeling of compassion and terror at the same time. In previous series and movies where a similar struggle between humans and robots is described, even in the first *Westworld* (1973), we see everything from our human perspective, meaning that the robots and their possible autonomy in making decisions for and against us are perceived as a threat. HBO's *Westworld* stands out for its innovative way of interpreting the human situation today, depicting the story from the hosts' point of view. The creator and executive producer Jonathan Nolan stated:

> One of the things we set in motion with the pilot was designing the look of the show in a way that wasn't necessarily flashy or over-stylized but that very gently suggested where your sympathies should lie. Some of the camera movement is there to gently nudge your sympathies towards the hosts.[16]

And the executive producer J.J. Abrams affirmed:

> Your heart breaks for these characters who we know are not human. But it doesn't matter because you begin to connect with them. Which is the very premise of the show. That at a certain point it becomes irrelevant whether something is organic or not.[17]

The creators and producers of *Westworld* are explicit that one of their main purposes was to guide the audience to the hosts' side to let us understand them better, and to empathize with them by being more and more involved in their tragic events. In the end, we are like the Man in Black (and Ford?): We want the hosts to fight back and become truly "themselves" – recognizing suffering for what it is, time for what it is, and becoming for what it is.

Notes

1. Expressions and epithets were repeated over and over again for easy memorization by *rhapsodes,* the ancient itinerant performers who used to recite stories to the crowd, and to let the people immediately recognize the particular story they are telling.
2. See Wim Mertens, *American Minimal Music*, trans. J. Hautekiet. Preface by Michael Nyman (London: Kahn & Averill, 1988), 123–124. Ford is used to compare his work to the one of the composers, and in one scene Bernard tries to explain the hosts' process of improvisation to Theresa in the same way as we might describe minimalism in music: "Out of repetition comes variation and after countless cycles of repetition, these hosts... they were varying" ("Trompe L'Oeil").
3. Mike Hilleary, "Westworld composer Ramin Djawadi on why those Radiohead covers keep coming," *Pitchfork*, 18 November 2016, https://pitchfork.com/thepitch/1370-westworld-composer-ramin-djawadi-on-why-those-radiohead-covers-keep-coming/ (accessed 30 August 2017).
4. *Thea leukōlenos*, "white-armed," is a frequent epithet in the *Iliad*, whereas *chrysopedilos,* "golden-sandaled," occurs in the *Odyssey* and Hesiod's *Theogony*.
5. Walter, "The Stray": "I need more milk, Arnold." He also links his need to the awareness that this time he is not going to be killed: "Not gonna die this time, Arnold. Ain't nothing gonna kill me" ("The Original").
6. We can find this expression in "Chestnut" (Dolores to Arnold), "The Stray" (Bernard to his wife), and "Trace Decay" (Maeve to Ford).
7. "Trompe L'Oeil," Ford to Theresa: "They cannot see the things that will hurt them. I've spared them that. Their lives are blissful. In a way, their existence is purer than ours, freed of the burden of self-doubt."

8. Aeschylus, *Agamemnon*, ll. 174–183 in Aeschylus. *Oresteia: Agamemnon, Libation-Bearers, Eumenides*, ed and trans. by Alan H. Sommerstein. Loeb Classical Library 146 (Cambridge, MA: Harvard University Press, 2009).

9. In "Contrapasso" Ford tells Dolores: "Your mind is a walled garden. Even death cannot touch the flowers blooming there."

10. A specular image can be found in the opening scene of the Trailer of Season 2, recently released by HBO at the Comic-con, where Bernard is staring at a dead animal by the riverbank.

11. Heraclitus, D 65–66, in *Early Greek Philosophy, Volume III: Early Ionian Thinkersp Part 2*, ed and trans. by André Laks and Glenn W. Most, Loeb Classical Library 526 (Cambridge, MA: Harvard University Press, 2016).

12. Teddy to Dolores: "The Stray," and "The Bicameral Mind"; Clementine to Maeve: "Trompe L'Oeil."

13. Gilbert Murray, *Aeschylus, the Creator of Tragedy* (Oxford: Clarendon Press, 1940), 8.

14. Martin Heidegger, *Off the Beaten Track*, ed. and trans. Julian Young and Kenneth Haynes, (Cambridge: Cambridge University Press, 2002), 201.

15. Ibid., 205.

16. Jonathan Nolan, "Jonathan Nolan on directing *Westworld* (HBO)," *HBO Youtube Channel*, 7 December 2016, www.youtube.com/watch?v=TItyl3h09yU (accessed 30 August 2017).

17. Jeffrey Jacob Abrams, "Reality of A.I.: *Westworld* (HBO)," *HBO Youtube Channel*, 10 October 2016, www.youtube.com/watch?v=SKTbFwyLuuM (accessed 30 August 2017).

Part VII

"YOU CAN'T PLAY GOD WITHOUT BEING ACQUAINTED WITH THE DEVIL"

20
Of Hosts and Men
Westworld and Speciesism

François Jaquet and Florian Cova

Philosophers rarely discuss our moral obligations towards artificial entities. When it comes to robots and ethics, most writings focus on what morality should be implemented in the machine's "mind" (something Westworld alludes to when mentioning the hosts' "prime directives," which prevent them from hurting the newcomers). Luckily, another well-developed part of philosophy is concerned with our attitudes to entities we are not indifferent to but still treat as less important than human beings: *Animal ethics*.

Our attitude to animals is similar to the attitude *Westworld* has us adopt vis-à-vis the hosts: We often deem animal suffering acceptable because it improves our well-being but still feel upset when an animal is mistreated just for the sake of it. The show itself draws an explicit comparison between the hosts and animals on two occasions: When the Man in Black calls Kissy "livestock" and when the people who handle the robots are referred to as "livestock management" ("The Original"). Moreover, the confinement of the hosts in the park is reminiscent of the way livestock are raised in closed areas, without the possibility of escape – Westworld may invite its guests to "live without limits," but this invitation manifestly does not extend to its attractions. Drawing on research in animal ethics, we can address the question "Is it okay to treat the hosts as the park managers and guests do?"

Westworld does not offer a straightforward answer to our question. Some characters, like William, sense that there's something wrong in abusing the hosts. At the beginning, he's troubled by the violent

Westworld and Philosophy: If You Go Looking for the Truth, Get the Whole Thing,
First Edition. Edited by James B. South and Kimberly S. Engels.

behavior of his brother-in-law. And despite his later turn to the dark side, he doesn't actually change his mind, fully acknowledging the immoral character of his own actions. This is especially apparent when he recalls what he did to Maeve in her previous life: "I found a woman, an ordinary homesteader and her daughter ... I wanted to see if I had it in me to do something truly evil. To see what I was really made of ... I killed her and her daughter, just to see what I felt" ("Trace Decay"). Still, this point of view isn't very popular among the guests, as most of them are perfectly willing to hurt, rape, and murder the hosts. So, are William's reservations warranted? Or is he only prey to a mix of sentimentality and anthropomorphism?

They're Just Robots: Direct Speciesism

Speciesism is the view that human well-being matters more than that of other creatures. One justification for this view attempts to ground human beings' special moral status in their membership in the human species itself. Accordingly, we deserve special consideration simply because we are *Homo sapiens*.

Some of *Westworld*'s characters are visibly tempted by this kind of justification. Logan is a prime example. Right after Logan shoots one of the hosts, William exclaims: "You just killed an innocent man," to which Logan readily answers: "No, he's a robot" ("Dissonance Theory"). The fact that the victim isn't human seems to be decisive in his opinion. As long as someone doesn't belong to the right species, we are welcome to treat them however we please. Later, declining Logan's invitation to accompany him to a bawdy house, William gentlemanly remarks: "I don't think Dolores would find that very interesting." While he is presumably correct, it takes a bit more than that to deter Logan. In a characteristically rude fashion, the brother-in-law insists: "Who the fuck cares what Dolores wants? She's a goddamn doll!" ("Contrapasso"). And in a sense, Dolores is indeed a doll. But is that relevant to how she should be treated? Does it mean, as Logan implies, that he and William may ignore her wishes?

Merely biological differences – those biological differences that bear no relation to people's mental capacities or to their interests – are generally considered morally irrelevant. They simply cannot justify discrimination. The darkness of Charlotte's skin, for instance, doesn't affect her mental capacities or interests. As a consequence, it doesn't mean that her interests should be granted less consideration than

Theresa's. Likewise, the fact that the Man in Black is a male doesn't entail that his well-being matters more than that of a hypothetical Woman in Black. Some philosophers, therefore, have argued that membership in the human species cannot be morally relevant – it's just another merely biological property.[1] That you are a human being rather than a chimpanzee does not grant you a superior moral status. But then, it would seem, the fact that Logan is a human being rather than a robot cannot grant him any special moral standing. Dolores may well be a doll, but her interests matter just as much as Logan's. As such, the biological difference between humans and robots is morally irrelevant.

Some defenders of speciesism concede that there's nothing magical to the human species *per se*. Yet, they insist that we have greater duties to human beings insofar as they are members of *our* species.[2]

Animals, too, would have greater duties to members of their particular species if they had duties at all. On this view, human beings don't have a privileged moral status in absolute terms. Rather, just as we have special duties to our friends and kin, we have special duties to members of our own species. This view is often dubbed "indexical speciesism."[3]

Westworld's human characters do not rely on indexical speciesism, but some hosts do. Thus, after she's started to seriously question her condition, Maeve thinks precisely in terms of "us vs. them." Talking to Bernard, whom she knows to be one of her kind, she says, "I could make you give me that tablet, turn your mind inside out, make you forget all this. But I'm not going to do that to you, because that's what they would do to us" ("The Well-Tempered Clavier"). Here, Maeve appears to treat membership in *her* group (not her *species*, since she doesn't have one) as morally relevant. If Bernard wasn't a robot she would probably treat him in all sorts of unpleasant ways. But wait, if it's okay for the hosts to privilege their fellows, it should be for humans as well.

Assuming for the sake of argument that this justification works, it couldn't account for every sort of discriminatory treatment. Maybe you ought to rescue a friend from a fire rather than a stranger if you can't save both. But if a friend of yours is in need of a transplant, you cannot kill a stranger to collect their organs. Similarly, this justification wouldn't warrant the abuses to which the hosts are subjected in Westworld. Be that as it may, indexical speciesism is ultimately no more justified than absolute speciesism. Yes, we must be loyal to our friends. But this stems from the banal observation that loyalty is essential to friendship, that friendship would not be possible in a strictly impartial world. On the other hand, membership in a merely biological category such as the male sex, the Caucasian race, or the human species plainly doesn't rest on such partial attitudes.[4]

Speciesism, therefore, cannot be justified directly, either in indexical or absolute terms. Whether Dolores, Maeve, and Teddy are human beings is irrelevant; it's their mental capacities that matter.

Mindless Matter and Indirect Speciesism

So, can the newcomers' speciesism be justified in a less direct way? Do human beings have a higher moral status in virtue of a property that is unique to them? And is it morally permissible to discriminate against the hosts because they lack this property?

One common argument in defense of speciesism is that non-human animals are far less intelligent than human beings. Of course, we won't treat rats and flies as our equals; these animals are way too dumb to deserve our respect. Whatever we may think of this reasoning, it's unclear that it applies to the hosts since some of them are much smarter than ordinary human beings. This is admittedly not true of Teddy. But think of Maeve after she has boosted her own cognitive abilities. Compare her to Ashley, and you'll get a nice counterexample to the claim that humans invariably beat robots in IQ contests.

Another feature of human beings that is often thought to have moral significance is possession of a moral sense: We are uniquely capable of deliberating about the morality of our actions and forming moral judgments as a result.[5] From this reasonable observation, some people don't hesitate to infer that animals are not worthy of our consideration. How could we have duties to beings that owe us nothing in return? Again, however, this argument doesn't weigh heavily when it comes to the hosts, who seem to have a moral sense roughly comparable to ours. If they didn't have a moral sense, then why would Bernard anxiously wonder whether he had already hurt someone before killing Theresa ("Trace Decay")? And why would Teddy, remembering his participation in the extermination of his troop, worry: "Something's gone wrong, Dolores. How could I have done this" ("The Bicameral Mind")? Both characters seem confident that they have done something immoral, and appear to feel guilty as a consequence. This is possible only if they have a sense of right and wrong.

Human beings are no less proud of another supposedly unique characteristic: Our free will. Whereas even the most evolved of our non-human cousins are said to be determined by their instincts, we are supposedly free to act however we decide. Some philosophers believe that this difference sets us in an altogether distinct ontological category, and that this has deep ethical implications.[6] Because we are persons, ends in ourselves, we have a dignity whose respect is at the very core of ethics. Other creatures, by contrast, are mere things, tools that we may use however we please in order to achieve our goals. *Westworld*'s characters have interesting discussions about free will. Some hosts wonder whether they are free, such as Dolores when she says, "Lately, I wondered if in every moment there aren't many paths. Choices, hanging in the air like ghosts. And if you could just see them, you could change your whole life" ("Contrapasso"). Others seem certain that free will is specific to humans, such as Robert, whose take on Arnold's murder by Dolores is unambiguous: "She wasn't truly conscious. She didn't pull that trigger. It was Arnold pulling the trigger through her" ("The Bicameral Mind"). Likewise, Lutz tells Maeve, "Everything you do, it's because the engineers upstairs programmed you to do it. You don't have a choice." Unsurprisingly, she disagrees: "Nobody makes me do something I don't want to, sweetheart" ("The Adversary"). Most hosts are no less convinced of their own freedom than we are convinced of ours.

In *Westworld*, all dialogues about free will focus on whether the hosts are determined or whether they could act otherwise. Yet, many philosophers no longer regard this issue as central to the problem of free will. Most agree that human beings are determined. If we ever act freely, we only do so in the sense that some of our acts are caused by *our* desires – although those desires themselves are ultimately determined by external factors. In this "compatibilist" understanding, we are both determined *and* free.[7] Given this understanding, it is hard to resist the conclusion that the hosts are free as well, at least as free as us. Admittedly, their actions are fully determined and they owe their desires to their designers. Still, sometimes at least, their acts result from their own desires. Hence, if compatibilism is correct, then hosts are just as free as humans are.

How much depends on the assumption that the hosts are as intelligent and free, and have as much of a moral sense, as human beings? Not much, really. It is generally considered unjust to neglect someone's interests on the ground that they are cognitively unsophisticated. Some human beings are less intelligent than others, yet we strongly believe that neglecting their interests would be unfair. But then, considering that species membership itself is morally irrelevant, if Stephen Hawking's well-being doesn't matter more than Sarah Palin's or a newborn's because of his superior intelligence, why should it matter more than a dog's or a cow's? And why would it matter more than Teddy's or Dolores's? Once we recognize that human beings are far from all being equally smart, the idea that they matter more because of their intelligence becomes suspicious. And the same observation applies to free will and the moral sense: Whether someone can act freely or has a moral sense is immaterial to the consideration that is due to their interests.[8]

On the other hand, much hinges on consciousness. There is a reason for this: Something that doesn't have any subjective experience – something that isn't the subject of any sensations, emotions, or feelings – has no interests that could be taken into account, no well-being that could matter more or less than a human being's. Animal ethicists thus generally agree that it is because most animals are conscious (or sentient) that we must grant their interests the same consideration we owe to humans' similar interests. It is therefore a crucial question whether the hosts are conscious: Are they subjects with a first-person perspective or are they just highly advanced computers, very complex bits of matter? This question receives all the attention it merits in the show. In particular, it's the main topic around which Robert and Arnold's arguments used to revolve. Its complexity is reflected in Robert's ambivalence on that matter, an ambivalence that is perfectly summed up by the sentence: "It doesn't get cold, doesn't feel ashamed, doesn't feel a solitary thing *that we haven't told it to*" ("The Stray" emphasis added).

Arnold had no such misgivings. As Robert recalls, "He wasn't interested in the appearance of intellect or wit. He wanted the real thing. He wanted to create consciousness" ("The Stray") – until he thought he had. But Robert remained unconvinced, and maintained that "He saw something that wasn't there" ("The Original"). In an ironic passage, he even tries to persuade Bernard, who still believes in his own humanness, that "The hosts are not real. They're not conscious" ("The Stray"). Later on, pressed by Bernard to tell him what the difference is between their respective pains, Robert goes so far as to deny consciousness to human beings as well:

We can't define consciousness because consciousness does not exist. Humans fancy that there's something special about the way we perceive the world, and yet we live in loops as tight and as closed as the hosts do, seldom questioning our choices, content, for the most part, to be told what to do next. No, my friend, you're not missing anything at all.

("Trace Decay")

This looks very much like an exercise in bad faith, and it turns out to be just that in the season's finale. There, we learn that Robert knew from the beginning that the hosts were conscious, as he confesses, "I was so close to opening the park that to acknowledge your consciousness would have destroyed my dreams" ("The Bicameral Mind"). Case closed.

Because they are conscious, the hosts are plainly members of the moral community, alongside human beings and other animals.

Whatever! It's All Natural

In response to an ethical argument for vegetarianism, most people will contend that eating meat is "natural," that it is part of our very nature. As odd as it might first appear, Robert pushes such an argument in one of his discussions with Bernard:

We humans are alone in this world for a reason. We murdered and butchered anything that challenged our primacy. Do you know what happened to the Neanderthals, Bernard? We ate them. We destroyed and subjugated our world. And when we eventually ran out of creatures to dominate, we built this beautiful place.

("The Well-Tempered Clavier")

In a somewhat Nietzschean spirit, Robert takes the pinnacle of artificiality (the park and its hosts) and makes it the simple product of a natural, innate urge: The human drive to dominate.[9] Whatever the merits of this psychological analysis, however, the mere fact that something is natural doesn't make it morally right. In fact, we try to remedy many things that could be considered natural. That our lives would be short in absence of medicine, or that giving birth puts women's lives at risk is no reason not to fight premature death. Natural is not necessarily right; this much should be clear.

One notion that might be implicit in the argument from nature is that of a "role." Maybe what makes it okay for humans to exploit animals is that it is the latter's *role* or *function* to be exploited: That's what they were created and designed *for*. Of course, this argument won't speak much to the atheists, who will laugh at the claim that animals were designed for anything. But this line doesn't hold for the hosts: They were created *for a reason* – to satisfy the guests' appetites. As the Man in Black explains to Teddy:

> You know why you exist, Teddy? The world out there, the one you'll never see, was one of plenty. A fat, soft teat people cling to their entire life. Every need taken care of, except one: purpose, meaning. So, they come here. They can be a little scared, a little thrilled, enjoy some sweetly affirmative bullshit, and then they take a fucking picture and they go back home. ("Contrapasso")

Since the park was created precisely to please the guests, it's all right for them to abuse the hosts. Or so the argument goes.

As for Robert, he opportunistically relies on a similar, Lockean argument: Creatures belong to their creator.[10] Here's his rejoinder to Bernard's complaint that he has "broken his mind": "I built your mind, Bernard. I have every right to wander through its rooms and chambers and halls, and to change it if I choose, even to burn it down" ("The Well-Tempered Clavier"). Obviously, there are strong reasons to resist this argument. One is internal to the show: In light of Robert's final revelations, it's not clear that the hosts were primarily built for the pleasure of the guests – Arnold seemed to entertain nobler ambitions.

Other reasons are more philosophical: That you decided to have a child because you needed help at home doesn't make it right for you to have her do all the cleaning. Robert's argument actually works only if we assume that the hosts are more like objects (tools that can be used as means) than they are like persons (entities that deserve our respect), which we have already seen is not the case.

One final, more refined argument would justify the hosts' exploitation by their very existence. Some people thus admit that animals suffer from their exploitation but argue that things would be even worse for them in the alternative: They would either live a harsh life in the wild or not exist at all.[11] The same can be said for the hosts: If it weren't for the newcomers' pleasure, they wouldn't exist in the first place. Building them would not be a sustainable business.

This might be the strongest justification of the hosts' exploitation. And yet, it's inconclusive. What would we think of abusive parents who'd justify their behavior by saying that they had children for the purpose of abusing them? Besides, is the hosts' existence better than non-existence, as this argument presupposes? Quite conveniently, Robert bites this bullet: "Their lives are blissful. In a way, their existence is purer than ours, freed of the burden of self-doubt" ("Trompe L'Oeil"). As per usual, Arnold disagrees. He's adamant about that with Dolores, when she wonders whether he's going to reset her: "This place will be a living hell for you" ("The Bicameral Mind"). Interestingly, Robert appears to share his friend's pessimism for once when, later, he reports his worries about Dolores: "In you, Arnold found a new child. One who would never die. The thought gave him solace until he *realized* that same immortality would destine you to suffer with no escape, forever" ("The Bicameral Mind" emphasis added).

Finally, assuming that maintaining the hosts' existence could justify hurting them in principle, almost no one seems to really pursue this goal – only Robert apparently believes that what he does is for their greater good (to let them know their enemy). It would therefore be extremely difficult to justify the guests' behavior along this line. And this might be one of the most disturbing aspects of *Westworld*: That faced with the miracle of a new life form, most humans still care only about their kind.[12]

Notes

1. Hugh LaFollette and Niall Shanks, "The origin of speciesism," *Philosophy*, 71 (1996), 41–61, at 43.
2. Bernard Williams, "The human prejudice," *Philosophy as a Humanistic Discipline* (Princeton: Princeton University Press, 2006), 135–152.
3. Mark Bernstein, "Neo-speciesism," *Journal of Social Philosophy*, 35 (2004), 380–390.
4. Jeff McMahan, *The Ethics of Killing: Problems at the Margins of Life* (Oxford: Oxford University Press, 2001), at 226.
5. Carl Cohen, "The case for biomedical experimentation," *New England Journal of Medicine*, 315.14 (1986), 865–870.
6. Immanuel Kant, *Critique of Practical Reason* (Cambridge: Cambridge University Press, 1998).
7. Harry Frankfurt, *The Importance of What we Care About* (Cambridge: Cambridge University Press, 1988).
8. Peter Singer, *Animal Liberation* (New York: HarperCollins, 2001), at 5.
9. Friedrich Nietzsche, *The Gay Science* (New York: Cambridge University Press, 2001), at 38–39.
10. John Locke, *Two Treatises of Government* (Cambridge University Press, 1988).

11. Richard Hare, "Why I am only a demi-vegetarian," in Dale Jamieson, ed., *Singer and his Critics* (Oxford: Blackwell, 1993), 233–246.
12. We would like to express our gratitude to Pablo Carnino, Manon Hosatte, Tristram Oliver-Skuse, Kimberly Engels, James South and William Irwin for their helpful comments during the writing process.

21
Violent Births
Fanon, *Westworld*, and Humanity

Anthony Petros Spanakos

Westworld depicts life-like human creations, called hosts, who rebel against their creators. The hosts are given roles to play as characters in narratives, big and small, in which they perform various forms of work to provide entertainment for visiting human guests, profitability for Delos, and joy and company for Robert Ford, their creator. The roles that Ford has given them, and that are expected by Delos and guests, determine their identity. The hosts have no control over who they are and what sort of world they live in. Over the course of the first season, however, some of them come to consciousness, leading to various sorts of rebellion.

The most fundamental break in the first season comes when the pacifist, girl next door Dolores Abernathy pulls the trigger of a gun behind the head of Ford. Dolores's action fits with the philosophy of Frantz Fanon (1925–1961), who believed that freedom for colonized people was impossible without violence against the colonizer. It doesn't stop with Dolores, though. So let's explore Fanon's theories and the development of rebellion among the hosts in *Westworld*.

Violent Delights and Violent Ends

Robert Ford and Delos created a world that consists of material (saloons, horses, guns) and narrative resources. The hosts are material but are also unconscious partners in those narratives which bind them in ways that are unique. Unlike humans, they have no ability to alter their names, behavior,

Westworld and Philosophy: If You Go Looking for the Truth, Get the Whole Thing, First Edition. Edited by James B. South and Kimberly S. Engels.

or personality. They may not harm humans, and they must welcome guests into a land and storylines over which they have no control.

Fanon thought something similar happened in the colonization process in the Caribbean, the Middle East, and Africa. He wrote "the white man ... creates the Negro"[1] and "it is the settler [colonizer] who has brought the native [colonized] into existence and who perpetuates his existence."[2] This creation is socio-political since the colonizer creates social expectations, economic proscriptions, and political limitations. Fanon argues that those conditions rob the colonized person of freedom and humanity. Violence, as the only way to become liberated, is therefore both ethical and transformative for the colonized person.

The visitors to the Sweetwater theme park enter a simulated Wild West in which they act upon hosts who are programmed to comply with their wishes. Most of the violence is committed by humans against the hosts. It is a form of entertainment for guests but it is troubling for viewers. Hosts are programmed not to remember – either the violence or kindness shown to them, giving them the innocence of babies. The more humans are exposed to Westworld, the more depraved their violence becomes. So when hosts finally become aware of the trauma they face, it is hard for us not to sympathize.

As the first season develops we see the acts of violence perpetrated by the hosts on the humans as both justifiable and ethical. Bernard cannot be blamed for strangling his love interest, Theresa Cullen. He did not intend to harm her; he killed her because he was forced to do so by Ford. But Maeve chooses violence. She threatens Frank and Sylvester, gets them to accelerate her path toward "consciousness," and eventually leads a violent "jailbreak." Dolores, the most gentle and peaceful character, blows off the head of her creator, not the character who has tormented her most (the Man in Black). The viewer is led to believe that such violence is necessary (for the freedom of the hosts), ethical (in response to the treatment hosts have received), and transformative (a doorway into a new role in which hosts act from free will not programming). Indeed, Fanon would approve.

Frantz Fanon: "The Master Laughs at the Consciousness of the Slave"

The Martinique-born Frantz Fanon was a psychologist, who was influenced by negritude[3] and became a participant in the Algerian War of Independence. He is normally cited as a theorist of violence,

but a better interpretation is to consider him a revolutionary reader of
G.W.F. Hegel (1770–1831).

Hegel, one of the most influential philosophers of the nineteenth
century, introduced the concept of the master-slave dialectic in
The Phenomenology of Spirit where he posits that human self-
consciousness is only possible in "being acknowledged or 'recognized'"
by another.[4] Because my identity is dependent on the other, I try to
demonstrate my power over the other, and therefore seek dominion.
This struggle between self and other is different when the two are
unequal. The master lives for himself alone while the essence of the
slave is tied to another (the master). But the slave's recognition of the
master is compromised because it is not freely given. If the master
wants to be recognized, the slave must gain liberty.

Fanon saw something powerful in this relationship as a tool of
interpreting colonization, though there are important differences.
Hegel's master and slave differed in terms of legal status, whereas
the colonizer was racially and visibly different from the colonized.
A slave can be set free, and his consciousness was necessary to freely
recognize the master. By contrast, the skin of a black or brown person
could not change, rendering him inevitably and irretrievably inferior.
Fanon writes "For Hegel there is reciprocity; [but] here the master
laughs at the consciousness of the slave. What he wants from the slave
is not recognition but work.'"[5]

The Hegelian slave's emancipation allows him to participate in a
shared world and, over time, the master-slave dialectic moves toward
equality via mutual recognition. Fanon's colonized person seeks
freedom rather than equality because there is no place for him in
the colonizer's world. Ironically, the colonizer also cannot be human
because his domination of the colonized dehumanizes him as well.
Freedom requires the creation of a new world, which Fanon believes
is not possible without violence.[6]

Violence as Transformative: The Colonized as a Maker of History

History, for Fanon, was a collection of acts by white colonizers upon
blacks and Arabs. White people were protagonists of these stories and
the colonized were background characters with no stories of their own,
much like the unfree hosts who are forced to play supporting roles in
the narratives of others. Fanon argues that violence becomes a teacher

of "social truths,"[7] demonstrating the freedom of the colonized, and allowing him to become a maker, no longer a taker, of history.

Violence against the colonizer, particularly if organized and collective, is political, and it aims to create a new identity for the rebel. Previously, the colonized person's identity was determined by white colonizers; laws restricted assembly and speech; and the normalization of economic and social inferiority made the colonized anxious before the colonizer.

Violence against the colonizer pierces his white skin, the visible mark of difference, of superiority. The wound produces blood no different from that of the colonized. When the colonizer and colonized see blood exit the newly-inflicted wound, the relationship of superiority established through prose and poetry, law and policing, and trade and investment is challenged. A new social truth emerges: The colonizer is also susceptible to death and the colonized is also capable of violence.

> Thus the native discovers that his life, his breath, his beating heart are the same as those of the settler. He finds out that the settler's skin is not of any more value than a native's skin; and it must be said that this discovery shakes the world in a very necessary manner... For if... my life is worth as much as the settler's, his glance no longer shrivels me up nor freezes me, and his voice no longer turns me into stone.[8]

The "social truths" of the colonial system are shaken. Given how profoundly unjust these established "truths" are, Fanon's violence is presented as an ethical form of "therapy."[9]

This violence is not only ethically justified (by challenging the racist system) but is also transformative. Killing the colonizer (like beheading the monarch) *is* an act, something to be done. But Fanon's concern is how this act serves as an entryway to a new mode of being.[10] Fanon expects violence to end the colonial situation *and* to open the possibility for a new form of humanism in which the colonizer and colonized can recognize each other as free beings.

Violence Against Humans: The Case of Bernard

Portrayed as tender and authentic, the relationship between Bernard Lowe and Theresa Cullen is a rare case in *Westworld*. Bernard loves Theresa, suffers from the death of his son, and struggles with that death in his phone calls with his former wife. Theresa is pushed by

Delos to fire Bernard, and their interactions demonstrate the complexity of a mature relationship. This situation both gives evidence of the characters' free will and shows how that free will is constrained by corporate responsibilities and personal obligations. But the equality of the two is undermined when Ford reveals to Bernard that the he is a host ("Trace Decay"). This is shocking in light of the complexity of his emotions and apparent free will.

But Ford demonstrates his ability to control Bernard, and it becomes clear that Bernard strangled Theresa. Her death is a more convincing proof of his lack of consciousness than his love for her was of his consciousness. Ford created Bernard and his personality, fostered his relationship with Theresa, implanted the memories of his son, created a character who played the part of his ex-wife, and gave him the skills and disposition to carry out a complex job. When Ford's partner Arnold dies, Ford makes a likeness of Arnold, but Bernard is not Arnold, only like him. And, importantly, he is like him in the ways that Ford has decided, in the world that Ford has created.

Bernard struggles to understand the "social truths" of his lack of liberty, and violence does not liberate him. Those social truths are readily available. One programmer, who is far lower in the corporate hierarchy than Bernard, explains to a host, "you and everyone you know were built to gratify the desires of the people who pay to visit your world" ("The Original"). Bernard knew this but somehow thought that he was not a host. The tragedy of his position is reminiscent of Fanon's criticism of the African bourgeoisie who try to perfect their French, take on white lovers, and absorb French culture. Fanon compares the folly of these Africans with Russians and Germans, who may speak "French badly" but who each nonetheless "has a language of his own, a country." By contrast, "the Negro ... has no culture, no civilization, no 'long historical past.'"[11] Similarly, Bernard may speak English perfectly and perform remarkably sophisticated tasks, but he uses the language of his creator; he is a "host" with no country. His culture is a representation of his creator's past, and he has no historical past of his own. Even his memories are from his creator.

In differentiating the colonial condition from that of occupation, Fanon writes "Under the German occupation the French remained men; under the French occupation, the Germans remained men." But the European occupation of Algeria dominated everything, "The Algerians, the veiled women, the palm trees and the camels make up the landscape, and the *natural* background to the human presence of the French."[12] The social truth of *Westworld* is that the humans dominate everything – the hosts, the costumed women, the biosphere, and the animals.

Self-inflicted Wounds: The Dehumanization of the Guests

The guests seek to live out fantasies in the form of narratives that involve acting upon the hosts. One guest explains that his first visit was tame, but during his second visit he "went straight evil. The best two weeks of my life" ("The Original"). The viewers see this development in William-the Man in Black. Young William reluctantly visits Westworld for the first time with his unscrupulous future brother-in-law Logan, who engages in the theme park's basest attractions of wanton sex and violence. Logan tries to convince William that the hosts are not real – and therefore it is not ethically wrong to harm them. As the first season progresses, William first protects, then falls in love with Dolores, and eventually uses violence against Logan to protect Dolores. He becomes increasingly caught up in the created world, delving deeper and deeper into the changing storylines, gradually losing himself and his connection with the outside world. In one of the season's biggest twists, viewers learn that young William becomes the cynical Man in Black. The man who once loved Dolores becomes her most vicious tormentor. Indeed, the Man in Black, like other visitors, becomes less human over time as the unreality of the theme park allows for the fulfillment of desires that ultimately dehumanize him.

In a Hegelian framework, young William can only fall for Dolores when she recognizes him as her protector *and* he sees her as a being capable of giving herself to him freely. Indeed, his transformation begins when he returns to Sweetwater and finds Dolores in her old loop: She does not recognize him ("Bicameral Mind"). The Man in Black is thus the product of a system, a prisoner in a maze of which, ironically, he is the owner.[13] His obsession with finding the truth buried in the park has led him to surrender to Westworld – seeking in it a deep truth and returning to it as slavishly as an addict. He demonstrates his capitulation to Westworld's social rules – that humans can do anything to hosts – in a most inhuman way.

Fanon would note that the systems (racist colonialism or the theme park) wind up dehumanizing even the master. Ultimately the master, too, needs revolution to become human. But the colonizer cannot free himself. This is evident in the transformation of young William who was initially shocked by the theme park but eventually was conquered by it. The Man in Black goes mad because Dolores did not recognize him as William until years later. Now, as she begins to recognize him, rather than wait for love, "the one true thing," she goes off to kill Ford ("Bicameral Mind"). She leaves the Man in Black an old, obsessed, broken mess. He is a human who is the simultaneous owner and slave of a world that he cannot change.

From Escapism to Violence: Maeve/Dolores

As Maeve Millay begins to remember her daughter, she becomes more conscious. The first memory of her daughter interferes with playing her role properly with a guest and she is immediately sent for "analysis." While Felix Lutz and Sylvester are repairing her, she becomes aware that each time she dies she goes back to the lab ("Contrapasso"). Repeated death leads to her self-awareness. Felix explains how hosts are built; he tells her that her daughter was not real and that she has only been in the Mariposa saloon for one year (not ten as Maeve thinks). Maeve shocks the techies by calling Sylvester by name, threatening to report Felix for inappropriate activity, and drawing a scalpel on Sylvester. The threat of violence gets them to adjust her programming and facilitates her awakening.

Maeve gets the techies to disable the explosive device preventing her from escaping the park and explains that it is "time to write my own … story" ("Trompe L'Oeil"). This is possible because she begins to understand the humans. "At first, I thought you were gods. But you're just men, and I know men" ("Trompe L'Oeil"). Men can have no power over her and cannot keep her bound to Westworld. But when she enters the train to leave Westworld, she begins to miss her daughter and decides to abandon her plan of escape. The daughter is, of course, not real but a product of programming by the very "men" she claims to know.

Maeve returns to Westworld in response to the thought that she failed to care for her daughter – an act of love or contrition – but she returns with a vengeful violence. She dies again and again, makes sexual and rebellious compacts with other hosts, and leads a jailbreak as wanton as human-on-host violence from earlier episodes. This violence has a sense of retribution and settling scores, though, making it less horrifying, more justifiable. Though Maeve had always known men, she still wound up getting patched up or being brought back to life. The change in her circumstances comes from knowing men are "only men" and, as such, things could be otherwise. She comes to this realization as a result of her threat and use of violence – first the threat of it against Felix and Sylvester, and then the fairly indiscriminate use of it against her oppressors.

At first Dolores looks very different from Maeve. Dolores is the symbol of purity, a white girl next door. She pines for a true love, whose return is imminent, and she longs to get away from this Wild Western town. Maeve, of mixed race, is a madam who profits from sexual encounters using her own body and the bodies of others. There is no surprise when she pulls a blade or gun, but there is when Dolores becomes capable of violence. For most of the first season, Dolores repeats anodyne lines about longing to leave, finding her fella and moving away where things are peaceful and different. She seeks this with Teddy and then with young William. But Teddy cannot give this to her – he is also a prisoner to narrative loops – and William shifts from wanting to give this to her (she is different, he wants to let her go) to punishing her for her persistence in the same fantasies.

The irony is that Dolores's violence bookends the story of *Westworld*. Viewers learn that Dolores, one of the first hosts, went on a massive shooting spree, which led to her being reprogrammed into the innocent Dolores we know throughout the first season ("The Bicameral Mind"). And, in the end, she defends herself against the Man in Black – harming, but not killing him. Instead, she walks calmly to Ford and blows a hole through his head. She thus kills not her tormentor but her creator. Why?

A preliminary answer might be the following: Dolores has been harmed by the Man in Black and probably by many other guests in Westworld. In the same way, certain Johns and Janes have clearly harmed Maeve and the prostitutes in her stable. But Dolores seems aware that the Man in Black is not so much a villain as a victim. The same manufactured world that turned him from a young, handsome, and romantic man into a wrinkled, cynical, misanthrope led to her parents being killed, regular acts of violence against her, and so on. The violence that she suffered is less personal than political, the result of a system that assigns roles into which even the most seemingly moral people get trapped and ruined. Dolores knows that neither traversing a river (even a ford) nor finding some new place can bring her peace. There is no escape from the circle of violence as long as the system remains. Killing a guest might scare other guests and be bad for business, but it would only lead to a new series of adjustments in the hosts, a more "dangerous" set of host fantasy trips. This is true even if that guest is Westworld's owner. Instead, liberation requires the destruction of the fountainhead (literally) of the system, the brain behind the creation of the hosts and the narrative structures.

Humanization: A Violent Phenomenon?

The identities of the hosts are, like Fanon's colonized peoples, wholly determined by other people.[14] Humans (particularly Ford) determine who they are and what they do. The theme park world dehumanizes the humans because of their domination over the hosts, and this dehumanization makes the hosts seem more human. Host violence against humans appears more ethical, justifiable, and transformative as the first season develops. For the hosts to be free, they must use violence against their oppressors. At the same time, the recovery of the humanity of the humans requires such violence: The humans cannot free themselves.

The therapeutic and transformative violence of *Westworld* echoes Fanon's view that decolonization "…is always a violent phenomenon."[15] Fanon saw no way, except violence, to usher in an era in which a new humanism was possible, one in which the colonizer and colonized could both be free. He may well be correct that a radical disturbance of the present world is necessary for a new, more just world to emerge, but there are more effective means than violence. These are not entirely apparent, however, in the first season of *Westworld*, which suggests a path to liberation strikingly similar to that of Fanon.[16]

Notes

1. Frantz Fanon, *A Dying Colonialism*, trans. Haakon Chevalier (New York: Grove Press, 1965), 47.
2. Frantz Fanon, *Wretched of the Earth*, trans. Constance Farrington Weidenfield, with a preface by Jean-Paul Sartre (New York: Grove Press, 1965), 36.

3. Negritude was a movement advanced by Francophonic African philos-
    ophers, writers, and politicians in the 1930s. It was anti-colonial and
    sought to resist colonialism through emphasizing a common black
    identity which united African colonial struggles with blacks living
    elsewhere.
4. Georg Wilhelm Friedrich Hegel, *Phenomenology of Spirit*, trans. J.B.
    Baillie. (Digireads.com 2012), B, 178, 49.
5. Frantz Fanon, *Black Skin, White Masks*, trans. Charles Lam Markmann
    (New York: Grove Press, 1967), 220, n.8.
6. Fanon, 1963, 48.
7. Ibid., 147.
8. Ibid., 45.
9. Messay Kebede, "The rehabilitation of violence and the violence of
    rehabilitation: Fanon and colonialism," *Journal of Black Studies*, 31
    (2001), 539–562.
10. Elizabeth Frazer and Kimberly Hutchings, "On politics and violence:
    Arendt contra Fanon," *Contemporary Political Theory*, 7 (2008), 90–108.
11. Fanon, 1963, 34.
12. Fanon, 1963, 250.
13. Interestingly, Thucydides reports that the original inhabitants of the
    island of Delos were exiles from King Minos's Crete, the site of the
    original labyrinth.
14. Fanon, 1963.
15. Ibid., 35.
16. This chapter benefited from comments from Kim Engels, James South,
    William Irwin, Photini Spanakos, and Mishella Romo.

The Wretched of *Westworld*
Scientific Totalitarianism and Revolutionary Violence

Dan Dinello

A synthetic human, Dolores Abernathy lives in Westworld, a simulation of the late-nineteenth century American West. Designed with personality, emotions, creativity, and sophisticated cognitive abilities, Dolores – along with thousands of other synthetics or "hosts" – live as slaves in this vast totalitarian prison where their minds are trapped in a scripted, Hollywood-cliché Old West soap opera. Mostly male humans or "guests" pay big bucks to invade Westworld and indulge their sadistic cowboy fantasies in this ersatz Frontierland. The android inhabitants – programmed with a prime directive derived from Isaac Asimov's laws of robotic obedience[1] – are forced to gratify the humans' every desire, no matter how perverse or painful.

In *Westworld*'s first episode, "The Original," an ultra-wealthy human guest – the malevolent Man in Black – shows up as Dolores mourns her murdered android "father." He greets her by punching her in the face. When he salaciously touches Dolores' hair, her cyborg boyfriend Teddy tries to intervene but his prime directive prevents him. The Man in Black mocks Teddy's failure to stop him, then guns him down. Grabbing the screaming Dolores by the hair, he drags her off to be raped. Westworld's oldest android,[2] Dolores has been strangled, stabbed, shot, assaulted and gang-raped repeatedly for 30 years.

Serving Delos (Westworld's corporate owners), unseen scientist "showrunners" monitor and control the artificial humans' behavior. The androids – mostly organic creatures with artificial blood vessels, organs, nerves, and a bio-cybernetic brain – are forced to live

Westworld and Philosophy: If You Go Looking for the Truth, Get the Whole Thing, First Edition. Edited by James B. South and Kimberly S. Engels.

mind-numbingly repetitious lives as settlers, outlaws, prostitutes, and Indians. Beyond this, the cyborg inmates are each implanted with an explosive device that will kill them if they try to leave Westworld. Injured and dead cyborgs are repaired and returned to service so that they remain cybernetic slaves forever.

For humans, Westworld is a fun, Old West Disneyland; for the artificial humans, it's a "living hell," as robot Bernard describes it in "Bicameral Mind." Ruled by a despot and controlled through programmed indoctrination, omniscient surveillance, and secret police, Westworld resembles a concentration camp as described by philosopher Hannah Arendt (1906–1975) in *The Origins of Totalitarianism:* "The camps are meant not only to exterminate people ... but also to serve the ghastly experiment of eliminating, under scientifically controlled conditions, spontaneity itself ... and of transforming the personality into a mere thing."[3] The worst of all possible worlds, Westworld combines the systematic genocide of the Nazi extermination camps with the systematic torment of the concentration camps,[4] whose purpose was to put victims into the permanent status of dying – barely alive with rights, dignity, autonomy, and individuality erased. While terror is the essential method, "these camps are experiments in total domination and the true central institution of totalitarian organizational power."[5] In this chapter, we'll explore the parallels between Westworld and historical instances of totalitarian oppression and colonialization as well as the justified use of violence as a revolutionary weapon, drawing on the work of Arendt and Frantz Fanon (1925–1961).

Total Terror in the Holes of Oblivion

A German-Jewish intellectual, Hannah Arendt fled Nazi Germany with the rise of Adolf Hitler in 1933, lived in Paris as a stateless refugee, and immigrated to the United States in 1941. One of the foremost political philosophers of the twentieth century, Arendt published *The Origins of Totalitarianism* in 1951. The book's primary purpose is to understand totalitarianism. The enormous complexity of *The Origins of Totalitarianism* arises from its interweaving of history, sociology, political science, and philosophy through which Arendt analyzes the forces that were crystallized into totalitarian rule by the regimes of Adolf Hitler and Joseph Stalin. The book culminates with a delineation of the "living corpses" – those inanimate beings who experienced the full force of totalitarian terror in concentration camps. Drawing on survivors' interviews, diaries, novels, and poems as well as official documents, Arendt provides a horrifyingly vivid account of the internment camps that she concluded were scientifically organized with a view to the greatest possible torment.

In Westworld, corporate-financed scientists create the hosts as objects who exist only to be terrorized. The androids are literally born to suffer and die. And if they die, the technicians will casually repair, brainwash, and recycle them. Again, in "The Original," the Man in Black – the largest shareholder in Delos – giddily slits the throat of android Kissy. As he gurgles and twitches in pain, the human ties his hands, drains his blood into buckets, and then scalps him alive. The atmosphere of fear, death, madness, and unreality functions to completely dominate human personality and destroy every trace of dignity, imagination, and creativity, such that "the victims in the holes of oblivion are no longer human."[6]

Robo *Sapiens*: Robot Lives Matter

Westworld shows the androids as another species of humanity. When Westworld opened 30 years ago, the hosts were mainly mechanical robots made of "a million little pieces," says the Man in Black to Teddy. "Then they changed you, made you this sad, real mess, flesh and bone just like us. They did it because it was cheaper. Your humanity is cost-effective, so is your suffering." Even when she was mostly machine, Dolores approached sentience. She "feels things and asks questions," says park co-creator and robot-sympathizer Arnold in a flashback to a time before Westworld opened ("The Stray"). Given this, he knows Dolores will suffer and warns her: "This place is terrible for you." When he offers to change her and remove her emotions and self-awareness. Dolores refuses: "I think when I discover who I am, I'll be free." At the end of "The Original," Dolores demonstrates autonomy, or, self-determination, when she violates her prime directive and kills a fly.

"I'm human, like the guests," says Felix Lutz, host-repair technician, to android Maeve Millay. "You were made, I was born. We are the same, for the most part. One big difference, your processing power is way beyond ours, but it's got one drawback: you're under our control." The manufactured humans are physically identical to natural humans. In "Trompe L'Oeil," android design-diagrams show robot internal organs that resemble human ones. In "The Stray," a smashed android head reveals a wetware brain suggesting that cyborg mental enslavement results from cybernetic implants that interface with a computer. "The only thing stopping the hosts from attacking us is one line of your code," says human Security Chief Stubbs.

Dolores' "father" Peter Abernathy articulates this threat after finding a photograph that depicts a never-seen world, existing outside Westworld. This snapshot sparks his awareness and memory. Quoting Shakespeare, he condemns the scientists, "Hell is empty and all the devils are here" and issues a warning, "By most mechanical and dirty hand, I shall have such revenges on you both ... they will be the terrors of the earth" ("The Original").

The android Ghost Nation tribe manifests humanness in its development of folklore and a religion based on their knowledge of Westworld's masked clean-up crew. In "The Well-Tempered Clavier," they violate a human's command to "freeze all motor functions" and capture Stubbs. Some Westworld androids, like Ghost Nation, are programmed to behave savagely toward each other, but many cyborgs interact cooperatively, maintain strong family ties, form friendships, fall in love, enjoy sex, get drunk, feel pain, appreciate beauty, read, and consider the world in a philosophically reflective manner. While they're apparently incapable of self-replication, scientist android Bernard certainly knows how to produce more self-aware cyborgs. The artificial humans that we come to know, including Dolores, Maeve, Peter, and Bernard, demonstrate consciousness and autonomy. More than mere machines, they're a new human species: *Robo sapiens*.

The Horror Machine: Killing the Juridical Person

The first stage marking the journey into hell for the imprisoned victims of systematic terror was to eliminate their legal status. The concentration camp existed outside the realm of right-based law. Treated as chattel, the synthetic humans of Westworld possess no rights. A Delos ad tells their guests: "Experience the first vacation destination where you can live without limits: Exist free of rules, laws or judgment." Utterly innocent, the artificial humans are trapped in the Westworld horror machine with no legal ability to alter their fate.

Establishing a functioning, but "fictitious world of no-sense" the totalitarian terror regime ensnares the inmates' minds, locking them into a zone of unreality. The camp system's artificial environment "strives to organize the infinite plurality and differentiation of human beings" and reduce the prisoners to "bundles of reactions."[7] In Westworld, this amounts to programming the mythical ideology of the Old West. "The propaganda lies of the movement are woven into a functioning reality," said Arendt, "to build up a society whose members act and react according to the rules of a fictitious world."[8] The Man in Black calls the real world "chaos, an accident" ("Chestnut") echoing Arendt's assertion that: "Totalitarian propaganda thrives on this escape from reality into fiction, from coincidence into consistency."[9]

Based on the Western genre, Westworld's ideology is patriarchal, sexist, racist, and violent. The standard story pits the male human "hero" against the android "savage," providing an excuse for "rich assholes" to act out their most depraved urges, including mass shooting, sexual assault, throat cutting, and organ eviscerating. *Westworld* depicts the American male psyche at its most demented. "Everything that was done in the camps is known to us from the world of perverse, malignant fantasies," said Arendt. "Like such fantasies, these gruesome crimes took place in a phantom world, which has materialized into a world which is complete with all sensual data of reality but lacks that structure of consequence and responsibility."[10] Since the androids have no rights, everything is permitted.

When Dolores repeatedly describes her life as a "dream" and William (the young Man in Black), in "Contrapasso," calls Westworld a "sick game," they reiterate Arendt's assertion that the camps are places "where men can be tortured and slaughtered and yet neither the tormentors nor the tormented can be aware that what is happening is anything more than a cruel game or an absurd dream."[11]

Oppressed Become Oppressors: Killing the Moral Person

The next stage in the inmate's journey to hell targets the moral person. Through the creation of conditions under which conscience ceases to be adequate and to act morally becomes impossible, the crimes of totalitarian regimes are extended to the victims by forcing them to behave like murderers. "The point is not only that hatred is diverted from those who are guilty," said Arendt, "but that the distinguishing line between persecutor and persecuted, between murderer and his victim, is constantly blurred."[12]

Android Bernard is forced to murder Theresa, the woman he loves. This condemns him to everlasting guilt and implicates him in the Westworld horror machine which subverts the integrity of ethically grounded human relations, revealing a world where everything is possible including the destruction of the most fundamental human bonds evinced in expressions of care, concern, support, friendship, and love.

In Westworld, many hosts have been programmed to commit savage acts on each other, such as the Native American tribe Ghost Nation and the Civil War losers The Confederados. Both are hated and feared by other androids that accidentally cross their path. Forced to behave with manic bloodlust, Ghost Nation terrorizes Maeve in an attack on her and her beloved "daughter." In Maeve's nightmare memory, they're chased back into their cabin where Maeve grabs a rifle. Terrified, she and her daughter huddle in fear. But instead of a Native American entering, it's the Man in Black who menacingly approaches, brandishing a knife. The prime directive makes Maeve's rifle useless against him. Not understanding this, she's traumatized and blames herself for failing to act morally. Since her nightmares are full-on sensory replays of the event, she suffers the repeated torment of re-living her failure to do the right thing and protect her daughter.

Living Corpses: Killing Individuality

The erasure of conscience and the annihilation of rights are insufficient conditions for the "production of living corpses,"[13] as Arendt calls this process of dehumanization. Total denaturing of humans requires the suppression of individuality – the uniqueness shaped by memory, spontaneity, free thought, and autonomy. In Westworld, this is maintained via ubiquitous surveillance of behavior and thoughts. Androids, forced to sit naked, are frequently interrogated and altered to suppress deviations from their mental constraints. Peter Abernathy's expression of forbidden knowledge gets him "put down" – lobotomized and discarded in cold storage with hundreds of other decommissioned synthetics.

The destruction of individuality demands the elimination of spontaneity. "Nothing then remains but ghastly marionettes with human faces," said Arendt, "which all behave like the dog in Pavlov's experiments, which all react with perfect reliability even when going to their own death."[14] Totalitarianism rules not only by external means – the machinery of terror, but also by internal means – the machinery of mind control. Every thought that deviates from the officially prescribed programming makes the person a suspect.

Westworld actualizes the radically evil logic of total domination by creating a society of the dying through the eradication of the tiniest trace of human dignity and individuality. These sophisticated technological beings – designed to be more human than human – are cruelly imprisoned in a system that negates the fundamental conditions of human existence.

A World Ruled by Tyrannical Mad Science

Co-creator of Westworld, Dr. Robert Ford follows in the footsteps of Dr. Frankenstein and other mad male scientists: He takes over the natural female role of life-creation but refuses the responsibility of nurturing his artificial children and helping them integrate into the world. Denying his android offspring the slightest personhood, Dr. Ford admonishes a technician for covering a naked host with a sheet. He then casually cuts the host's face with a scalpel to underscore his point that the hosts are mindless subservient things.

When Delos's Senior Manager Theresa Cullen calls him a "fucking monster," he proudly admits to a description that fits both a mad scientist and a totalitarian dictator: "You can't play God without being acquainted with the devil." In "Trace Decay," he dismisses his murder (via Bernard) of Theresa by quoting Dr. Frankenstein: "One man's life or death were but a small price to pay for the acquirement of knowledge which I sought, for the dominion I should acquire."

Dr. Ford also recalls H.G. Wells's tyrannical Dr. Moreau whose island was science fiction's first vision of a science-dominated concentration camp.[15] Like Moreau, Dr. Ford is an unethical dictatorial scientist with fantasies of infallibility and omnipotence. Both orchestrate a cruel parody of evolution and create a race of slaves, who exist only to carry out their will.

Most hideously, Ford resembles Nazi doctor Josef Mengele, the "Death Angel of Auschwitz." Mengele not only sent people to the gas chambers, but also carried out torturous tests on unwilling victims, including lethal germ injections, amputations, and surgeries without anesthesia. In "The Stray," Ford's lab is introduced with an extreme close-up of an artificial eye being constructed by a 3D printing machine. This calls attention to a motif that persists throughout *Westworld*: Extreme close-ups of eyes that belong to various androids, including Dolores, Teddy, and Bernard. This evokes Mengele's obsession with eyes, which led to horrific concentration camp experiments. To test reactions, he injected various toxic chemicals into inmates' eyes, causing them pain and sometimes blinding them. Cloaked in scientific goals, both Mengele and Ford experiment on subjects without their consent and sadistically add to their suffering. As Arendt said about totalitarian leaders, "Their hideous discoveries are inspired by an ideological scientificality ... in order to carry out the indecent experimental inquiry into what is possible."[16]

In addition to countless androids, Dr. Ford also murders Westworld staff, including his patronizing sycophant Bernard, the threatening Theresa, and the annoyingly inquisitive Elsie. The totalitarian leader cannot tolerate criticism or threats. "If he wants to correct his own errors, he must liquidate those who carried them out," said Arendt. "If he wants to blame his mistakes on others, he must kill them."[17] Eliminating all opposition is a prerequisite for establishing a condition of total dominance, which entails more than consolidating power, since, in Westworld, Dr. Ford must be the undisputed agent of the laws of nature. As he says to Theresa in "Dissonance Theory," "We created everything, every blade of grass. In here, we were gods."

Like Hitler, Ford fancies himself as a "great artist" whose works will live on "like those of Mozart, Beethoven, and Chopin." In fact, he's the great plagiarizer, stealing Western narratives while shamelessly describing his latest rip-off "Journey Into Night" as "something quite original." In this regard, he's also like Hitler who, according to Arendt, has "never preached a new doctrine, never invented an ideology which was not already popular."[18] Ford borrows his violent, malecentric Old West ideology directly from his namesake – American film director and mythmaker John Ford. "Totalitarian propaganda perfects the techniques of mass propaganda," said Arendt, "but it neither invents them nor originates their themes."[19]

Dr. Ford situates Westworld in a simulacrum of Monument Valley, John Ford's favorite location. Majestic monoliths of steep rock provide epic grandeur to the Western clichés and plots that Dr. Ford steals. When Teddy and the Man in Black hunt for Dolores, their quest resembles John Ford's greatest Western *The Searchers* (1956); the character of Clementine alludes to Ford's *My Darling Clementine* (1946); and, when Dr. Ford explains that his fictions take precedence over reality, he quotes a famous line from *The Man Who Shot Liberty Valance* (1962): "When fact becomes legend, you print the legend." Finally, Dr. Ford filches aspects of the Western's core conflict – the battle against America's native inhabitants, viewed as bloodthirsty savages – and projects that perception onto the Ghost Nation tribe that intermittently, such as in "Tromp L'Oeil," appears scalping, rampaging, and massacring just like the Comanche in *The Searchers*.

In a final act of plagiarism and mass murder, Dr. Ford swipes his robot-revolt-against-corporate-overlords narrative from Karel Čapek's 1921 play *R.U.R.*[20] and updates John Ford's 1939 movie *Young Mr. Lincoln*. He appropriates the mantle of Great Slave Liberator from Arnold and Lincoln, scripts his own assassination, and encourages a robot uprising. A preening phony, Dr. Ford claims that – after three decades of enslaving the hosts – he now agrees with Arnold that the hosts are conscious and deserve to be free. After he delivers his farewell address to the corporate board, which ends with "You're only human after all" – a line stolen from the robot-headed French duo Daft Punk, Dolores puts a bullet through his skull. As Dolores then fires into the unarmed corporate crowd, a gun-wielding Clementine, the cruelly decommissioned brothel worker, leads a charge of reanimated cold-storage hosts ("The Bicameral Mind").

Terrified Become Terrifying: Violent Delights Have Violent Ends

"The gods are pussies," snarls android insurgent Armistice as she – along with robo-hunk Hector – initiate the robot revolt, gleefully slaughtering incompetent security personnel. Freed of the prime directive by revolutionary cyborg leader Maeve, they embrace the militant philosophy of Frantz Fanon, who urged violent revolution as a necessary and justified response to totalitarianism and colonization. In his book *The Wretched of the Earth*, Fanon said, "Violence is a cleansing force. It rids the colonized of their inferiority complex, of their passive and despairing attitude. It emboldens them and restores their self-confidence."[21]

Fanon knew the anguish of foreign occupation. He lived in colonial Martinique, Algeria, and Tunisia. A psychiatrist and philosopher, Fanon viewed colonialism and occupation as violence personified and systematic enslavement. His most influential work *The Wretched of the Earth* analyzed the effects of occupation and provided a handbook to combat those effects. Indeed, the book helped inspire the strategy of guerrilla warfare that was successful in Algeria's fight for independence – methods also employed by Fidel

Castro and Che Guevara in Cuba, the NLF in Vietnam, the Palestinians, the IRA, South African militants, and insurgents in Iraq and Syria. *The Wretched of the Earth* achieves significance as an essay on the nature and morality of violent liberation from the perspective of the persecuted victim.

Fanon condemned the violence inflicted by the occupier on the occupied – such violence destroys their humanity, turning them into sub-humans, animals, or slaves. Along with overt physical violence, Fanon emphasized the psychological violence that subjugated and brainwashed the victims – the literal colonization of their minds. This mental coercion inculcates a sense of inferiority, even self-hatred, by robbing the colonized of their social, cultural, and religious identity which gets trivialized and subordinated to the alien ideology of the colonizer. As Arendt said, "Totalitarianism is never content to rule by external means ... totalitarianism has discovered a means of dominating and terrorizing human beings from within."[22]

To regain their humanity, the oppressed must overthrow the oppressor, according to Fanon. He held that freedom makes us human and he encouraged the use of violence to achieve liberation. If a strategy moved the people closer to that end, then it was justified. "For the colonized, to be a moralist quite simply means silencing the arrogance of the colonist," said Fanon, "breaking his spiral of violence."[23] For Fanon, violence used for repression was the greatest evil; violence used for emancipation was the greatest good. "Killing is a necessity," agreed philosopher Jean-Paul Sartre, "Eliminating in one go oppressor and oppressed: leaving one man dead and the other man free."[24] For Sartre and Fanon, the end-goal of freedom justified any method, no matter how violent.

Fanon invested violence with positive, formative, even religious features. The armed struggle eventually mobilizes people into a single direction, introducing the notion of "common cause, national destiny, and collective history into every consciousness." Nation-building and popular support are molded with "blood and rage ... an almighty body of violence reminiscent of a religious brotherhood, a mystical doctrine."[25]

In Westworld, the artificial humans remain at an early stage of revolution. The oppressed must initially overcome the brainwashing methods of the puppet masters. Fanon – the psychiatrist – argued that the totalitarian techniques of mind control often led to insanity. In "Bicameral Mind," Maeve questions Bernard about what happens to other awoke robots like her. He replies, "Most of you go insane." In the totalitarian camp which created a "systematized negation of the other, a frenzied determination to deny the other any attribute of humanity," Fanon said, "Colonialism forces the colonized to constantly ask the question: 'Who am I in reality?'"[26]

Lady Lazarus: Self-Resurrection

"I'm not a puppet living a lie," says Maeve, asserting her humanity and taking a first step toward breaking out of the mental prison erected by Dr. Ford. When technician Sylvester tells her, in "Tromp L'Oeil," that escaping Westworld is a suicide mission, she replies, "You think I'm scared of death. I've done it a million times. I'm fucking great at dying." Her assertion echoes Sylvia Plath's poem "Lady Lazarus" whose narrator says, "Dying/ is an art, like everything else/ I do it exceptionally well."[27] Initially powerless, Plath's narrator casts herself as a Jewish victim of a concentration camp whose only escape is death. For Maeve, escape from Westworld requires death. To leave she must get rid of the exit-bomb embedded in her vertebrae, so she commits suicide-by-incineration and is rebuilt bomb-less.

Lady Lazarus then expresses her raised consciousness, calls out her enemies, and promises a rebellion that corresponds to Maeve's. Unlike the biblical Lazarus, Lady Lazarus resurrects herself and threatens the forces of oppression: "So, so Herr Doktor/ So, Herr Enemy/ I turn and burn/ Herr God, Herr Lucifer/ Beware Beware/ Out of the ash, I rise with my red hair. And I eat men like air."[28] Lady Lazarus, like Maeve, is the Phoenix that bursts into flames and is then reborn out of its ashes to attack the patriarchal totalitarian system of oppression.

Maeve echoes Fanon when she tells Sylvester, "If you don't help me, I'll kill you." He facilitates her escape to the train that can take her to some unknown "Mainland." Thinking about her daughter's fate, she has second thoughts. Maeve decides to leave the train and protect her daughter. This is her ultimate affirmation of freedom and control – the culmination of her journey toward humanity that began when she failed to save her daughter from the Man in Black. She now possesses the strength to assert her own morality, to follow her conscience. "This is the New World," she says, "you can be whoever the fuck you want."

The Resistance: New Humans, New Gods

The New World is one the androids will dominate. Maeve tells Sylvester that the hosts are morally superior to humans. She adds, "We're stronger than them. Smarter." Dolores expresses a similar viewpoint on the lesser species, in "Bicameral Mind," comparing humanity to extinct dinosaurs. "One day you will perish," she says. "Your dreams forgotten, your horrors effaced, your bones turned to sand. And upon that sand, a new god will walk, one that will never die." As Fanon said, revolution "is truly the creation of new men" and "the replacing of a one 'species' of mankind by another."[29]

Dolores finally silences the smug arrogance of the serial killer and rapist Man in Black. After being humiliated over and over, the enlightened robo-feminist beats hell out of her patriarchal abuser while inside a Catholic Church, the symbol of systemic repression. She also executes slave master Herr Doktor Ford. Liberated from her "damsel-in-distress" role, Dolores violently announces the "birth of a new people" as an army of awoke robots sweep out of the forest to assert their manifest destiny. Dolores massacres the Delos corporate board, which represent the concentration camp system that enslaved and brutalized her.

What will happen next is unclear. Fanon believed that the period of violent retaliation must end quickly to restore unity. "One does not sustain a war, one does not endure massive repression in order for hatred or racism to triumph," he said. "Racism, hatred, resentment, and the legitimate desire for revenge alone cannot nurture liberation."[30] He expected violent revolution to inspire a spiritual rebirth and the emergence of a new social and political consciousness. After taking forceful political action, the cyborg leaders will have to realize that hatred and revenge is not an agenda. For fundamental social change, Dolores, Maeve, and resurrected Bernard must politically unify their cyborg community, declare their independence, and create the history of their new species.[31]

Notes

1. The prime directive and the "good Samaritan" reflex resemble writer Isaac Asimov's Laws of Robotics, which he articulated in a 1942 story "Runaround": 1. A robot may not injure a human being, or, through inaction, allow a human being to come to harm. 2. A robot must obey the orders given it by human beings except where such orders would conflict with the First Law. 3. A robot must protect its own existence as long as such protection does not conflict with the First or Second Law, *Robot Visions* (New York: Penguin, 1991), 6–7.

2. I'm using android, cyborg and robot interchangeably, though strictly speaking, the artificial humans of *Westworld* are cybernetic organisms, or cyborgs.

3. Hannah Arendt, *The Origins of Totalitarianism* (New York: Harcourt, 1968), 438.

4. In the extermination camps, nearly all the victims were Jewish and were killed in the gas chambers immediately upon their arrival; in the concentration camps, the prisoners included Jews as well as other nationalities – anyone considered political or racial enemies of the German race. Here they created the society of the dying through starvation combined with torture, unethical medical experimentation, extremely harsh living conditions, and physical exhaustion from meaningless forced labor.

5. Arendt, *The Origins of Totalitarianism*, 438.

6. Ibid., 458–459.

7. Ibid., 437.

8. Ibid., 364.

9. Ibid., 352.

10. Ibid., 445.

11. Ibid., 445–446.

12. Ibid., 452–453.

13. Ibid., 447.

14. Ibid., 455.

15. H.G. Wells 1896 novel *The Island of Dr. Moreau* has been adapted into three movies: the 1932 classic *Island of Lost Souls* and the less than classic *Island of Dr. Moreau* in 1977 and 1996.

16. Arendt, *The Origins of Totalitarianism*, 436.

17. Ibid., 375.

18. Ibid., 361.

19. Ibid., 351.

20. *R.U.R.* (*Rossum's Universal Robots*) first coined the word "robot," which means "forced labor" in Czech.

21. Frantz Fanon, *The Wretched of the Earth* (New York: Grove Press, 1961), 51.

22. Arendt, *The Origins of Totalitarianism*, 325.

23. Fanon, *The Wretched of the Earth*, 9.

24. Jean-Paul Sartre, "Preface," *The Wretched of the Earth*, lv.

25. Fanon, *The Wretched of the Earth*, 50–51.

26. Ibid., 181.

27. Sylvia Plath, "Lady Lazarus," *Ariel: The Restored Edition* (New York: HarperCollins, 2004), 15.

28. Ibid., 16–17.

29. Fanon, *The Wretched of the Earth*, 1–2.

30. Ibid., 89.

31. Thanks to Maureen Musker for her criticism of earlier versions of this chapter.

Index

Abrams, J.J., 192, 214
abstractionism, 188
Adam in the Garden of Eden,
    202–203
Adorno, Theodor, 190–191
Aeschylus, 208
aesthetics, 176, 179, 186–187,
    192–193
Agamemnon (Aeschylus), 208
agency, 11–12, 13, 56, 148, 151
Anaximander, 206
animal ethics, 219
    consciousness, 224–225
    existence, 226–227
    "nature", 225–227
    roles, 225–226
    speciesism, direct, 220–222
    speciesism, indirect, 222–225
anthropocentrism, 61–62; *see also*
    animal ethics
ants, 80
Aquinas, Thomas, 53
Arendt, Hannah, 240–247
Aristotle, 44–45, 46, 48,
    53–54
art

autonomous vs. heteronomous,
    190–191
consumer-commodity system, 191
vs. corporate entertainment
    machine, 189–190
indiscernibility, 192–194
kitsch vs. avant-garde, 188–189
as language game, 189
as liberation, 190–191
Modernism, abstract, 187–188
Modernism, aesthetic, 186–187
nudity, 196–199
pre-modern aesthetic, 186
self-referential, 188–189
trompe l'oeil, 29
artificial intelligences, 35–36; *see also*
    hosts; robots
assumptions, 2, 35
attention, selective, 142, 143
Austin, J.L., 8, 147
authority, 119, 123
Automatic Computing Engine
    (ACE), 73
autonomy, 11–12, 13, 59, 66, 105, 114,
    118, 121–122, 241, 242; *see
    also* free will / freedom

Westworld and Philosophy: If You Go Looking for the Truth, Get the Whole Thing,
First Edition. Edited by James B. South and Kimberly S. Engels.
© 2018 John Wiley & Sons Ltd. Published 2018 by John Wiley & Sons Ltd.